# NOT JUST A NAME

# Not Just a Name

by

Roger Bullen

MERSEA ISLAND MUSEUM PUBLICATIONS

Published by Mersea Island Museum Publications
High Street, West Mersea, Colchester, Essex.

Produced with the aid of a grant from the
Millennium Festival Awards.

First published 2000

Copyright © Roger Bullen 2000

All rights reserved
Without limiting the rights under copyright
reserved, above, no part of this publication may be
reproduced, stored in or introduced into a retrieval system
or transmitted in any form or by any means (electronic, mechanical
photocopying, recording or otherwise) without the prior
written permission of both the copyright owner and
the above publisher of this book.

ISBN 0-9537322-1-5

Printed by Page Bros (Norwich) Ltd.,
Mile Cross Lane, Norwich, Norfolk, NR6 6SA

*This book is dedicated
to the memory of all those who sacrificed their lives
for their country in the First World War*

# Contents

| | Page |
|---|---|
| Acknowledgements | ix |
| Introduction | xi |
| Author's Note | xiii |
| | |
| The First Casualties | 1 |
| Yeoman of Signals Ralph Cutts Avis | 6 |
| Leading Stoker Thomas Edward Funnell | 9 |
| Private Albert Jordan | 12 |
| Leading Seaman Frederick Funnell Mussett | 16 |
| Private Hugh Smith | 19 |
| Private Frederick Beckett Bennett | 26 |
| Private Rowland Cook | 31 |
| Private Bertie Cundy | 34 |
| Private Arthur Wade | 39 |
| Sergeant George Walter Hewes | 43 |
| Private Harry James Cottrell | 49 |
| Private Stanley Mason | 52 |
| Private James Frederick Cutts Avis | 55 |
| Rifleman Harold Mole | 59 |
| Rifleman Harris William Hoy | 61 |
| Private Alfred Lewis Pullen | 65 |
| Private Harry Victor Gardner | 68 |
| Gunner Nathan Cudmore, East Mersea | 71 |
| Private George Cudmore, East Mersea | 73 |
| Gunner Ernest Green | 77 |
| Private Frederick Samuel White | 80 |
| Private John D. Howard | 89 |
| Private Sidney Elijah Wright | 94 |
| Acting Sergeant Clifford Farthing | 97 |
| Private Thomas Marriage, East Mersea | 101 |
| Acting Bombardier Bertie Woods, East Mersea | 113 |
| Deckhand/Sea Gunner Albert Victor Juba Cudmore | 115 |
| Deckhand Frederick Joseph Cutts Avis | 117 |
| Rifleman Edward Oscar Green | 120 |
| Lieutenant Edmund Percy Roberts | 123 |
| Gunner Joseph Stacey | 133 |
| Private Christopher Pullen Brand | 136 |
| Private Alfred Bertie Thursby | 142 |

## Contents

| | Page |
|---|---|
| Private Arthur David Pullen | 146 |
| Bombardier Charles Thomas Powell, East Mersea | 152 |
| Private Edward Parkin | 156 |
| Private Bertie Lee | 160 |
| The Royal Fleet Auxiliary Industry | 163 |
| Able Seaman Archibold Percy Green | 167 |
| Fireman Alfred John Mole | 170 |
| Cook/Able Seaman Frederick Westhorpe Mole | 172 |
| Able Seaman Reginald John Mole | 174 |
| Quartermaster Henry William Pullen | 176 |
| Able Seaman Harold Frederick Stoker | 178 |
| Second Lieutenant Ernest Hart | 180 |
| Leading Seaman Walter James Beynon | 186 |
| Private Percy Louis Whiting | 195 |
| Deckhand/Sea Gunner Percy French | 199 |
| Private Alfred Edward Russell, East Mersea | 201 |
| Deckhand Albert Hewes | 205 |
| Private Ezra John Mussett | 207 |
| 'Aftermath' by Siegfried Sassoon | 209 |

Cover illustrations
Front: Faubourg d'Amiens Cemetery and Arras Memorial
Back top left: West Mersea War Memorial
Back top right: East Mersea War Memorial
Back lower and frontispiece: Map of Mersea Island which is situated 8 miles. south of Colchester in Essex. Reproduced from Ordnance mapping by permission of Ordnance Survey on behalf of the Controller of Her Majesty's Stationery Office, © Crown Copyright MC 100031450

# Acknowledgements

The research for this book has taken place over the last three years. During that period, I have received the help and co-operation of a large number of organisations and individuals and without their input this publication would not have been possible.

The relatives of those named on the War Memorials of West and East Mersea are mentioned individually in the 'Sources' at the end of each entry. The information and photographs supplied by them were invaluable and were very much appreciated.

My thanks to fellow members of the Western Front Association, Essex Branch, especially Monique Bailey, Brian Clayton and Doug Rowe. A special thanks to the last named, who has accompanied me on numerous visits to the Public Record Office at Kew. Assistance was also given by the national body of the Association in providing the majority of the trench maps.

The Commonwealth War Graves Commission and the Ministry of Defence Records Department are also due thanks for the way they dealt with my enquiries in a professional and efficient manner.

All Regimental Museums contacted were very helpful in providing information especially the Essex Regimental Museum at Chelmsford under their curator, Ian Hogg, who allowed me access to their records.

The Public Record Office at Kew has been visited on a regular basis for the past few months, and their staff have been invaluable in pointing me in the right direction, even if at times looking for that piece of elusive information has proved very frustrating. Extracts appear in the book from previously unpublished sources such as Battalion War Diaries, Trench maps and reports from Courts of Inquiry.

The Local Studies section of Colchester Library provided access to census returns and past issues of local newspapers, while Essex University Library allowed me to view their mighty volumes of the *East Anglian Daily Times* from 1914-1918.

Fellow local historians on the Island, Ron Green and Brian Jay, have provided me with photographs from their respective collections. Also thanks to those who took photographs on my behalf of memorials and graves in Plymouth, Melksham, Norway and Germany.

The Mersea Island Museum Trust have been very supportive and it was through their sponsorship that the Millennium Festival Award was received which made the publication of this book possible. On the practical side, I owe thanks to John Coulson for his proof reading and Facsimile Graphics of Coggeshall for supplying the cover film.

A final thanks go to my wife Linda, who has always navigated me successfully around the highways and byways of France and Belgium while visiting the war graves and battlefields of the Western Front.

# Introduction

War against Germany was declared on 4th August, 1914, and in the countryside there was an enthusiasm among menfolk to join up and 'do their bit' before it was all over, probably by Christmas. The Mersea men were no exception. This report appeared in the *Essex County Telegraph* on 8th August, 1914.

*'The call to the Naval Reservists brought a number of strangers into Colchester from the Colneside towns and Mersea. A party of nine came by waggonette from the latter district on Tuesday night and on the journey the axle gave way under the weight of the men. They soon hopped overboard, and sorting out their bundles completed the distance on foot.'*

Regional newspapers were soon compiling lists of those men from each town and village, who had answered the call to volunteer. Families were encouraged to send in names of their menfolk so they could be added to the list. The *Essex County Telegraph*, dated 17th October, 1914, listed 78 names of those from Mersea who had joined up. By 14th November, 1914, this had risen to 94 who were listed in the *Essex County Standard*. Two were already dead and one was a prisoner of war.

But there were other lists, those of the casualties. It was also becoming painfully obvious that the war would not be over by Christmas. The need for more and more men meant that at the beginning of 1916 conscription came into force and a second wave of men from Mersea left to enlist.

There were a number of applications by Islanders for exemption, due either to ill health, their marital situation or that they felt they could not be spared from their current occupation. At the Tribunals there was a growing feeling that men from Mersea were trying 'to dodge the draft', as extracts from a local newspaper shows.

*Lexden and Winstree Authority Meeting, 27th April, 1916*
*Mr Fairhead remarked that if the Council wanted any men at all, it was for scavenging West Mersea (laughter).* (This was to replace men conscripted to the army.)
*Lexden and Winstree Tribunial, 14th October, 1916*
*Mr Prior also appeared for a West Mersea coal merchant who claimed his carman, aged 35, and married, stating that he had been unable to get another man.*
*Mr Cross: 'There is a lot of young fellows walking about Mersea, why can't you get them?'*
*The Employer: 'I don't know of any do you?'*
*Mr Cross: ' Yes I do, and I think its a disgrace that young fellows should be walking about Mersea at times like this.'*
*The Employer: You won't get fellows at Mersea off the water for any money.*
*Mr Prior: ' Those fellows ought to be 'somewhere in France.'*
*The Military were recommended not to call the man up until 1st December.*

However, the majority of those called up enlisted and did their duty, some never to return. By the end of the war, approximately 320 Mersea men had served in the Forces, and of those fifty had been killed. Forty four from West Mersea and six from East Mersea.

There are two poems in this book which I feel are particularly relevant, Siegfried Sassoon's *Aftermath* at the end of the book, and this one written in 1919 by a mother or father grieving the loss of their son.

They are speaking, best beloved, of erecting you a shrine
That your death may live for ever there, immortal son of mine.
They will deck your name with laurels for the price that you have paid
To deliver us for freedom - for the sacrifice you made.

For you went out in the darkness, smiling gaily from the train.
We did our best for you, and hoped to see you soon again.
Sadly home we went without you, all your chances to review
While you entered that mad maelstrom, made by others, not by you.

And we waited - waited - waited - for the scanty news that came
While your bed and chair were empty and the home was not the same.
The blow fell soon and swiftly, for we learned that you had died;
But you knew then how we sorrowed - you were with us as we cried.

Though the days to years are turning, you we never can forget,
And the heavy aching sorrow in our hearts is living yet,
But we feel that in the spirit you are with us once again,
Telling us our earthly loss is to your eternal gain.

They are speaking, best beloved, of erecting you a shrine,
That your death may live, forever there, immortal son o'mine;
And in all the future ages when we see you near to God,
Men will read your name and bless you, for the narrow path you trod.

A.R.P.

(Credit: Reprinted from *If you want the old battalion*, the newsletter of the Essex Branch, Western Front Association).

# Author's Note

Inevitably, I have managed to discover more information on some individuals than others. This has been due to a number of factors. Where relatives have come forward, they have provided me with background information, and sometimes the 'key' to unlock other sources that I was not previously aware of. Official Records have sometimes been disposed of, or are not available. For instance all the First World War records for the Mercantile Marine Reserve were thrown away in the 1960s.

Each plea in the local newspapers has resulted in people coming forward with information, and I am sure there is more to come. Even the smallest piece of information can sometimes lead to bigger things. Even though this book has been published, I shall continue to add to my archive, hopefully for a reprint in the future. So please contact me or the Museum if you can help.

A photograph of the grave or a memorial inscription accompanies each entry. The condition of the original varies and hence the reproduction in this book. However, it was felt that it was better to include them to show their last resting place or the memorial that commemorates them.

It is suggested that it would be helpful to have Michelin Map 236 by your side while reading this book, as it shows the locations where many of the Mersea men served.

Roger Bullen
June 2000

# The First Casualties

# Two Mersea Men die in Naval Disaster

On 22nd September, 1914, the three armoured cruisers, HMS *Aboukir, Hogue*, and *Cressy* were on picket duty in the sea area known as the Broad Fourteens off the Dutch coast. They were there to ensure the presence of armoured ships in the southern approaches of the North Sea, and the eastern entrance to the Channel, and to keep the area clear of enemy torpedo craft and minelayers.

The patrol had commenced at the outbreak of war with a destroyer escort, but because the weather in September was so bad the escort had been withdrawn. Because it was felt that the German U-boats would also be unable to operate in these conditions, no precautions were taken against such an attack, and the cruisers were steaming at a steady ten knots in line astern, without even bothering to zigzag. Disaster struck in the early morning, when the *Aboukir* was struck by a torpedo fired from the German submarine U9, commanded by Lieutenant Weddigen. Thinking he had struck a drifting mine, the captain of the *Aboukir* ordered the *Hogue* and *Cressy* to come about to rescue survivors. As they approached and stopped they were torpedoed in turn, and all three ships sank with a loss of 1,459 out of 2,200 men on board the three ships. Amongst those lost were two men from Mersea, Yeoman of Signals Ralph Cutts Avis (Ralph Mussett) on the *Cressy*, and Leading Stoker, Thomas Edward Funnell on the *Aboukir*.

A contemporary report taken from the *Essex County Chronicle* describes the sinking of the three cruisers and the subsequent rescue of survivors. Its reporter and the victims of the attack were obviously unaware at the time, that only one submarine was involved.

**NAVAL REVERSE IN THE NORTH SEA**

**GERMAN SUBMARINES AT WORK**

**THREE BRITISH CRUISERS SUNK**

*The Secretary of the Admiralty reported on Tuesday that 'His Majesty's ships Aboukir (Capt. John E. Drummond), Hogue (Capt. Wilmot S. Nicholson), and Cressy (Capt Robt. W. Johnson) have been sunk by submarines in the North Sea'.*

*The Aboukir was torpedoed, and while the Hogue and Cressy had closed in and were standing by to save the crew, they were also torpedoed.*

*A considerable number were saved by H.M.S. Lowestoft (Capt. Theobald W.B. Kennedy) and by a division of destroyers, trawlers, and boats.*

*The Cressy, Aboukir, and Hogue were sister ships-armoured cruisers of a comparatively old type, built fourteen years ago.*

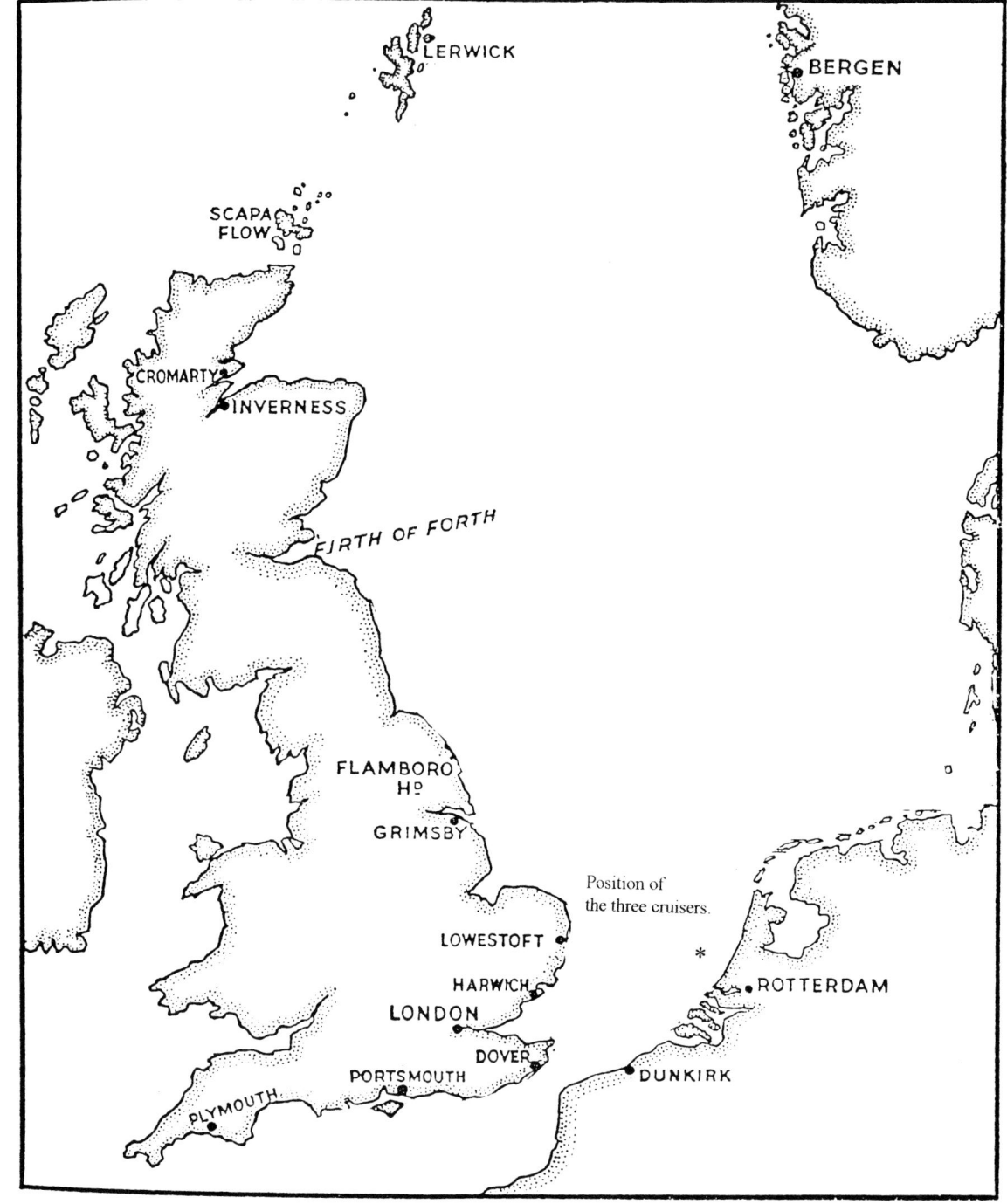

Map showing position of the three British cruisers, *Aboukir*, *Hogue* and *Cressy* when they were attacked by the German submarine U9.

*All three ships belonged to the Third Fleet. The loss of life has been heavy. There were about 2,000 men on board the three vessels, of which the following have been accounted for:-*

*Landed at Harwich.................. 470*
*Landed at Lowestoft................ 84*
*Landed at Ymuiden.................. 287*
*Landed at Rotterdam................ 25*
*Still aboard ships..................... 218*
*   Possible total............. 1,034*

*Many survivors were landed by warships at Harwich on Tuesday night.*

*Of those brought ashore, eighty were received on board the Woolwich, the depot ship for submarines, and a number of wounded were taken to Shotley Barracks.*

*Thirty officers were included among the survivors. Bodies were also brought ashore.*

*Nineteen unwounded and one wounded man were landed at the Hook of Holland on Tuesday by the Dutch steamer Titan, which rescued in all 114 of the drowning blue-jackets and transferred most of them to a British torpedo-boat.*

*The disaster is stated to have occurred at half-past seven on Tuesday morning. Information from Amsterdam states that the Dutch steamer Flora, while en route for Rotterdam, sighted several boats with sailors and officers on board. These proved to be survivors of the British cruisers Hogue, Aboukir, and Cressy.*

*A telegram from Ymuiden states that the Dutch steamship Flora arrived there on Tuesday night, having on board 857 English sailors, some of whom were wounded. They were survivors from the two British cruisers which the Dutch steamer reports to have been torpedoed off the Dogger Bank by German submarines.*

*The third British cruiser, the Cressy, was sunk twenty miles off the Hook of Holland.*

*The crews of the Aboukir, Hogue, and Cressy were composed mainly of reservists. The Aboukir was the first to be struck, at about six o'clock. A terrific explosion followed, and the ship began to sink rapidly.*

*Seeing the ship sinking, and believing she had struck a mine, the Hogue lowered her boats, and began to save the swimming survivors. The Hogue herself was, however, shortly afterwards torpedoed. Both vessels appear to have sunk very rapidly. No sooner had the Cressy began to put out her boats than she was also torpedoed.*

*Harwich was in a state of great excitement on Tuesday evening. During the day the harbour was denuded of warships, but at about seven o'clock in the evening one by one the Harwich vessels of the flotilla began to return, and in some cases, they were flying the flag at half-mast, which told its own tale.*

*On the arrival of H.M.S. Lowestoft abreast of the pier, the little Red Cross boat could be seen gliding to and fro between the warships and Shotley Barracks, where the wounded were being landed.*

*Crowds of people gathered on Harwich pier and quayside, and shortly after eight o'clock the first batch of survivors came ashore at Harwich. They seemed to be all officers. They appeared in odd garments, some wearing large wraps, others a piece of sacking round their loins, and for the most part they were barefooted. It is estimated that thirty in all came ashore. They walked to the hotel hospital, where they received every comfort and attention. As each little batch of the rescued came ashore a loud cheer was given by the spectators. For the most part the survivors appeared wet through and it seems certain that all had been recovered from the water.*

*It is stated that the Dutch military authorities have decided that survivors of the British cruisers landed in Holland must remain there during the war.*

*Twenty-one of the men who are wounded, one seriously, will remain in Ymuiden.*

*Twenty officers, including a medical officer and one chaplain, are among those rescued*

## THE STORY OF THE ATTACK

*From interviews with some of the rescued, it is possible to weave together the story of the Naval reverse inflicted by a German Submarine Flotilla.*

*It appears that the attack was made about 6.30 on Tuesday morning, and there seems no doubt that the British ships were taken by complete surprise. A flotilla of German submarines, said to be five in number, formed the attacking party. These submarines seem to have had their base at Borkum, under the shelter of the Frisian Islands. They had doubtless observed the English warships engaged on patrol duty and waited their time and opportunity for attack. The parent ship of the German flotilla was, it is stated, flying the Dutch flag, and she made no pretence whatever to participate in the rescue of any of the survivors of the disaster.*

## BOTTOM RIPPED OUT

*The Aboukir was undoubtedly the first cruiser to be struck. She was, it is stated, struck by two torpedoes and sank in the brief space of six or seven minutes. The Cressy and the Hogue were some distance from the Aboukir, and, seeing their sister ship in distress, they hurried to the scene, and it was while engaged in assisting in the work of rescue that they themselves were torpedoed by the enemy's submarines. The Cressy was struck aft. It was not thought at the time that she was badly damaged, but after a brief interval she was torpedoed again, and the bottom of the ship was practically ripped out. Almost immediately the Hogue was torpedoed, and she settled down very quickly.*

## SAFETY IN SPEED

*Meanwhile warships of all kinds steamed up with all possible speed to take part in the work of rescue, and also to beat off the enemy. H.M.S. Lowestoft, which arrived soon after the disaster, saw two German submarines, and it is said that her speed saved her from a like fate. The Lowestoft did not fire on the submarines for fear of striking the men in the water, but she steamed over the spot in the hope of running them down. The Cressy, however, is said to have sunk two submarines before she herself was torpedoed and sunk.*

*H.M.S. Fearless, when she left Harwich on Wednesday, steamed at 29 knots for three and a half hours without finding trace of the enemy. Destroyers also reached the scene in four and a half hours, but they observed nothing in the vicinity, although other destroyers earlier on the scene described large quantities of wreckage floating about.*

## SAILOR'S EXPERIENCE'S

*One of the crew of the Aboukir who was rescued and brought into Harwich gave a short history of the disaster. He said that at 5.15 a.m. on Tuesday they were in company with Hogue and Cressy. Suddenly they were torpedoed. His opinion was that the torpedo got the cruiser amidships. He saw no periscope of the German submarine. The Cressy and Hogue came smartly to the rescue. An hour had elapsed when the Aboukir disappeared.*

*Whilst the crews of the Cressy and Hogue were searching for the survivors of the Aboukir those in the boats saw two German submarines. They fired two torpedoes at the Hogue, and the cruiser sank in less than thirty-five minutes.*

*The scene was indescribable. It was an hour afterwards, he said, that the Cressy was torpedoed by four torpedoes. He thought the German submarines were in strong force, and he should say they were about 20 of them. The Cressy fired the first shot, but he could not say whether any damage was done.*

*Signaller Frank William Grocott, a survivor of the Hogue, who has returned home to Newcastle (Staffs), in an interview stated that when the Hogue was torpedoed, the commander called out 'keep a cool head signaller', and immediately ordered the crew to look out for themselves. Next Captain Nicholson instructed Grocott to signal to the Cressy, which was standing by, 'submarines on starboard side'.*

*'We had got the flags half way up'* continued Grocott, *'when the Hogue lurched and suddenly turned turtle, throwing us into the water. I made for the Cressy, which was blazing away at the submarine and was only two hundred yards off, when she too was struck. She heeled over and righted herself, but the Germans fired another torpedo which sealed the Cressy's doom'.*

*Grocott was eventually picked up by the Hogue's picket boat after being in the water two and a half hours, and was transferred to a Dutch steamer which landed him at Ymuiden.*

*Grocott says 'the Dutch were splendid and could not do too much for them'. He declared that he is certain that six submarines were attacking and that five were sunk. Seven torpedoes in all were fired in rapid succession. He is anxious to be afloat again 'to wipe off the score of my lost comrades.'*

Photograph of HMS *Cressy* taken in 1906. She was one of six ships in the *Cressy* class, launched on 4th December, 1899, one of two built by Fairfield. The other was HMS *Aboukir*. Ralph Cutts Avis served on HMS *Cressy* as Yeoman of Signals. *(Photograph courtesy of the Imperial War Museum Q21127)*

**SURNAME: Cutts Avis**

CHRISTIAN NAME(S): Ralph

AGE: 35

SHORE BASE: Chatham

SERVICE NO: 191425 (RFR/CH/B/6683)     RANK: Yeoman of Signals

SERVICE/REGIMENT: Royal Navy

DECORATIONS EARNED: Unknown

DATE KILLED/DIED: 22nd September, 1914   LOCATION: North Sea

MEMORIAL IF NO KNOWN GRAVE: Chatham Naval Memorial

---

**BACKGROUND AND SERVICE HISTORY:**

Ralph Cutts Avis was born on 15th May, 1880, the son of Hope Cutts Avis, a sewing machinist, who lived with her parents, Issac and Susannah Cutts Avis in The Square, West Mersea. On 20th June, 1880, she married Ralph's father, Alfred Mussett, a mariner, who was now living with the family, and Ralph became known on the Island as Ralph Mussett, although in official circles he was known as Ralph Cutts Avis, the name he was baptised with on 8th September, 1880.

In 1896, at the age of sixteen, he enlisted in the Royal Navy and on 17th November, 1896, he joined HMS *Impregnable*. On his eighteenth birthday, 15th May, 1898, he signed on for twelve years. He served on a number of ships until he left the Navy on 25th June 1910, remaining on the Royal Naval Reserve (see Naval Service Record).

He returned to Mersea to take up fishing again, the occupation quoted on his enlistment papers. Also by then he had married Ann Elizabeth (maiden name unknown). In 1913, he was serving on the jury (committee) of the Tollesbury and Mersea Oyster Fishery Company.

At the outbreak of war, being part of the Royal Naval Reserve, he was called up and posted to HMS *Cressy* as a Yeoman of Signals. HMS *Cressy* was one of six ships in the *Cressy* class and was launched in 1899. They were 472ft long with a beam of 69.5 ft, displacement of 12,000 tons. Maximum speed was 21 knots. They were armed with 2 x 9.2 inch and 12 x 6 inch guns, and had 2 x 18 inch torpedo tubes. Total crew was 760.

On 22nd September, 1914, three armoured cruisers of the *Cressy* class, the *Aboukir*, *Hogue* and *Cressy* herself were on patrol in sea area known as the Broad Fourteens off the Dutch coast, when they were discovered by the German submarine U9, which sank each one of them in turn. Ralph Cutts Avis was not one of the survivors, having gone down with the ship.

He is commemorated on the Chatham Naval Memorial as Ralph Cutts Avis, and on the West Mersea War Memorial as Ralph Mussett.

| 191425 | Chatham | 191425 |

**Name in full:** Ralph Cutts Avis

**Date of Birth:** 15 May 1880
**Place of Birth:** W. Mersea, Essex
**Occupation:** Fishing

| Date and Period of C. S. Engagements. | Age. | Height. Ft. in. | Hair. | Eyes. | Complexion. | Wounds, Scars, Marks, &c. |
|---|---|---|---|---|---|---|
| 15 May 1898 – 12 yrs | 28 / 18 | 5:8½ / 5:9 | Lt Brn | Blue | Fresh | |

| Ships, &c., served in. | List and No. | Rating. | Sub-ratings Rating. From To | Badges. | Period of Service. From To | Character. | If Discharged, When and for what Cause |
|---|---|---|---|---|---|---|---|
| Impregnable | 15ᵃ 7672 / 15 5607 | B2C / B1C | Sig. ✓ ✓ | G¹ 15.5.01 17 Nov 06 | | | |
| " | " " | | J.M. 27.8.99 | G² 15 5 02 29 Aug 97 | 12 Apl 98 | VG | |
| Agincourt | 15ᶠ 230 | " | H.S.2cl. 23.11.05 | 13 Apl 98 | 13 May 98 | | |
| Pembroke I | 15ᵘ 203 | | | 14 May 98 | | VG | |
| | | Sign ᵐ | | 15 May 98 | 30 Sep 98 | VG 31.12.98 | |
| Gibraltar | 15 82 | " | | 10 Oct 98 | 5 Feb 99 | VG 31.12.99 | |
| Scylla | " 57 | " | | 6 Feb 99 | 7 June 99 | VG 31.12.00 | |
| Aebe | 15 11 | " | | 8 June 99 | | VG 31.12.01 | |
| | | 2d. Sig. | | 19 June 00 | 22 Dec 00 | VG 31.12.02 | |
| Pembroke I | 15 1253 | " | | 23 Dec 00 | 7 Feb 01 | VG 31.12.03 | |
| Wildfire | 5ᵗ 54 | " | | 8 Feb 01 | 1 Dec 02 | VG 31.12.04 | |
| Pembroke I | 15ᵘ 2069 | – | | 2 Dec 02 | 9 June 03 | VG 31.12.05 | |
| Irresistible | 5 432 | | | 10 June 03 | | VG 31.12.06 | |
| | | Lg. Sig. | | 18 Oct 03 | 30 Nov 04 | VG 31.12.07 | |
| Pembroke I | 15 1061 | " | | 1 Dec 04 | 2 Jan 05 | VG 31.12.08 | |
| Diadem | 5 66 | " | | 3 Jan 05 | | VG 31.12.09 VG | |
| " | " | 2 Yeo Sig | | 4 mch 05 | | | |
| | | Yeo Sig. | | 31 Dec 06 | 8 Apl 07 | | |
| Pembroke | 5ᵗ 10 / 15ᵘ 2477 | – | | 9 Apl 07 | 1 Sep 07 | | |
| Charybdis | 5ᵗ 12 | | | 2 Sep 07 | 4 Sep 08 | | |
| Astraea | 5ᶠ 6 | Q(11) | | 5 Sep 08 | 31 mch 10 | | |
| Edgar | | | | 1 Apl 10 | 25 May 10 | VG VG | |
| Pembroke | 15ᵘ 671 / 203 | R.F.R. "Chatham" B 6683 | | 26 May 10 24 June 10 / 25 June 1910 | | | 5yrs C.S. Expired. Accord for R.F.R. |
| Cressy | | | | 2 Aug 14 | | | |
| Cressy | R⁴ 216 | Yeo Sig (4 yrs) | | 2 August | 22 Sep 14 | | DD |

N.P. 2269
DD 22 Sep 1914
Drowned in North Sea when H.M.S. Cressy was sunk by German Submarine

PAID WAR GRATUITY
Refer to [illegible]

**Clothing and Bedding Gratuities.**
£6 J.C.
R¹ 9 C Sep 97
L 3 June 98

**REMARKS.**
10/ Grat for raising V. 68 Impreg. Dec.
(1) O.S. from 1-10-07.
(2) over 4 yrs 30.12.09.

The Naval Record of Yeoman of Signals, Ralph Cutts Avis (PRO, Kew ADM188/327).

By the end of the war, his wife had remarried, becoming Mrs Robins and lived with her husband William Herbert Robins in New Captains Road, West Mersea. The house was named *Cressey Ville*, no doubt in memory of her first husband.

**Sources**
*1881 and 1891 Census*
*Commonwealth War Graves Commission*
*Naval Service Record, PRO, Kew, Ref no: ADM188/327*
*Essex Record Office, Colchester*
*Imperial War Museum*

The panel on the Chatham Naval Memorial on which is inscribed the name of Ralph Cutts Avis, under the heading 'Yeoman of Signals'.

**SURNAME: Funnell**

CHRISTIAN NAME(S): Thomas Edward

AGE: 33

SHORE BASE: PORTSMOUTH

SERVICE NO: 299136          RANK: Leading Stoker

SERVICE/REGIMENT: Royal Naval Reserve

DECORATIONS EARNED: Unknown

DATE KILLED/DIED: 22nd September, 1914   LOCATION: North Sea

MEMORIAL IF NO KNOWN GRAVE: Portsmouth Naval Memorial

---

**BACKGROUND AND SERVICE HISTORY:**

Thomas Edward Funnell was born on 12th December 1881 in Burwash, Sussex. After leaving school he worked as a labourer until a month before his twentieth birthday on 12th November, 1901, when he joined the Royal Navy, enlisting for a term of 12 years, commencing as a Stoker, second class. He finally completed his service as a Leading Stoker, having served on a number of ships (see Naval Service Record).

On 14th February, 1913, he signed on for a further period of service, transferring to the Eastern West Mersea Battalion of the Coastguard on 25th March of that year.

A local newspaper reported that on Saturday 13th December, 1913, he participated in a walking race which was organised by Mr John Wood of the Nook, to settle an argument as to the lowest possible time in which one could walk round Mersea Island by the sea wall. The 23 entries started at 1.10pm from the Victory, and the winner, Chas Prigg, completed the course in 2 hrs 39 mins with Thomas Funnell coming in fifth. It was reported that seven handsome walking sticks were given as prizes.

On 1st August, 1914, with the outbreak of war imminent, he received orders to join HMS *Aboukir* as a Leading Stoker. On 22nd September, 1914, she was patrolling the North sea off Holland with her sister ships, *Cressy* and *Hogue* when she was torpedoed by the German submarine U9. He was drowned and his body was never recovered.

On 31st October, 1914, the following report appeared in the Essex County Standard

*'Coast Guard Funnell of West Mersea, who went down with the Aboukir was well known and very popular locally. He had joined the Aboukir as one of the Royal Naval Reserve.*
  *On arrival of the news of his loss at West Mersea and that of Ralph Mussett who went down with 'The Cressy' all Mersea mourned the loss of two gallant sailors and heroes'.*

Portsmouth — 299136 — 299136

**Name in full:** Thomas Edward Funnell
**Date of Birth:** 12 December 1881
**Place of Birth:** Burwash, Sussex
**Occupation:** Labourer

| Date and Period of C. S. Engagements. | Age. | Height Ft. in. | Hair. | Eyes. | Complexion. | Wounds, Scars, Marks, &c. |
|---|---|---|---|---|---|---|
| 12 November 1901 – 12 yrs | 16 | 5 6 | Dk Brn | Hazel | Dark | |
| 14 February 1913 – to comp. | — | 5 7½ | | | Fresh | Tattooed right forearm |
| Vol — | | | | | | |

| Ships, &c., served in. | List and No. | Rating. | Sub-ratings Rating | From | To | Badges. | Period of Service From | To | Character. | If Discharged, Whither, and for what Cause. |
|---|---|---|---|---|---|---|---|---|---|---|
| Duke of Wellington II | 15a⁴ 4995 | Sto 2c | J.M. | 31.3.05 | 6.6.06 | G¹ 1.11.04 | 12 Nov 01 | 15 June 02 | V.G. 31.12.01 | |
| Prince George | 5a 336 | | | | | G¹ 10.11.07 / 2 | 13 June 02 | | V.G. 31.12.02 | |
| | | Stoker | | | | | 1 Nov 02 | 30 Jan | V.G. 31.12.03 | |
| Fire Queen | 18a² 1511 | " | | | | | 31 Jan 04 | 9 Mch 04 | V.G. 31.12.04 | |
| Vernon | 16 3919 | | | | | | 10 Mch 04 | 24 Mch 04 | V.G. 31.12.05 | |
| Fire Queen | 15a² 1511 | " | | | | | 25 Mch 04 | 6 Ap 04 | V.G. 31.12.06 | |
| Pembroke II | 15a³ 3049 | | | | | | 7 Ap 04 | 17 May 04 | V.G. 31.12.07 | |
| Pr of Wales | 5a 149 | | | | | | 18 May 04 | 28 May 06 | V.G. 31.12.08 | |
| Victory II | 15a² 5887 | | | | | | 29 May 06 | | V.G. 31.12.09 V.G. | |
| | | Stoker | | | | | 1 July 06 | 10 Oct 06 | V.G. 31.12.10 V.G. | |
| Majestic | 5a² 10 | " | | | | | 20 Oct 06 | 25 Xb 07 | V.G. 31.12.11 Sat. | |
| Albion | 5a² 80 | " | | | | | 26 Xb 07 | | V.G. 31.12.12 Supr. | |
| | | " Act. Lg. Sto (1) | | | | | 24 Dec 08 | 24 Aug 09 | V.G. 31.12.13 Sat. Rm1. | |
| Victory | 15a² 2580 | " | | | | | 25 Aug 09 | 15 Oct 09 | | |
| Fisgard | 15a 821 | | | | | | 16 Oct 09 | | | |
| | | Ldg. Sto (2) | | | | | 26 Jan 10 | 4 Feb 10 | | |
| Victory II | 15a² 2928 | " | | | | | 5 Feb 10 | 12 May 10 | | |
| Halcyon | 6a¹¹ 38 | " | | | | | 13 May 10 | 10 Ap 11 | | |
| Victory II | 15a² 3953 | " | | | | | 11 Ap 11 | 7 Aug 11 | | |
| Egmont | 13a² 64 | " | | | | | 8 Aug 11 | 10 Oct 11 | | |
| Swiftsure | 5a² 200 | " (3) | | | | | 11 Oct 11 | 7 May 12 | | |
| Victory II | 15a² 5200 | " | | | | | 8 May 12 | 30 July 12 | | |
| Blenheim | 12a² 117 | " | | | | | 31 July 12 | 10 Feb 13 | | |
| Victory II | 15a² 6141 | " | | | | | 11 Feb 13 | 24 Mch 13 | | |
| Eastern West Mersea Btn. | | | | | | | 25 Mch 13 | 31 July 14 | | |
| Aboukir | 5a 114 Ldg. Sto (not 4 yrs) | | | | | | 1 Aug 14 | 22 Sept 14 | | D.D. |

N.P. 2259/14
D.D. 22 Sept 1914
Lost in North Sea when H.M.S. "Aboukir" was sunk by a German submarine.
(A.C.R. ref. N.P. 397/17)

**Clothing and Bedding Gratuities.**
£3.10.7½
£2/10/- G.C. V.67 Eastern Dist. Nov. 13

**REMARKS.**
10/- Grat. for re-issuing of Duke of Well¹¹ Nov 01. S.B. to E. Section 2/3/17 9.6. N.30/17
(1) Per M.S. 06 Ledger
Failed educationally for Sto. P.O. but passed for Ldg. Sto. on 26 Jan. t.o. at expiration of 3 months M.T.C. N.P. 1312/10 and N.P. 3352/10
(2) Per "Victory" Lady 10. Qd for Ldg. Sto. 26.1.10
(3) Over 3 yrs 24.12.11

PAID WAR GRATUITY

The Naval Record of Leading Stoker Thomas Edward Funnell (PRO Kew ADM188/485)

He is commemorated on the Portsmouth Naval Memorial and on the West Mersea War Memorial.

**Sources**
*Commonwealth War Graves Commission*
*Essex County Standard*
*Essex Regiment Museum*
*Naval Service Record, PRO, Kew, Ref no: ADM188/485*

A contemporary postcard of HMS *Aboukir*, a *Cressy* class armoured cruiser, built by Fairfield, and launched on 16th May, 1900.

Leading Stoker Thomas Edward Funnell's name inscribed on the Portsmouth Naval Memorial

**SURNAME:** Jordan

CHRISTIAN NAME(S): Albert

AGE: 22

RECRUITMENT OFFICE: Stratford, Essex

SERVICE NO: 3/2122  RANK: Private

SERVICE/REGIMENT: 1st Battalion Essex Regiment

DECORATIONS EARNED: 1914/15 Star, War Medal, Victory Medal

DATE KILLED/DIED: 6th August, 1915  LOCATION: Gallipoli

MEMORIAL IF NO KNOWN GRAVE: Helles Memorial, Turkey

---

**BACKGROUND AND SERVICE HISTORY:**

Albert Jordan was born in 1893, in Canning Town, the son of John William and Mary Ann Jordan. At the outbreak of war they were living at the Coast Guard Station, West Mersea.

He had already served in the army before the war and as a reservist he was recalled in 1914, and re-enlisted at Stratford, Essex, joining the 1st Battalion, Essex Regiment.

On 25th April, 1915, the Battalion was part of the 29th Division that landed on the Gallipoli peninsula, the Battalion going ashore at Cape Helles on 'W' Beach. The landing is described in the Battalion War Diary as follows:

*9.00 am - The Battalion less 2 Coy transhipped from HT Dongola to a minesweeper and was conveyed as close to the shore as possible, when they were transferred to boats. The landing was carried out under fire and there were several casualties in the boats which took place on W. Beach about 9.30 am.*

*9.30am - As soon as the first boats were landed, we received orders to connect between the Royal Fusiliers on right and Lancashire Fusiliers on left, and as many as were available were sent to fill this gap, reinforcing as men arrived on the beach. On reaching the crest it was found that no one was on our right.*

*11.35am - A message was received from G.H.Q to report progress and reasons for not pushing on. Reply was sent, that we were waiting for our left to move up and would then advance. This was attempted, but the advance was held up by very heavy fire and many casualties occurred.*

*12.30pm - Supported by 4th Worcesters and after bombardment by navy, which drove out the enemy, the Battalion took Hill 138 and redoubt beyond.*

*07.00pm - Received orders to connect with Worcesters on right and 1st Hampshires on left and entrench position.*

*Enemy attacked at night, and came to close range with a machine gun, but inflicted no loss and were driven off.*

*Casualties during day: 2 Officers killed, 4 wounded, 1 since died. Other ranks 15 killed, 87 wounded.*

Also on the beaches that day from Mersea, were Private Hugh Smith also of 1st Battalion, Essex Regiment, who landed with Private Albert Jordan, and Private George Hewes who landed with the Australians at Anzac Cove.

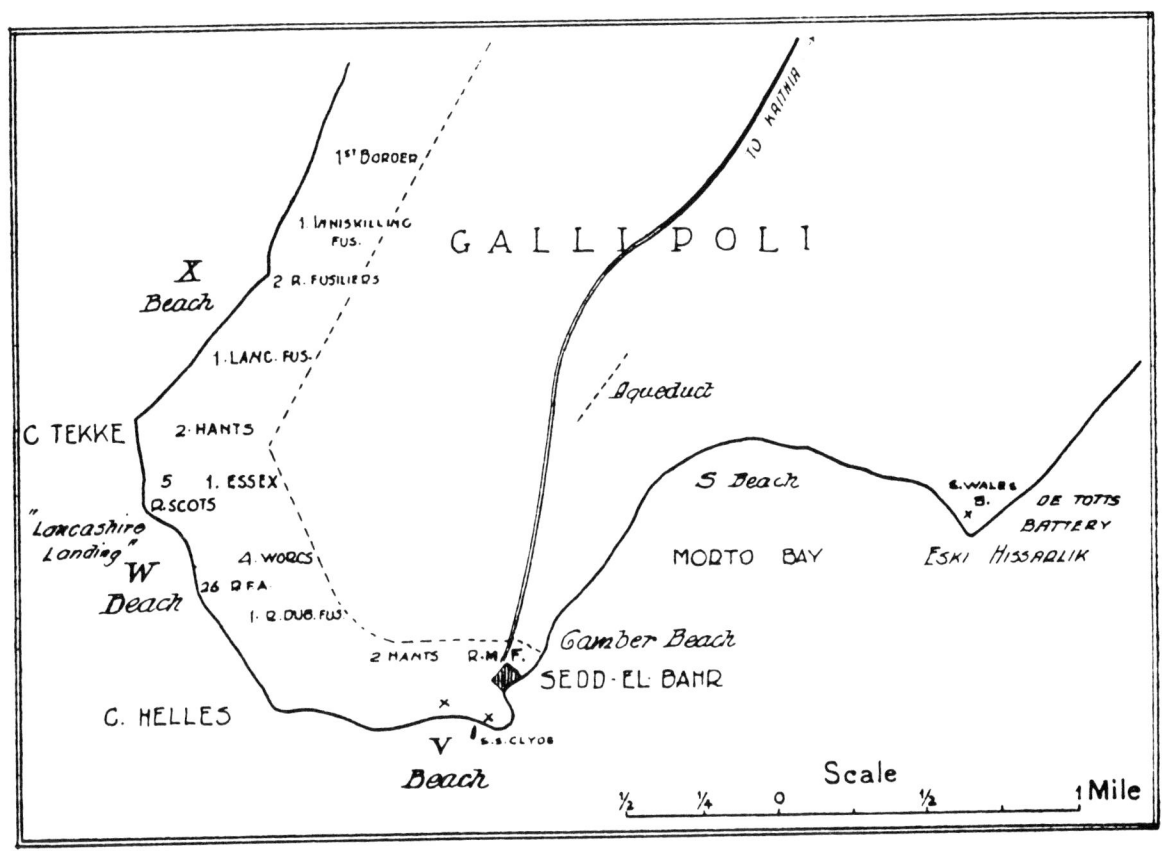

Position of 29th Division, Gallipoli, 26th April, 1915

On 5th August, 1915, the Battalion was involved in operations to aid the landing at Suvla Bay, by taking part in one of two diversionary actions to draw the Turks attention from the landings, one at Helles, and one at Anzac. The former operation involved the 42nd (East Lancashire) Division and 88th Brigade of the 29th Division. The latter were ordered to take 1,200 yards of Turkish trenches named H 13 and H 12, which were opposite the British right and right centre, 4th Worcesters being on the right, 2nd Hampshires in the centre, and the 1st Essex on the left, with 5th Royal Scots in reserve.

The preliminary bombardment was by machine guns as well as by artillery. Both Worcesters and Hampshires were met with heavy fire, and although small parties reached their objectives, they could not hold them. The 1st Battalion, Essex Regiment were detailed to attack the trenches called H 12a, H 12 and trenches under construction, north-east of H 12, near Krithia. The artillery opened at 2.30 pm, but the Turks replied with shrapnel and high explosive on the British trench system, in particular the reserve trenches, causing many casualties. At 3.50 pm, the Battalion advanced in two lines, two companies, 'Y' and 'Z', moving on H 12a from the south west, having 200 yards to cross before reaching the enemy's trenches. 'W' Company attacked H 12 and the connection with H 12a, each company finding its own supports. 'X' Company was in reserve.

The advance on H 12 was initially very successful. The position was taken with few casualties, but very heavy shrapnel fire opened up as the men moved forward again. With great gallantry, they took the next trench H 12a, but they were then held up by machine gun, rifle fire and bombs. The Companies were so weak that on the Turks counter attacking with bomb and bayonet, they were driven back to H 12a and its approaches, and then to the corner of the Southern Barricade. 'W' Company on the left reached the trench in continuation of the Southern Barricade and that leading north from it, but they were unable to secure the continuation of the Northern Barricade. In the section between the two Barricades, serious casualties were sustained, six officers alone being killed.

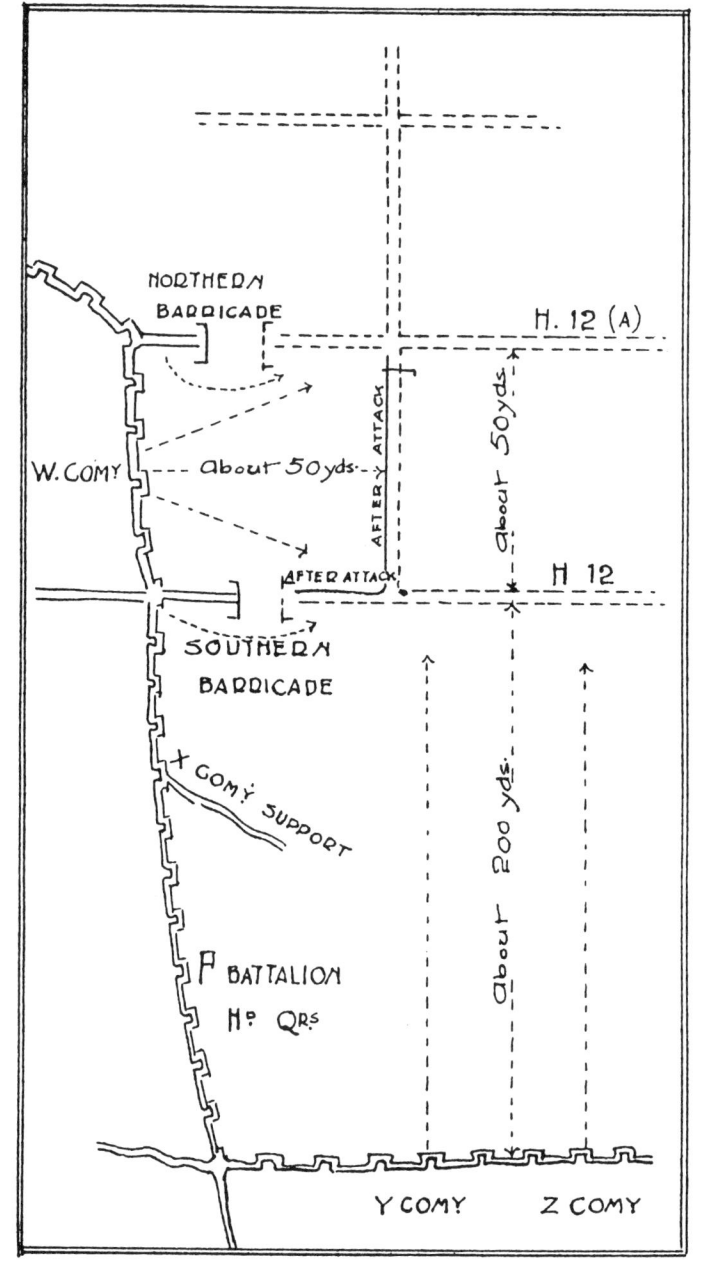

Diagram showing the attack by the 1st Battalion, Essex Regiment in Gallipoli on 5th August, 1915, in which Private Albert Jordan took part and was killed.

By nightfall, the Battalion had secured as a result of heavy fighting, the corner formed by H 12 and the trench connecting that point and H 12a, the only means of communication being a small tunnel under the Southern Barricade. Part of 'X' Company was sent forward with men of other Companies during the night, as the position was difficult to hold on account of its being exposed on three sides to enemy fire. The order had, however, been issued that the trench was to be held at all costs. This they did, staying there all through the next day, 6th August, although suffering considerably from thirst, supplies reaching them by means of petrol tins. At daybreak on 7th August, the Battalion was moved out of the line to Gully Beach, having suffered very heavy casualties, totalling 432, consisting of 50 killed, 202 wounded and 180 missing.

Albert Jordan was killed in action on 6th August, 1915. A contemporary newspaper dated 24th September, 1915, reported him as wounded, although it is likely that he was wounded and missing, as his body was never recovered.

He is commemorated on the Helles Memorial on the tip of the Gallipoli peninsula, Turkey, and on the West Mersea War Memorial.

**Sources**
*Commonwealth War Graves Commission*
*Essex Regiment Museum*
*Essex Chronicle*
*Essex Units in the War, 1914-1919 by J.W. Burrows*
*1st Battalion, Essex Regiment War Diary, PRO, Kew, Ref no: WO95/4312*
*Medal Index Card, PRO, Kew*
*William Fulton, WFA Essex Branch - photograph of inscription on Helles Memorial*

Private Albert Jordan's name inscribed on the Helles Memorial, Gallipoli.

**SURNAME:** Mussett

CHRISTIAN NAME(S): Frederick Funnell

AGE: 34

SHORE BASE: Chatham

SERVICE NO: 191969 (RFR/CH/B/8540)    RANK: Leading Seaman

SERVICE/REGIMENT: Royal Navy

DECORATIONS EARNED: Unknown

DATE KILLED/DIED: 7th October, 1915

MEMORIAL IF NO KNOWN GRAVE: Chatham Naval Memorial

---

## BACKGROUND AND SERVICE HISTORY:

Frederick Funnell Mussett was born on 6th September, 1881, in Upchurch, Kent, the son of Frederick and Mary Mussett. The family later moved to Rainbow Road, West Mersea.

On 6th September, 1899, on his eighteenth birthday, he joined the Royal Navy, completing his service on 5th September, 1911 as a Leading Seaman (see Naval Service Record).*

On leaving the Royal Navy he joined the Royal Fleet Reserve and returned to Mersea to resume his occupation as a fisherman. At the outbreak of war, he was recalled to duty and joined HMS *Pyramus* on 11th August, 1914 as a Leading Seaman.

He sailed with the ship to New Zealand, and in 1915 she was on the East African coast and in the Indian Ocean. While on board he contracted bronchial pneumonia and died on 7th October, 1915, and was presumably buried at sea.

He is commemorated on the Chatham Naval Memorial and on the West Mersea War Memorial.

**Sources**
*Commonwealth War Graves Commission*
*David Mussett*
*Essex Regiment Museum*
*Naval Service Record, PRO, Kew, Ref no: ADM188/328*

---

*At the bottom of the Naval Service Record is the outline of a poignant note - 'In event of any casualty answering to the above name. Please contact his fiancee: Miss E. Heard, Near the Schools, Tollesbury, Essex, for enquiries 19123'. No doubt she held out a forlorn hope that he was still alive.

191969  Chatham  191969

**Name in full:** Frederick Funnell Mussett
**Date of Birth:** 6 September 1881
**Place of Birth:** Upchurch, Kent
**Occupation:** Fishing

| Date and Period of C. S. Engagements. | Age. | Height Ft. in. | Hair. | Eyes. | Complexion. | Wounds, Scars, Marks, &c. |
|---|---|---|---|---|---|---|
| 6 September 1899 – 12 yrs | 18 18 | 5'3 5'4 | Brown | Hazel | Fresh | |

| Ships, &c., served in. | List and No. | Rating. | Sub-ratings Rating. | From | To | Badges. | Period of Service From | To | Character. | If Discharged, Whither, and for what Cause. |
|---|---|---|---|---|---|---|---|---|---|---|
| Impregnable | 15ᵃ 7983 | B 2cl | J/n | 17.1.01 | 31.12.02 | 91.6.9.02 | 14 Jan 97 | 20 Jan 97 | | |
| Lion | 15a 3443 | " | AC | 1.1.03 | 30.11.08 | 91.5.9.07 | 21 Jan 97 | | | |
| " | " | B/c | S.G. 1.12.08 | | | 2. | 4 Nov 97 | 5 Aug 98 | VG | |
| Agincourt | 15c 270 | " | | | | 9.9.8.15 | 6 Aug 98 | 13 Oct 98 | | |
| Resolution | 15 364 | " | | | | 3 | 14 Oct 98 | | VG | |
| " | " | (ord) | | | | | 6 Sep 99 | 30 Jan 00 | VG 31.12.99 | |
| Pembroke I | 15² 7661 | " | | | | | 31 Jan 00 | 14 Feb 00 | VG 31.12.00 | |
| Ringarooma | 5 17 | " | | | | | 15 Feb 00 | | VG 31.12.01 | |
| " | " | AB | | | | | 17 Jan 02 | 7 Dec 03 | VG 31.12.02 | |
| Pembroke I | 15² 6615 | " | | | | | 8 Dec 03 | 2 Jan 04 | VG 31.12.03 | |
| Repulse | 5. 54 | " | | | | | 3 Jan 05 | 5 June 05 | VG 31.12.04 | |
| Dominion | " " | " | | | | | 6 June 05 | | VG 31.12.05 | |
| " | " | " | Ldg Sea | | | | 1 Oct 05 | 31 Mch 07 | VG 31.12.06 | |
| Hannibal | 16² 229 | " | | | | | 1 Apl 07 | 9 June 07 | VG 31.12.07 | |
| Dominion | 5² 54 | " | | | | | 10 June 07 | 1 June 08 | VG 31.12.08 | |
| Pembroke I | 15¹⁽²⁾ 1248 | " | | | | | 2 June 08 | 4 Jan 09 | VG 31.12.08 | |
| Hawke | 16ᴵᴵ 292 | " | | | | | 5 Jan 09 | 28 Feb 09 | VG 31.12.10 VG | |
| Tamar | 12c² 121 | " | | | | | 1 Mch 09 | 31 Mch 10 | | |
| Minotaur | 16cᵗ 8 | " | | | | | 1 Apl 10 | 15 Aug 10 | | |
| Tamar | 12c² 8 | " | | | | | 16 Aug 10 | 31 Mch 11 | | |
| Crescent | 15² 209 | " | | | | | 1 Apl 11 | 21 June 11 | | |
| Pembroke I | 15¹ 2560 | " | | | | | 22 June 11 | 6 Sep 11 | VG VG Shore b.S Exp | |
| | | | | | | | | | VG 31.12.14 Sep Rec R.F.R. | |

Joined R.F.R. Chatham B 8540, 23 March 1912

PAID WAR GRATUITY BY No. 87

| Pyramus | RFR 14 | 1 Ldg. Sea | | | | | 11 Aug 14 | 7 Oct 15 | VG – Sup DD |

N.P. 5228/15
DD. 7th October 15
Bronchial Pneumonia

**Clothing and Bedding Gratuities.**
£6
£1/8C Dec 97
£3/C – Sep 98

**REMARKS.**
10/ Grat for saving of SS Mersey June
(per Xmas 14 ledger)
A57/45/15

PAID WAR GRATUITY.

The Royal Naval Record of Leading Seaman Frederick Funnell Mussett (PRO Kew ADM188/328)

Photograph of HMS *Pyramus* taken in 1898. She was *a Pelorus* class (*third class cruiser*) built by Palmer of Jarrow and was launched on 15th May, 1897. She was completed and ready for service in 1900.
(*Photograph courtesy of the Imperial War Museum Q43286*)

Frederick Funnell Mussett's name inscribed on the
Chatham Naval Memorial.

**SURNAME:** Smith

CHRISTIAN NAME(S): Hugh

AGE: 27

RECRUITMENT OFFICE: Hastings, Sussex

SERVICE NO: 3/2720     RANK: Private

SERVICE/REGIMENT: 1st Battalion, Essex Regiment transferred to 9th Battalion, Essex Regiment

DECORATIONS EARNED: 1914/15 Star

DATE KILLED/DIED: 15th February, 1916   LOCATION: France

LOCATION OF GRAVE: Vermelles British Cemetery, Pas de Calais

---

**BACKGROUND AND SERVICE HISTORY:**

Hugh Smith was born in 1889, one of six sons born to George Frederick and Mary Overall Smith of Sunset House, Mill Road, West Mersea.

In 1902, his father George died at the age of 53, leaving his mother to bring up the boys and run the family milling and bakery business.

Before the war, Hugh went to Reading and then to Brighton where he worked in a gentlemen's outfitters. At the outbreak of war, Hugh was one of those who volunteered, enlisting in Hastings, where he joined the 1st Battalion, Essex Regiment. Hugh was initially based at Bury St Edmunds and then moved in December to Dovercourt for basic training. Here he wrote to his sister Eva:

*2720 Lance Corporal H. Smith*
*c/o Mrs Seabourne*
*1 Deanview*
*Upper Dovercourt*
*9/12/1914*

*Dearest Eva,*
*Very many thanks dear for letter of today, so you had to get home for Rehearsal* (both Hugh and his sister took part in amateur dramatics) *after all the Landlady said that you had told her that you would call back again but owing to weather I think you done the wisest thing in phoning after all no card came. Well dear I really meant to write before this thanking you all for the lovely cakes you brought me, they are very nice and go down well for tea, the celery too I enjoyed much and tell Blanche the pudding was lovely have not quite finished it yet. Glad you enjoyed yourself I am sure I enjoyed the company of you 3 very much, hope they did not rush ???? too much for rooms. Yes it was rather a rough night for ??? but still did not notice it much tonight, we are on Guard but I am in charge of waiting Guard and tomorrow morning.*

Enlargement of a postcard sent by Hugh to his sister, Daisy, showing the Battalion marching through Bury St Edmunds. The message on the back reads: 'Thank mother for letter, was sorry to hear that you were queer hope that this will find you better. This is a photo of our Company just leaving our barracks on going to camp, you can hardly see me, I am just behind Claude. Will write to mother tonight or tomorrow. The guv is away at Felixstowe for the day. Going to London tomorrow, so I'm afraid much work won't be done. Love Hugh.

*I shall have to be checking people passing through here from 5.30 until 7. I hope your affair will go off alright tonight I should very much like to see you in your part. Starting Friday morning with other Lance Cpl I have to start on 10 days classes of Infantry and musketry training, do not know how I shall get on, a lot to learn in 10 days, but shall do my best, we shall be at it from 9 to 12.30 every morning and from 2 until 3.45 but struck off all other duties. Today the major had the Company on the field for Company drill, I had to take charge of a section, felt rather small for the first time. Have also been up as evidence against a chap for refusing to carry out an order. The Colonel gave him 168 hours field punishment, that is the beauty of taking a stripe, one gets a lot*------- (rest of letter missing)

On 25th April, 1915, he landed with the Battalion on the Gallipoli peninsula, and after a period of eight days fierce fighting, Hugh was wounded. He was evacuated to Malta, where he wrote the following letter to his brother Edward.

*St George's Military Hospital,*
*Ward 4 Block D*
*Malta.*
*12/6/15*

*Dear Edd,*
*Just a few lines to let you know I received the small parcel on behalf of the Brotherhood in my last parcel from home. I am sure all the members will appreciate the kind thoughts of your Brotherhood and it will also cheer them to think of their arduous but noble work. I wish your Brotherhood every success, and may your prayers for us never cease. I shall never forget the Sunday we landed on the Peninsula, we were taken off a minesweeper, about 400 yards from the beach, and transferred to rowing boats manned by our brave sailors. Bullets flying all round us, our boat was hit 5 times, our Lieut was hit in the back, and died I heard afterwards the same night. During that few minutes, the thought flashed through my mind 'Have faith in God' and he has indeed been good. In closing I ask once again for your prayers.*

*Believe me*
*Your affectionate brother*
*Hugh*

He eventually arrived back in England at the beginning of July, 1915, where he was sent to Graylingwell Military Hospital in Chichester, from where he wrote to his mother.

*Queen's Section B2*
*Graylingwell Military Hospital*
*Chichester,*
*Surrey*
*3/7/15*

*Dear Mother,*
*No doubt you were surprised to hear that I had arrived in England, could not possibly let you know as I had no idea I was coming myself until about 2 days before the Boat sailed. We are in a fine place here, really the County asylum turned into a Hospital, the grounds too are very nice quite a pleasant change to the white walls of Malta. Last night a party came over from Arundel to give us a concert, they were very good. Of course you will not need to send me any eatables here, just a few cigs occasionally, although they do issue those out to us. We arrived in England on Wednesday night, came on here the following morning only about hour and a half run from Southampton, they have accommodation for about a thousand here, I*

*believe, certainly an ideal spot for the purpose. Various owners of private cars, send them up to the hospital each afternoon to take the patients for a trip, which I am told are usually very enjoyable. I think this is about all I can talk about this time will write again shortly. Hoping that this will find you and all at home well. Heaps of love to self and all.*

*Yours, your loving boy*
*Hugh*

A group of wounded soldiers recovering at Graylingwell Military Hospital Chichester.
Lance Corporal Hugh Smith can be seen in the middle row on the extreme right.

It was not until the end of the year that he had recovered from his wounds and was able to rejoin the Regiment. At the beginning of 1916 he returned to France, and on 15th January he was drafted to the 9th Battalion, Essex Regiment, joining 'A' Company. The Battalion entered the front line trenches on 14th February, near Vermelles, and participated in what was known as the 'Battle of the Craters'.

The Battalion held trenches from Devon Lane to St Elie Avenue, the chief defensive points being Lookout Crescent and Brook Wood Street. Two companies were in the front, one in support and one in reserve; Battalion headquarters were just south of the Fosseway. The enemy had sprung several mines during the previous month or so, and these with the counter mining, conducted from the British positions, had considerably altered the appearance of the landscape since the Battalion was there in October, 1915. The detection of hostile mining was constantly in mind. Holding the line when tunnelling was being frequently reported. This presented a problem and was a severe strain. All the communication trenches were guarded with bombing stops and loopholes. Saps ran out to all the craters in No Man's Land and they were held as bombing posts, permanently manned by thirteen bombing squads, five each from the front line companies and three from the support company. In addition, a squad was stationed on each flank of the support company, and five squads of the reserve company remained with that unit to be used as required. The hold on the front system was strengthened by twelve Lewis guns and four Vickers machine guns.

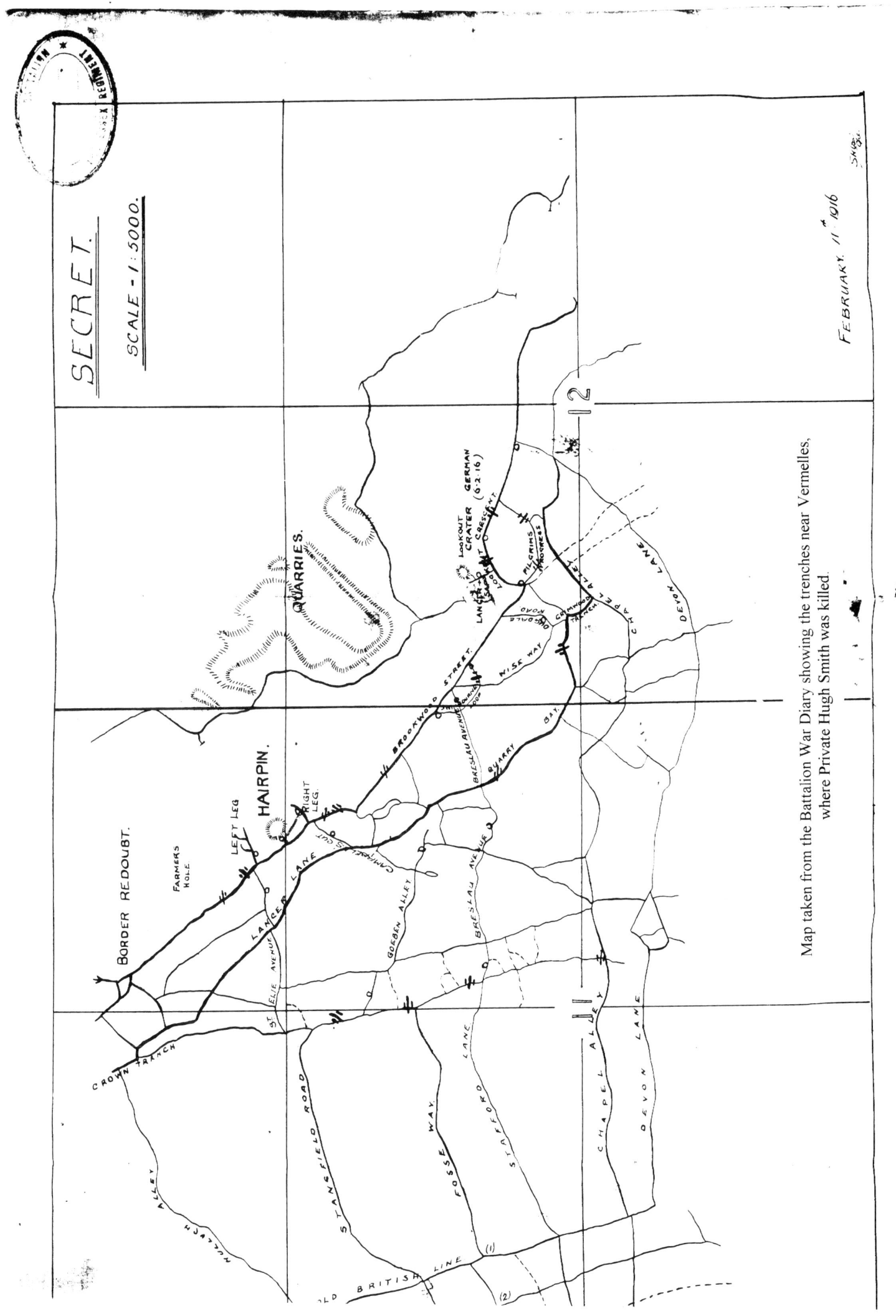

Map taken from the Battalion War Diary showing the trenches near Vermelles, where Private Hugh Smith was killed.

Private Hugh Smith,
9th Battalion, Essex Regiment

On 15th February, Private Hugh Smith's first day back in the trenches, the Battalion War Diary reported that *'the day was quiet except for slight shelling with shrapnel on the front line. A very successful reconnaissance of the enemy's wire was carried out by 6 patrols from 'A' and 'B' Companies, going out consecutively after the return of the first, and useful information was obtained'*. It was during one of these patrols, that Hugh Smith was killed by a shell, death being instantaneous. He was buried in Vermelles British Cemetery, near Bethune, and is commemorated on the West Mersea War Memorial.

The following letter was sent to Mrs Smith from his friend, Albert Branch.

*Dear Mrs Smith,*
*Undoubtedly, you have by now been notified of the death of your son Hugh. He was killed by a shell on Tuesday last, February 15th, while doing his duty as a true Englishman. It may slightly comfort you to know that death was instantaneous. He was carried back to a village near the trenches and properly buried in a British cemetery. The N.C.O.s and men of the platoon join with me in expressing our very deepest sympathy. He was liked and respected by all who knew him, and for myself, he was my chum, and I loved him almost as a brother. I am afraid there is nothing I can say to comfort you, but the One above who ordains all things for our good also gives us strength to bear these terrible burdens. His personal property, less his*

*watch and cigarette case, which of course were smashed, were handed in at headquarters, and will be forwarded on to you shortly. I can assure you I sympathise with you with all my heart, as I myself miss him terribly.*
*Believe me to remain*
    *Yours respectively*
        *ALBERT A. BRANCH*

With Hugh dead, and another one of her sons having lost a leg on the Western Front, Mrs Smith appeared a number of times at the local Tribunal, to stop her other sons being conscripted. There is some evidence that she was successful.

In May, 1919, the War Office returned to Mrs Smith, the sum of 8s 3d, which Hugh had left with the Battalion before he was killed.

**Sources**
*Commonwealth War Graves Commission*
*Essex Units in the War, 1914-1919 by J. W. Burrows*
*1st Battalion, Essex Regiment War Diary, PRO, Kew, Ref No: WO95/4312*
*9th Battalion, Essex Regiment War Diary, PRO, Kew, Ref No: WO95/1851*
*Essex County Chronicle*
*Mr Hubert Cock*

Private Hugh Smith's grave in Vermelles British Cemetery

**SURNAME: Bennett**

CHRISTIAN NAME(S): Frederick Beckett

AGE: 20

RECRUITMENT OFFICE: Chelsea, S.W.

SERVICE NO: 2063          RANK: Private

SERVICE/REGIMENT: 2nd/6th London Field Ambulance, Royal Medical Corps, attached to 2nd/3rd London Field Company, Royal Engineers.

DECORATIONS EARNED: 1914/15 Star, War Medal, Victory Medal

DATE KILLED/DIED: 3rd May, 1916    LOCATION: France

LOCATION OF GRAVE: Cabaret-Rouge British Cemetery, Souchez, Pas de Calais

---

**BACKGROUND AND SERVICE HISTORY:**

Frederick Beckett Bennett was born in 1896, in Loughton, Essex, the son of Frederick Adolphus and Mary Ann Bennett.

Soon after the outbreak of war, Frederick enlisted in Chelsea and joined the 2nd/6th London Field Ambulance Corp, Royal Army Medical Corps. According to the Unit's War Diary, it carried out a training role in the Chelmsford area. On completion of his training he was sent to France and arrived on 22nd June, 1915.

Meanwhile, his family left Loughton and moved to West Mersea, to live in Kingsland Road. The 1891 census recorded that his father's occupation as a corn merchant's clerk, but is not known whether this was the employment he undertook after arriving on the Island.

While in France, Frederick became attached to the 2nd/3rd London Field Company, Royal Engineers who were posted to the area around Vimy Ridge, assisting with mining operations and the construction of defensive earth works. It was during one of these missions that Frederick was killed. The Unit's War Diary describes the events surrounding his death.

*Villers au Bois 1.5.1916 - 2.5.1916*
*2nd Lieutenant Douglas consolidating on near lip of enemies crater at S8.b.9.0 (36 degrees) with details from No. 1 and 4 Sects. (on 2.5.16) 9.30 pm to 1 am.*
*Large carrying parties were employed throughout the night (96 men) from SOUCHEZ CORNER to FRONT LINE and advanced SUPPORT LINES forming engineering dumps for special work in connection with the firing of mines and the consolidation of craters.*
*No 4 Sections - was relieved by No. 2 after night work of the 2nd inst.*
*Lieut Frachi proceeded on leave 3.30 pm 2.5.16.*

Opposite page: Sketch taken from the Royal Engineers War Diary showing the three craters and their defensive works.

# WAR DIARY
## or
## INTELLIGENCE SUMMARY

*(Erase heading not required.)*

| Date | Hour | Summary of Events and Information | Remarks and references to Appendices |
|---|---|---|---|
| 8.5.16 | | Craters here keys were constructed on the inner lips of craters surmounted by communication trenches to the FRONT LINE of TANCHOT and Sap 3. Covering parties were established on North lip of LOVE, on inner lip of MOMBt. | |

*Villers au Bois 3.5.1916*

*In accordance with operational orders to the effect that mines would be exploded in RIGHT SECTOR, Capt Love proceeded at 2.30 pm from VILLERS to advanced H.Q. in time to take command of R.E. operations.*

*No 1 Sect, Lieut Knuth, No 2 Sect, Lieut Douglas stood by at CABARET ROUGE. No 3 Sect marching from VILLERS to undertake in conjunction with No 1, the work of consolidation of craters. No 1 and 3 Sections with 2nd Lieut's Culliford and Knuth moved forward to advanced SUPPORT LINE and stood by.*

*At 4.45 pm (3.5.16) 3 mines were fired forming craters now known as KENNEDY (36 degrees) S9c.1.2 - LOVE (36 degrees) S15a.1.8 - MOMBER (36 degrees) S15a.1.7. An intense bombardment followed immediately after the mines were fired.*

*At 6.45 pm Captain Love ordered reconnaissance to be carried out and reports submitted of all three craters.*

*2nd Lieut Culliford taking LOVE and MOMBER and 2nd Lieut Knuth taking KENNEDY. This being carried out during night by following parties:-*

*No 1 2nd Lieut Culliford with No 3 Sect R.E. - 3 officers with 40 O/Rs R.W.F. + 50 infantry*
*(carrying)*
*No 2 2nd Lieut Knuth with No 1 Sect R.E.     "     "     "     "     "     "*

*Each party working with covering party of 10 bombers from 21st Battalion of infantry plus Lewis gun detachment.*

*Seven fire bays were constructed on the new lips of craters connected by communications trenches to the FRONT LINE at TANCHOT and Sap 3.*

*Bombing posts were established on north side of LOVE, on rear lip of MOMBER and on the north of KENNEDY. Thus consolidating and putting in a state of defence almost the entire near lips of the 3 craters. Peep holes were made as shown in sketch.*

*Sergt Lacy and details of No 2 Sect working on the right and Corp Bellis on the left with the flanks of LOVE - MOMBER, Lance Corp Mclean on the left of KENNEDY.*

*During the work the parties were subject to intermittent attacks from bombers, rifle grenades and machine gun fire. The following casualties were sustained during the undertaking.*

*Killed 1068 L/c SEARLE A.J. - R.E. No 1 Sect*
*1123 Sap STOUT G.R. - R.E. No 1 Sect*
*2063 Pte BENNETT F.B. attached R.A.M.C.*

*Wounded: 1018 2nd Corp WOODLANDER R. R.E. No. 2 Sect.*

Frederick was buried in Cabaret-Rouge British Cemetery, Souchez, and is commemorated on the West Mersea War Memorial.

His family left Mersea Island in 1929 and moved to Herne Bay in Kent.

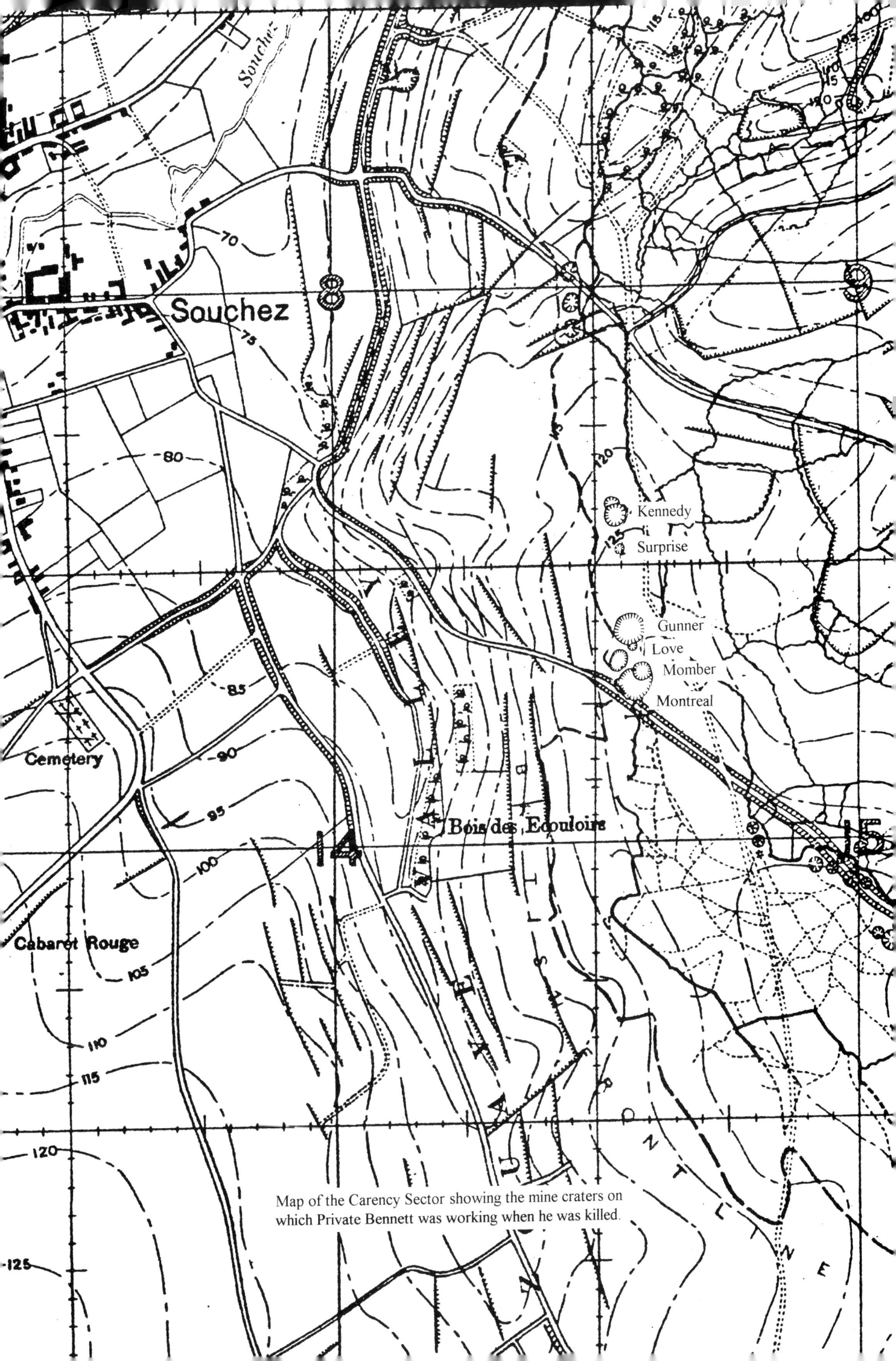

Map of the Carency Sector showing the mine craters on which Private Bennett was working when he was killed.

**Sources**
*Commonwealth War Graves Commission*
*1891 Census*
*2nd/6th London Field Ambulance Corp War Diary, PRO, Kew, Ref No WO95/3029*
*2nd/3rd London Field Company, Royal Engineers War Diary, Royal Engineers Museum, Chatham.*

The grave of Private Frederick Beckett Bennett in
Cabaret-Rouge British Cemetery, Souchez.

**SURNAME: Cook**

CHRISTIAN NAME(S): Rowland

AGE: Unknown

RECRUITMENT OFFICE: Colchester

SERVICE NO: 12803        RANK: Private

SERVICE/REGIMENT: 9th Battalion, Essex Regiment

DECORATIONS EARNED: 1914/1915 Star

DATE KILLED/DIED: 3rd July, 1916    LOCATION: France

LOCATION OF GRAVE: Ovillers Military Cemetery

---

**BACKGROUND AND SERVICE HISTORY:**

Rowland Cook was born on Mersea Island and nothing is currently known of his early life or occupation. On 26th December, 1913, he took part in the Island's Boxing Day running races and took first place in the men's race.

He was one of many men from the Island who responded to Kitchener's call to arms. He enlisted in Colchester, and by the end of October, 1914, had joined the 1st Battalion, Essex Regiment.

In late August, 1914, the 12th (Eastern) Division was formed as part of the First New Army, mainly recruited from the Eastern and Home Counties. It comprised the 35th Brigade, 36th Brigade, 37th Brigade and Pioneer Battalion (5th Battalion, Northamptonshire Regiment). Part of the 35th Brigade was the 9th Battalion, Essex Regiment, which was formed at Warley, Essex, and to which many new recruits including Rowland Cook were transferred.

The Battalion disembarked in France on 24th August, 1915, and joined the Division in a section of the front line north-west of Armentieres and extending through Ploegsteert Wood.

The Battle of Loos began in late September and the Battalion was in the line when the attack commenced. On September 25th, at 5.55 am, after an hours bombardment, a smoke curtain was created, part of co-ordinated move all along the front in order to conceal the points where the British offensive would be launched. Bundles of wet straw were soaked in paraffin, ignited and then thrown over the parapet, one bundle being used to every yard of trench. This was supplemented by a discharge of smoke bombs. In a few minutes a dense cloud of smoke was produced, rising to a height of 50ft, and then blown by a favourable wind slowly towards the enemy lines. This alarmed the Germans, who at the ringing of a bell opened up with rapid rifle and machine gun fire, to which the Battalion replied. Following a red signal rocket, the enemy artillery opened up with steady fire on the front and support trenches and various other points. Lawrence Farm East was hit by a 15 cm high-explosive shell which set the building on fire and burnt it to the ground, resulting in a number of packs and stores being lost. The enemy guns continued their accurate fire, scoring several direct hits, which caused a number of casualties. Firing died down after 130 shells had been discharged. In the afternoon, the 9th Battalion, Essex Regiment, harried the Germans with short bursts from rifles and machine guns. They responded with another 30 shells in the evening, and then early the next morning with trench howitzers. The Battalion casualties comprised two other ranks killed and 22 wounded.

On September 26th, in the evening, the Battalion were relieved by the 15th Canadians and marched into billets at Westhof Camp, which they reached early on the following morning. In the afternoon of 27th, the Battalion moved to billets in Merris, where the Brigade was concentrated on Corps reserve. The 35th Brigade was conveyed south, by bus, the Battalion resting the night in billets at L'Ecleme. Next day, in wet and cold weather, La Bourse was reached by route march, with a bivouac in a field for two companies and close billets in a girl's school for the rest. On September 30th, the Battalion marched with the Brigade along the Lens Road and took over the second line of defence, north of Loos, from the Scots Guards. Headquarters and 'A' and 'C' Companies were in this second line (Rowland Cook was in 'A' Company), with 'B' and 'D' Companies in the third line at Loos Road redoubt, and Brigade headquarters in a house on the west side of the Loos-la Bassee road.

The Battalion now had its first view of the battlefield before clearing. Bodies of men lay strewn about, with dead horses and limbers smashed to pieces, leaving an indescribable muddle and an odour which would remain in the men's memory. On the night of October 1st, the whole Division marched up to take over the line. The march seemed never-ending with the darkness and confusion making it very difficult. Their destination was finally reached at 2 am.

The first day was spent in clearing the battlefield and improving the trench, which was merely a 3 ft ditch dug in chalk. During the night of October 2nd-3rd, a working party of 400 men under Major Copeman commenced a new trench on the western side of Chalk Pit. Several casualties ensued from the enfilading of the second line trench by shrapnel from a field gun battery south-east of Loos on October 3rd, on the night of which the Battalion went into the front line, with headquarters in an old kiln near the Chalk Pit. One of the casualties of the shelling was Rowland Cook, who was wounded.

Having recovered from his wounds, he rejoined his Regiment and was to lose his life in the Battle of the Somme on July 3rd, 1916. The action in which he was killed is described in the Regimental History (See Private Bert Cundy's biography). He was buried in Ovillers Military Cemetery, and is commemorated on the West Mersea War Memorial

**Sources**
*Essex Regiment Museum*
*Kitcheners Army by Ray Westlake, Nutshell Publishing Co. Ltd*
*Essex Units in the War 1914-1919 by J.W. Burrows*
*Commonwealth War Graves Commission*
*9th Battalion, Essex Regiment War Diary, PRO, Kew, Ref no: WO95/1851*

Standing: Rowland (Dick) Cook, Bert Wright
Sitting: Unidentified, Horace Whiting
*(Ron Green Collection).*

The grave of Private Rowland Cook in Ovillers Military Cemetery.

**SURNAME: Cundy**

CHRISTIAN NAME(S): Bertie

AGE: 26

RECRUITMENT OFFICE: Colchester

SERVICE NO: 12801                    RANK: Private

SERVICE/REGIMENT: 9th Battalion, Essex Regiment

DECORATIONS EARNED: Military Medal, 1914/1915 Star

DATE KILLED/DIED: Died of wounds 5th July, 1916   LOCATION: Ovillers, France

LOCATION OF GRAVE: Boulogne Eastern Cemetery Part II

---

**BACKGROUND AND SERVICE HISTORY:**

Bertie Cundy was born in West Mersea in 1890, the son of Charles John and Eliza Harriet Cundy. He was baptised on 14th September, 1890. He had three sisters and two brothers. Before the outbreak of war, he lived with his mother in The Lane, his father having died. He was a member of the church choir. On 10th May, 1913, it was reported that Bert Cundy, a labourer, was summoned for cycling without a light at West Mersea on 27th April, 1913. Sergeant Putman said the defendant was riding without a light just behind another cyclist who had a light. He was ordered to pay costs of four shillings.

Like many other Mersea men, he responded to Kitchener's call for volunteers in September 1914, and enlisted in Colchester, joining the 1st Battalion, Essex Regiment, transferring on 15th January, 1915 to the 9th Battalion, Essex Regiment, which trained at Reed Hall in Colchester.

As member of 'A' Company, he was posted overseas on 24th August, 1915. On the 18th April, 1916, while in the Loos area, the enemy sent bombing parties against 'A' Company working on saps (extensions out into No Man's Land from the main trench). They were quickly dispersed by Corporal Digby and his party which included Bertie Cundy who was decorated for his part in the incident. The *London Gazette* of 2nd June lists him as being awarded the Military Medal for repulsing a night German raid, an extract from the citation reading *'Private Cundy managed almost single-handed on a very wet night to drive a number of Germans back, and his gallant and successful action was favourably reported by his Officer Commanding'*. This action earned him the nickname of 'Bomber' Cundy in the local press.

Private Bertie Cundy, seen here on the right of the photograph

With his fellow soldiers from Mersea, Rowland Cook and Albert Hewes, he marched with his Battalion to occupy the line opposite Ovillers on the Somme on 2nd July, 1916. On the night of 3rd July, they took up their positions for the assault to come.

This part of the Battle of the Somme is described in the Regimental History as follows:

*'The march of the Battalion'* wrote a member of the 9th, *' to take up position for the first Somme battle will ever be remembered by those engaged. Countless gun flashes lit the darkness of the night; they seemed endless and as one approached the line, the noise was deafening. After what appeared to be endless marching, we reached the trenches in front of Ovillers. They were of hard chalk and with the bad weather not at all easy to negotiate without trench boards. In moving to positions for attack, the congestion in the trenches was awful and mortally wounded men could not be moved. Zero hour arrived when it was raining, visibility was poor, with bitter retaliation by way of machine gun fire from the enemy'.*

At 2.15 am, everything was ready, when a message was received that zero hour had been changed to 3.7 am. The attack took place promptly to time after a heavy bombardment and at 3.20 am the leading lines of the Battalion followed in support. Considerable difficulty had been experienced in reaching the front line and the last of the Berkshires and Suffolks had disappeared into the darkness before the first Company had leapt the parapet in support. The direction of the attack was in a quarter left direction from the front line. Direction was not well maintained, chiefly because the objectives were indistinguishable and the jumping off

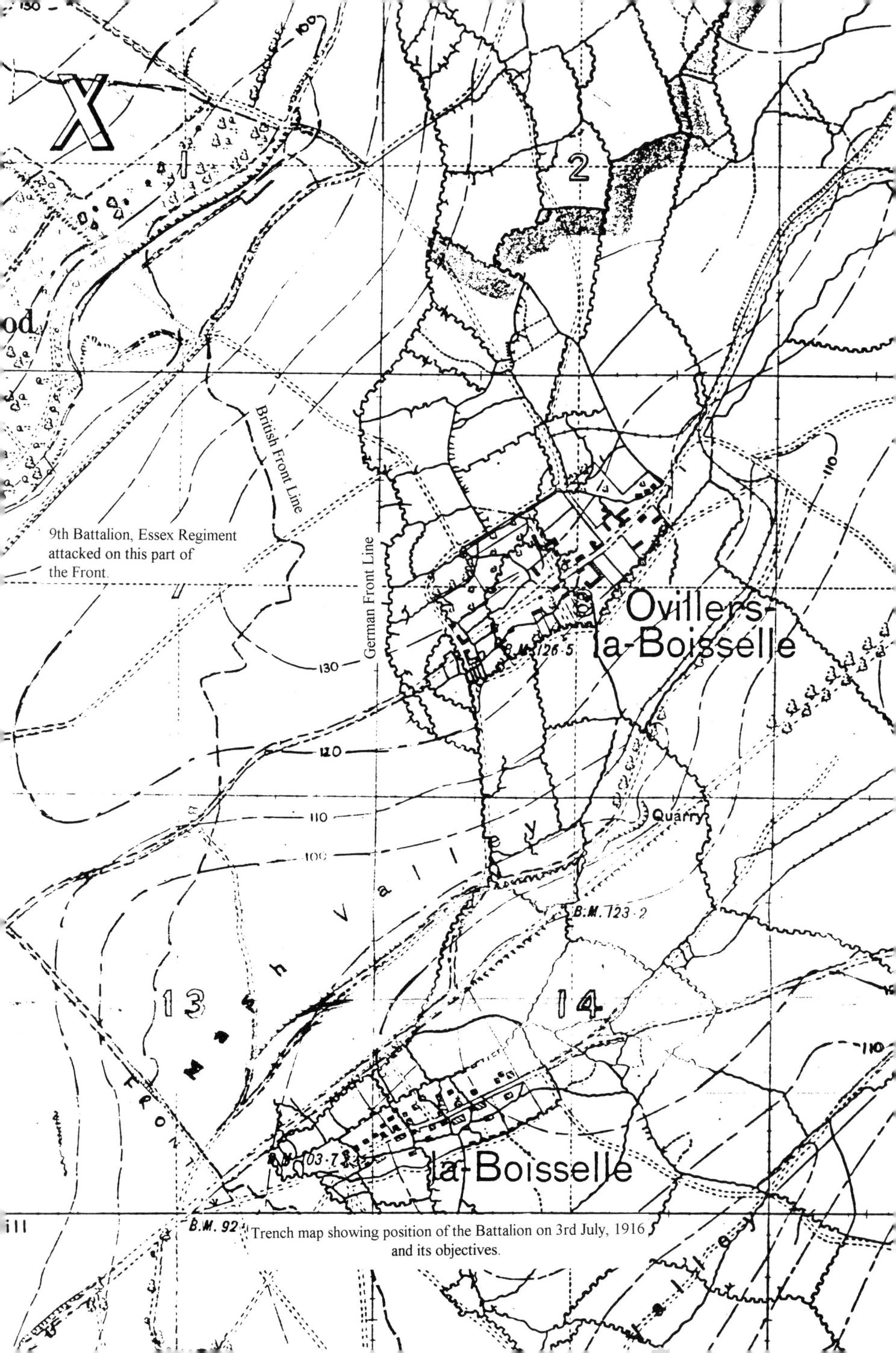

Trench map showing position of the Battalion on 3rd July, 1916 and its objectives.

places were not square to the enemy line. This difficulty notwithstanding, however, the leading battalions overran the enemy's front and support lines and parties entered Ovillers, together with men of the 9th Essex who had suffered severely whilst crossing the open ground due to machine gun fire from the flanks and the village, and the waves became a series of detached parties under either an officer or N.C.O.

'A' (including the men from Mersea), 'D' and three platoons of 'B' Company had advanced in platoon waves, but the lines were not always in touch, the initial cause being the difficulty of getting the companies deployed along the front trench so as to move simultaneously owing to their damaged condition and the number of wounded and other details making their way back by the communication trenches up which the 9th Essex had groped their way. Two platoons of 'B' Company got over the German front line and were then held up by a high command Circular Trench which overlooked the ground which had been won. The remainder of 'B' Company and 'A' Company almost reached the German line and were then held up by machine gun fire from Circular Trench, which had stopped the advance of the other portion of 'B' Company. 'D' Company also made progress on the left, but they too were stopped by the machine guns of Circular Trench, the wire of which had been renewed after the British bombardment had ceased. Survivors from the enemy front line had sought shelter in this miniature fortress when the Brigade advanced and from that position delivered the bombing attacks which were to have a potent effect in halting the Brigade's offensive. The first to feel the influence of this counter attack were the two platoons of 'B' Company, who were forced back, sadly depleted, to the German front line. Battalion headquarters had in the meantime moved to the junction of St Vincent Street and Border Street, and no information having come to hand, Lieutenant Colonel Lewes and the Adjutant went forward to ascertain the situation. Parties could be seen coming back on the right of the 37th Brigade, which had attacked with the 35th Brigade and other parties later sought to return on the right flank of the Brigade. A small detachment of the Essex Regiment, about fifty men, started digging in on a small ridge or bank which overlooked the enemy's first line and extra tools for that purpose were sent up by the 7th Battalion, Norfolk Regiment. Information was very difficult to obtain and there was no news of the exact whereabouts of the Berkshires and the Suffolks. At about 4.00 am the attack came to a standstill and the survivors withdrew again to the front line, where the 7th Battalion Norfolk Regiment took over, allowing the Essex Regiment to reorganise in Ribble Street.

Bertie Cundy was fatally wounded, Rowland Cook was killed, and Albert Hewes was shot in the eye*. The stretcher bearers got Bertie out but he died of his wounds on 5th July, 1916.

When the news of his death reached Mersea, it was reported that during a Sunday evening service the Vicar, Reverend C. Pierrepoint Edwards, made a touching reference to the death of this young soldier, who was one of the first to respond to the call for recruits. The Vicar, who was wearing his own Military Cross, quoted him as a noble example- *'one who had given his all. Greater love hath no man than this, that he lay down his life for his friends'*

He is buried in Boulogne Eastern Cemetery, Part II, and is commemorated on the West Mersea War Memorial.

---

*Albert Hewes was evacuated back to England to the London General Hospital, where he recovered to survive the war.

**Sources**

*Commonwealth War Graves Commission*
*Essex Regiment Museum*
*Essex County Standard*
*Essex County Telegraph*
*Doug Rowe*
*Essex Units in the War 1914-1919 by J.W. Burrows*

The grave of Private Bertie Cundy in
Boulogne Eastern Cemetery, Part II.

**SURNAME:** Wade

CHRISTIAN NAME(S): Arthur

AGE: 21

RECRUITMENT OFFICE:

SERVICE NO: 19576                    RANK: Private

SERVICE/REGIMENT: 6th Battalion, Bedfordshire Regiment

DECORATIONS EARNED: 1914/15 Star, War Medal, Victory Medal

DATE KILLED/DIED: 9th July, 1916          LOCATION: France

LOCATION OF GRAVE: Gordon Dump Cemetery, Ovillers - la Boisselle

---

**BACKGROUND AND SERVICE HISTORY:**

Arthur Wade was born on 21st June, 1895, the son of Arthur William and Elizabeth Ann Wade of Birch. He had one brother and six sisters.

He attended Birch School and became a member of the church choir. On leaving school, he gained employment at Layer Marney Tower as a gardener.

In 1914 he was the first man from Birch to join the army when he volunteered and enlisted at Colchester, joining the 6th Battalion, Bedfordshire Regiment. He embarked with the Battalion to France on 30th July, 1915, sailing on the *Empress Queen* arriving at Le Havre the next day.

During June 1916, he returned to Birch, on leave to celebrate his 21st birthday, and left with the foreboding that he would never come home again.

On 7th July he was with the Battalion, moving to the Front on the Somme. The Battalion War Diary describes that they moved to the Usna-Tara line east of Albert, and then on the 8th July they went into the front line trenches, forming a defensive flank in the event of a hostile attack from Contalmaison. On the next day, the Battalion suffered the following casualties, fourteen killed and one missing, with five officers and seventy other ranks wounded.

Arthur Wade was one of those killed and his obituary appeared in the *Birch, Layer Breton, and Layer Marney Parish Magazine*.

*We have to announce, with great sorrow, that Private Arthur Wade, 6th Bedfordshire Regiment was killed in action on the night of July 9th. He had the distinction of being the first man in this Parish to join the Army, immediately after the outbreak of the War, and now he has won the supreme honour of dying for his King and Country. Arthur Wade was a boy of*

(4 27 1) W 8687—1338 250,000 11/14 H W V 21/796

Army Form B. 104—82.

No. 19546 BEDFORDS
(If replying, please quote above No.)

Record Office,

_____ Station,

_____, 191_

Madam,

It is my painful duty to inform you that a report has this day been received from the War Office notifying the death of

(No.) 19546 (Rank) Private

(Name) A. Wade (Regiment) 6th

BEDFORDS which occurred in the Field on the 9th

of July 1916, and I am to express to you the sympathy and regret of the Army Council at your loss. The cause of death was

Killed in Action

If any articles of private property left by the deceased are found, they will be forwarded to this Office, but some time will probably elapse before their receipt, and when received they cannot be disposed of until authority is received from the War Office.

Application regarding the disposal of any such personal effects, or of any amount that may eventually be found to be due to the late soldier's estate, should be addressed to "The Secretary, War Office, London, S.W.," and marked outside "Effects."

I am,
Madam,
Your obedient Servant,

Mrs Wade
Layer Breton
Nr Kelvedon
Essex

F. P. Winter, Captain
For Officer in charge of Records,
NO. 9 DISTRICT.

The official notice from the War Office informing Mrs Wade of hers son's death.

*quiet, steadfast character and high principles-the sort of boy who would always go straight for the path of duty without any fuss and without any waste of words. We are proud of his example, and his name will always be honoured in this Parish with others who have died in the Service of their Country. His Company Officer in a very kind letter, written on the battlefield to Mrs Wade, says of him,*

*'His loss is very keenly felt throughout the whole Company, as he was a great favourite with them all. I hope it will comfort you to know that he died bravely, as so many other good soldiers have already done'.*

He was buried in Gordon Dump Cemetery on the Somme. Later in the war, his parents moved to West Mersea and at their request his name was inscribed on the West Mersea War Memorial.

**Sources**

*Commonwealth War Graves Commission*
*Mrs Ethel Carter, Mrs Ann Wiles (Arthur Wade's sisters)*
*Birch, Layer Breton and Layer Marney Parish Magazine*
*6th Battalion, Bedfordshire Regiment War Diary, PRO, Kew, Ref no: WO95/2537*

Below: The area around Contalmaison on the Somme.

Private Arthur Wade (sitting).

The grave of Private Arthur Wade in Gordon Dump Cemetery on the Somme.

**SURNAME:** Hewes

CHRISTIAN NAME(S): George Walter

AGE: 20

RECRUITMENT OFFICE: Enlisted in Australia

SERVICE NO: 515          RANK: Sergeant

SERVICE/REGIMENT: 54th Battalion, 1st Infantry Brigade, Australian Imperial Force

DECORATIONS EARNED: 1914/15 Star, British War Medal, Victory Medal

DATE KILLED/DIED: 20th July, 1916     LOCATION: France

MEMORIAL IF NO KNOWN GRAVE: Villers-Bretonneux Memorial, The Somme

---

**BACKGROUND AND SERVICE HISTORY:**

George Walter Hewes was born in September, 1893, the son of Harry George 'Hoppy' and Maria Hewes of Walmer Cottage, St Peter's Road, West Mersea. He was baptised on 25th March, 1894.

He attended West Mersea school and after leaving was employed by the Blackwater Oyster Fishery Company.

In 1914 he was an Able Seaman in the Royal Naval Reserve. When war broke out, he was on a merchant ship which had docked in Australia. He volunteered immediately and on 18th August enlisted in the Australian Imperial Force joining 'B' Company, 2nd Battalion, 1st Infantry Brigade.

On 18th October, 1914, he embarked from Sydney, sailing on HMAT *Suffolk* to Alexandria in Egypt, where he arrived on 8th December, 1914.

On 5th April, 1915, the Battalion left Alexandria as part of the Mediterranean Expeditionary Force on HMT *Derfflinger*, and on 25th April, 1915, they took part in the landings on the Gallipoli peninsula. Conditions on the peninsula were not good, due particularly to the terrain, heat, flies, and lack of water, and George was admitted to the 3rd Ambulance Unit on 22nd May with impetigo.

He returned to his unit on 29th May and a letter from Edwin Chatters, a Mersea Naval seaman, describes meeting him on the beaches.

*'I saw Walter Hewes (son of Mr George Hewes, chauffeur at the White Hart, West Mersea) on shore, he was alright when I left him the other day. We had a good old yarn with each other several evenings about old times such as the Dabchick Races at Mersea. We were talking one afternoon when suddenly a big shrapnel shell burst about ten yards from us, but*

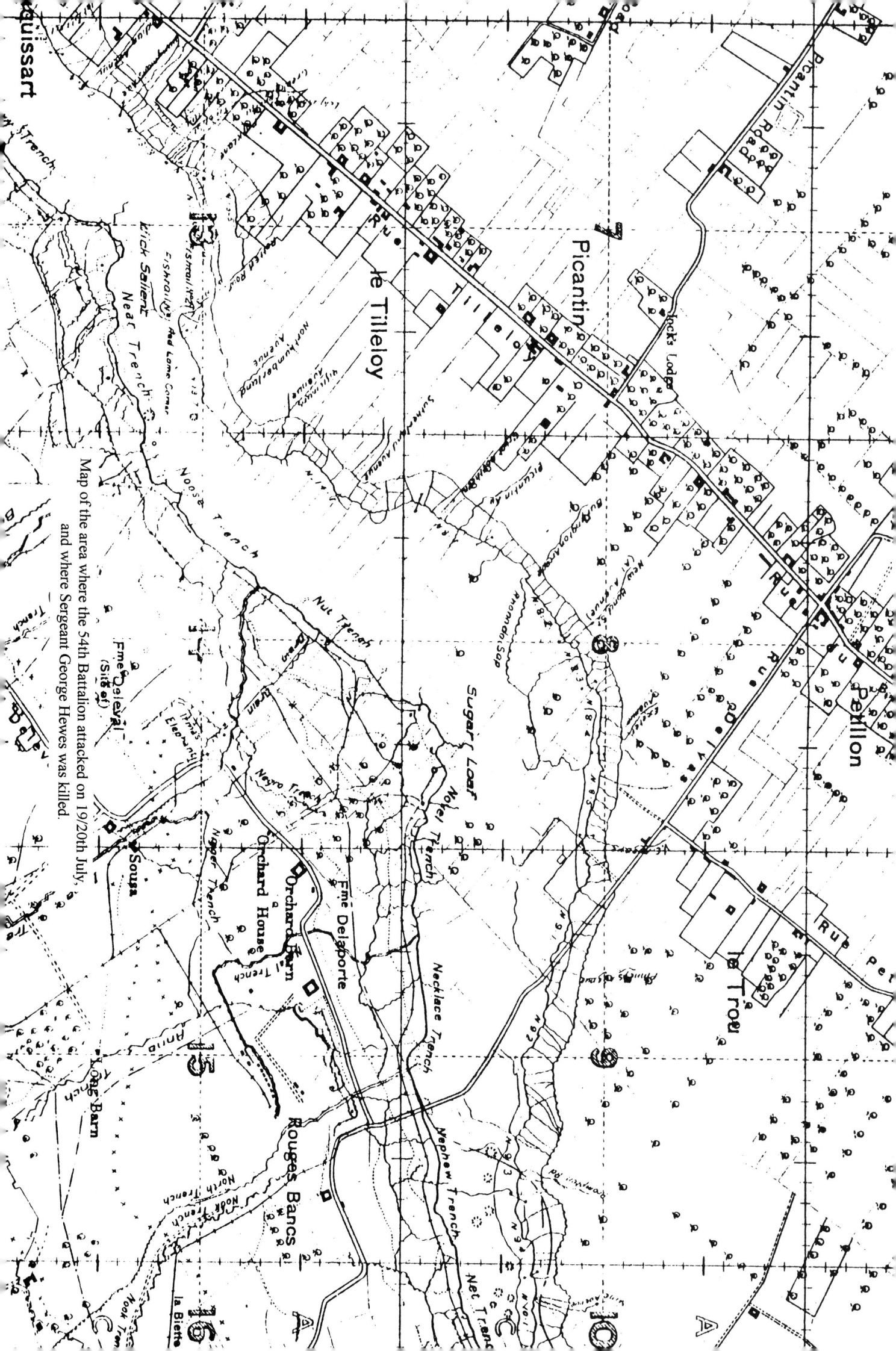

Map of the area where the 54th Battalion attacked on 19/20th July, and where Sergeant George Hewes was killed.

*we managed to swing clear alright. Bullets were whistling over our heads like rain, but it was a bit of a change after being on board so long'.*

In July he caught influenza, which was serious enough, for him to be evacuated and sent to hospital in Alexandria. He did not recover sufficiently for him to rejoin his unit at Gallipoli until 12th October.

On 28th November he was promoted to Lance Corporal and on 28th December, 1915, he took part in the general evacuation of the peninsula, leaving on the *Huntsgreen*, and returned to Alexandria.

On 18th January, 1916, he was promoted to Corporal and was transferred to 54th Battalion, Australian Imperial Force, where further promotion followed when he became a Sergeant on 1st March, 1916.

The Battalion were to become part of the British Expeditionary Force and they embarked from Alexandria on the HMS *Caledonian* on 19th June, 1916, arriving at Marseilles on 29th June. They then travelled by train, the length of France to join the British Forces on the Western Front.

After a period of training and familiarisation, the Battalion moved to the Front in the area of Aubers Ridge, as described in the Battalion War Diary.

*11/7/16 Sailly - The Battalion moved from billets in Sailly to a section of the trenches in Fleurbaix area. One company taking over a portion of the 2nd line, one company at Elbow Farm and the remaining two companies with Battalion H. Q. occupied billets in Fleurbaix, these two companies finding all guards, fatigues etc, the health and spirits of the troops is good.*
*14/7/16 - The Battalion was withdrawn from the trenches and moved into new billets at Bac St Maur commencing at 22.00 in the following order C,D,A, and B companies, the Battalion being relieved by the Shropshire Light Infantry.*
*17/7/16 - The Battalion moved from Bac St Maur to front line trenches with a view to developing an attack - Casualties: killed 1 Officer, wounded 5 other ranks.*
*18/7/16 - The Battalion was relieved in the front line trenches by the 53rd Bn and returned to billets in Bac St Maur.*
*19/7/16-20/7/16 - The Battalion moved from Bac St Maur at 2 pm to front line trenches. The Battalion attacked the enemy trenches at 5.50 pm, and occupied his front line trenches. At about 6 pm the Battalion withdrew from its new position and returned to billets at Bac St Maur at 7.30 am (20/7/16). Our casualties were killed 3 officers, 70 other ranks, wounded 11 officers, 277 other ranks, missing 4 officers and 169 other ranks.* \*

The Germans had taken reinforcements for the continuing Battle of the Somme from the Aubers Ridge Front. To counter this the British concentrated a limited attack at Fromelles, using the 61st (South Midland) British Division and the 5th Australian Division which included the 54th Battalion, on a front stretching for 4 kms. The action came to be known officially as the 'Attack at Fromelles'. The attack commenced with a long allied artillery bombardment, and in the afternoon the troops advanced from the Rue Tilleloy, near Picanton.

---

\*The entry in the War Diary for 19th/20th July, is but a summary of what really happened on those two days. The events were described in detail in an Appendix A which is missing from the duplicate copy of the War Diary held by the PRO. On contacting the Australian National Archives, it was discovered that it was also missing from their original.

Records due exist from the 54th Battalion's sister Battalion, the 53rd. They both advanced into the attack together and the latters' War Diary describes the action.

*19th July*
*11.00: Heavy bombardment by our guns on enemies' trenches and equally heavy bombardment by enemy on our trenches and communications.*
*16.00: 54th Battalion took over again the left 300 yds of our trenches and Battalion closed in on its original front of 300 yds with right on River Laies.*
*17.43: Battalion moved to attack in four waves.* (Included in the fourth wave was the Battalion HQ). *First wave moved out from our trenches, followed at 100 yds distance by second wave - lay down near German wire till 6 pm, then charged followed third and fourth waves. Took German first and second line trenches and pushed on parties about 200 yds further on to hold back enemies' bombers who were counter attacking on front and right flank, while the remainder proceeded to consolidate the position on the German 1st and 2nd line trench.* (It was reported that the captured German trench system was surprisingly inadequate with most support areas flooded). *Touch was obtained with the 54th Battalion on our left but none could be found on our right.*
*19/20th July*
*The line was held throughout the night against violent attacks, until orders were received (about 9 am) from O.C. 14th Brigade to retire from position won - our right flank being in the air, enemy had already turned it and re-established themselves in their 1st line trenches in rear of our right.*
*9.30: Retired though with very heavy loss. Covered by fire from own front line.*

The Germans fought against the withdrawal and 470 Australians and 51 British were taken prisoner. The 61st Division had lost over 1,000 officers and men out of 3,410 that took part and the 5th Australian Division had lost over 5,000 officers and men. One of these was George Walter Hewes who was reported missing and his body was never recovered. He is commemorated on the Villers-Bretonneux Memorial on the Somme, and on the West Mersea War Memorial.

**Sources**

*Commonwealth War Graves Commission*
*Essex County Standard*
*Mr Minter*
*Mr Owen Fletcher*
*Australian Archives*
*54th Battalion, Australian Imperial Force War Diary, PRO, Kew, Ref no: WO95/3629*
*53rd Battalion, Australian Imperial Force War Diary, PRO, Kew, Ref no: WO95/3628*

Sergeant George Walter Hewes's name inscribed on the Villers-Bretonneux Memorial on the Somme. The Memorial is dedicated to the Australian soldiers who fought in France and Belgium, to their dead, and especially those with no known grave.

23rd Battalion, Royal Fusiliers (Sportsmen's Battalion) at Greyfriars Hall, Hornchurch.

**SURNAME: Cottrell**

CHRISTIAN NAME(S): Harry James

AGE: Unknown

RECRUITMENT OFFICE: Hornchurch

SERVICE NO: SPTS/1594     RANK: Private

SERVICE/REGIMENT: 23rd (Sportsman's) Battalion Royal Fusiliers

DECORATIONS EARNED: 1914/15 Star, War Medal, Victory Medal

DATE KILLED/DIED: 27th July, 1916     LOCATION: France

MEMORIAL IF NO KNOWN GRAVE: Thiepval Memorial, The Somme

---

**BACKGROUND AND SERVICE HISTORY:**

Harry James Cottrell was born in Reading, his parents later moving to live on Mersea Island. He enlisted at Hornchurch, joining the 23rd (Sportsman's) Battalion, Royal Fusiliers. Initial training was at Greyfriars Hall, Hornchurch. He landed in France with his Battalion on 17th November, 1915.

On 26th July, 1916, the Battalion moved up to Delville Wood and occupied South St. and the front line facing north from Campbell St. westwards. The next day as part of 99 Brigade, it took part in an attack on Delville Wood on the Somme battle front. The attack was described in detail by the Battalion War Diary:

*5.10 am - Artillery bombardment by Division on our left commenced.*
*6.10 am - Our Artillery barrage commenced. Our first wave B & D Companies formed up in front of existing trenches.*
*7.10 am - Artillery barrage lifted to lines marked Red in annexed Map and N of it. Our first wave assaulted the Princes St. line and took it without much resistance. Meanwhile our second wave, A & C Companies occupied the line vacated by the first wave.*
*7.19 am - Message was received from officer commanding B Coy. that Waterford (i.e. Princes St. line) was reached and consolidation was proceeding.*
*7.40 am - Barrage lifted and second wave passed through the first to line marked Red on Map.*
*8.10 am - Barrage lifted to line marked Blue and second wave advanced to assault final objective, line marked green and clear the wood.*
*8.30 am - Advance was reported to be held up by heavy machine gun fire from Redoubt on our left. 2 Lewis guns were sent up and these in conjunction with Bombers captured the Redoubt putting 2 machine guns out of action and turning a third on the retreating enemy.*
*9.40 am - Second wave was reported at final objective and consolidation was proceeding.*
*11.00 am - Report was received from 1st K.R.R.C. that their right was being bombed in and B Company Bombers and a Lewis gun were sent over to assist.*

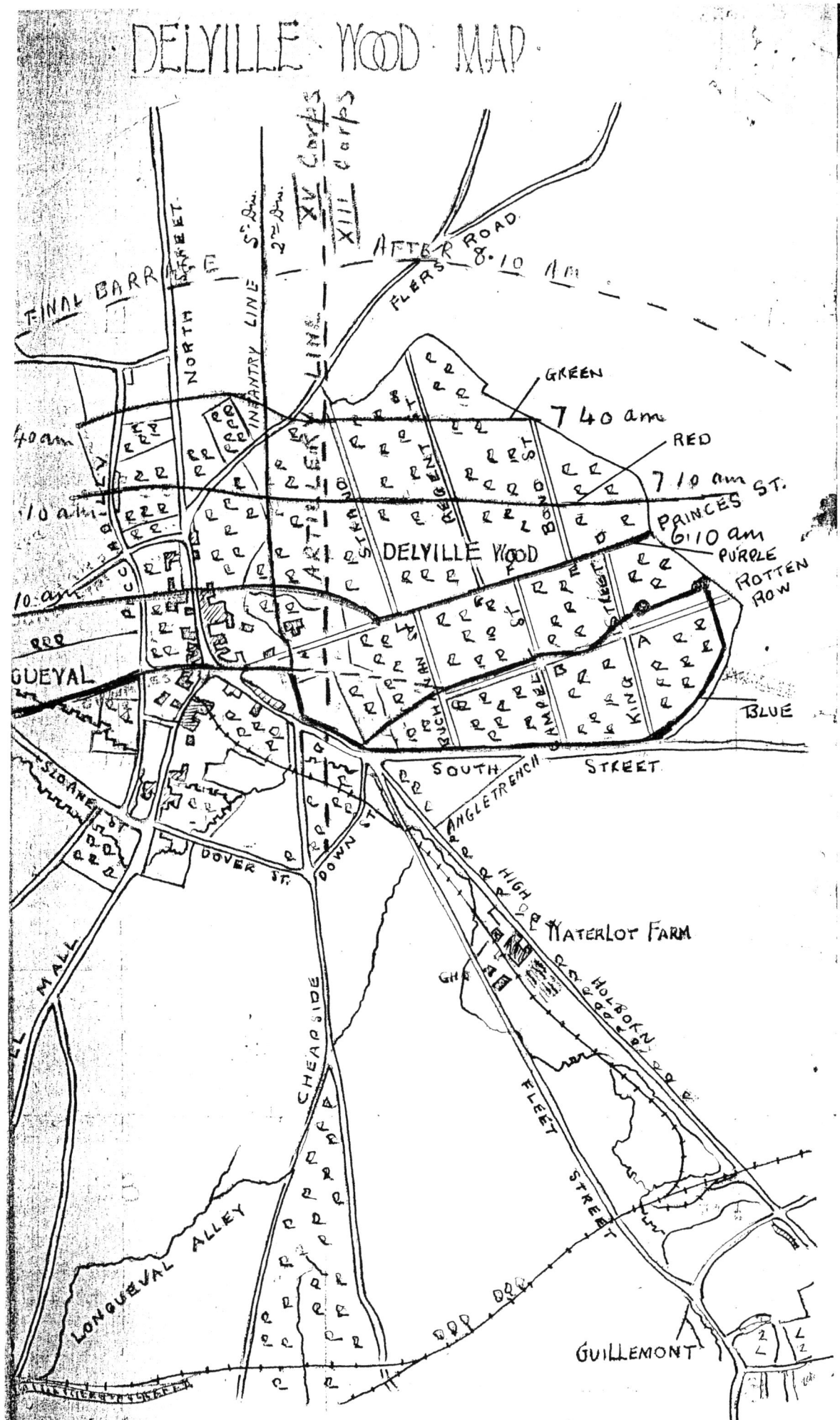

The map referred to in the Battalion War Diary account of the attack on Delville Wood by the 23rd Battalion, Royal Fusiliers.

*3.30 pm - Report of a strong counter attack was received from the Battalion on our right (1st.R.R.C.) and this was successfully dealt with by them assisted by our bombers.*

*7.00 pm - 1st South Staffords relieved our companies and these returned to the positions occupied before the attack. From 11.00 am, the enemy artillery heavily bombarded the whole of the wood until midnight and this bombardment was responsible for the bulk of our casualties.*

*We captured 6 machine guns.*

*Over 160 prisoners passed through the Cages captured partly by ourselves, partly by 1st K.R.R.C. and a few by the Division on our left.*

*Our casualties were: 5 officers killed, 7 officers wounded, 51 other ranks killed and 225 other ranks wounded.*

One of the victims of the intense enemy bombardment was Private Harry James Cottrell who was reported wounded and missing. His body was never found.

He is commemorated on the Thiepval Memorial, the Somme, France and on the West Mersea War Memorial.

**Sources**
*Commonwealth War Graves Commission*
*Essex Regiment Museum*
*The Somme, The Day-by-Day Account by Chris McCarthy, publish by Arms & Armour Press*
*Mr Hubert Cock*
*23rd Royal Fusiliers War Diary, PRO, Kew, Ref no: WO95/1372*

Private Harry Cottrell's name inscribed on the Thiepval Memorial on the Somme.

**SURNAME: Mason**

CHRISTIAN NAME(S): Stanley

AGE: 22

RECRUITMENT OFFICE: Colchester

SERVICE NO: 2386                    RANK: Private

SERVICE/REGIMENT: 8th Battalion (Cyclists), Essex Regiment, attached to the 7th Battalion, Northamptonshire Regiment.

DECORATIONS EARNED: War Medal, Victory Medal

DATE KILLED/DIED: 2nd September, 1916      LOCATION: France

MEMORIAL IF NO KNOWN GRAVE: Thiepval Memorial, The Somme, France

---

**BACKGROUND AND SERVICE HISTORY:**

Stanley H. Mason was born in 1894, the second son of Alfred Allen and Nellie Mason of Kingsland Road, West Mersea.

He enlisted at Colchester, and joined the 2nd/8th (Cyclist) Battalion, Essex Regiment.

He was sent to France, and during the early Autumn of 1916 was attached to the 7th Battalion Northamptonshire Regiment.

On 2nd September, 1916, the Battalion was in action around Delville Wood on the Somme.

The following extract from the Battalion War Diary describes events:

*'Major T.H.S. Swanton, 1st Bn. East Surrey Regiment joined for duty today and assumed Command.*
  *The Battalion* (7th Battalion, Northamptonshire Regiment) *relieved the 9th Bn Royal Sussex Regt and the 2nd Bn. Leinsters in the front line. C Company returned to SAVOY TRENCH. One Lewis Gun team was knocked out on the way up. No other casualties during relief. D Company accounted for 2 Germans on left of TEA LANE. Night quiet except for our own Artillery that constantly fired short'.*

As no other casualties were recorded, it is assumed that Stanley Mason was one of the Lewis Gun team. His body was never recovered and he is commemorated on the Thiepval Memorial on the Somme, also on the West Mersea War Memorial.

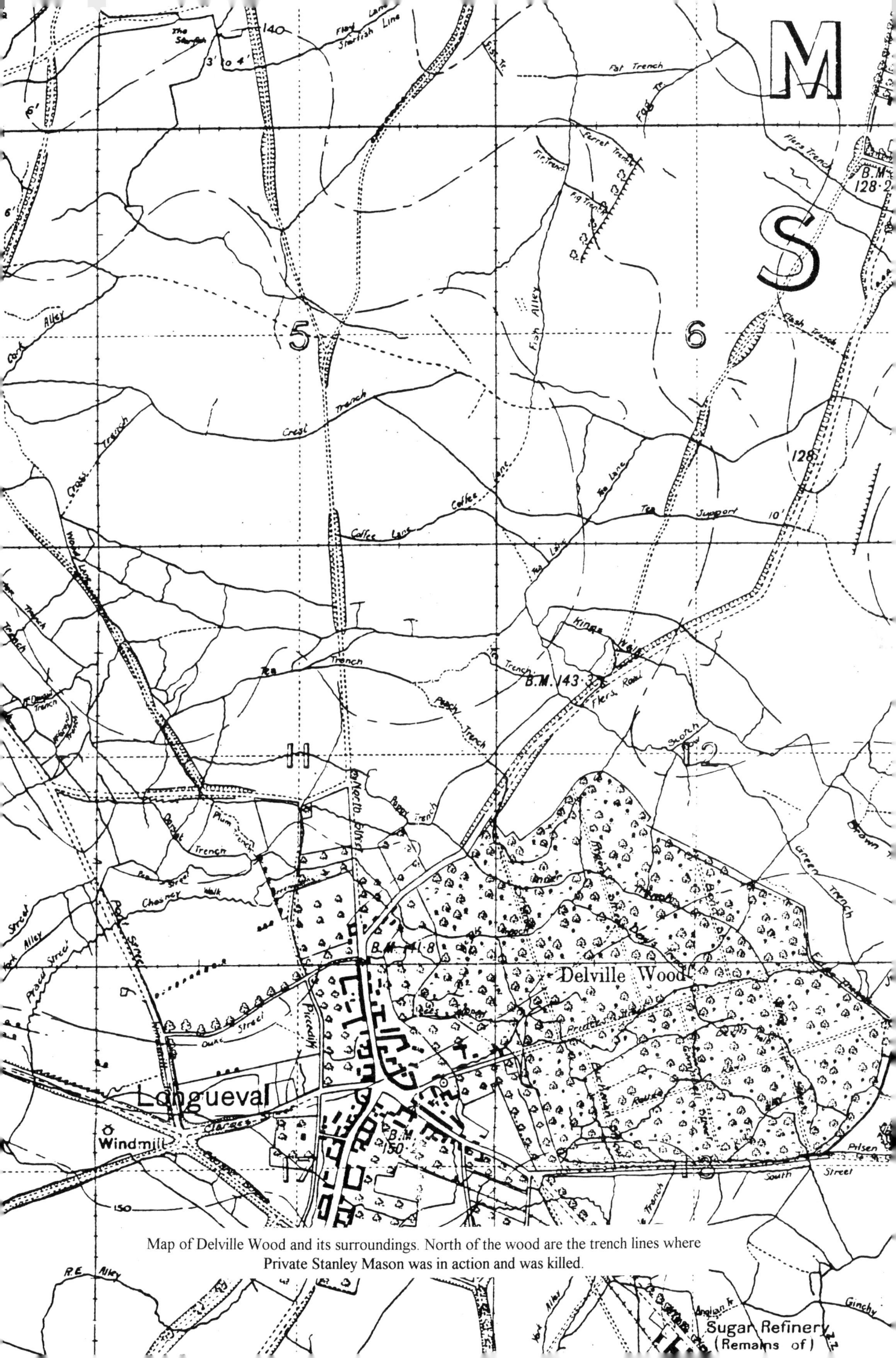

Map of Delville Wood and its surroundings. North of the wood are the trench lines where Private Stanley Mason was in action and was killed.

## Sources

*Commonwealth War Graves Commission*
*Essex County Standard*
*The Museum of the Northamptonshire Regiment*
*Essex Regiment Museum*
*7th Battalion, Northamptonshire Regiment War Diary, PRO, Kew, Ref no: WO95/2218*

Private Stanley Mason's name inscribed on the Thiepval Memorial on the Somme

**SURNAME:** Cutts Avis

CHRISTIAN NAME(S): James Frederick

AGE: Unknown

RECRUITMENT OFFICE: Warley

SERVICE NO: 40074     RANK: Private

SERVICE/REGIMENT: 8th Battalion, Bedfordshire Regiment (Transferred from Essex Territorial Force, Service no: 3827)

DECORATIONS EARNED: War Medal, Victory Medal

DATE KILLED/DIED: 25th September 1916     LOCATION: France

MEMORIAL IF NO KNOWN GRAVE: Thiepval Memorial, The Somme

---

**BACKGROUND AND SERVICE HISTORY:**

James Frederick Cutts Avis was born at West Mersea.

He enlisted at Warley, and initially joined the Essex Territorial Force, but was later transferred to the 8th Battalion, Bedfordshire Regiment.

At the end of July, 1916, the Battalion finished their long tour on the Ypres Salient. The next scene of operations was the Somme, where the Battle of the Somme had been in progress since 1st July.

On 25th September, 1916, the Battalion was involved in the Battle of Morval on the Somme, and the day's action is described in the Battalions War Diary.

*Guillemont - 25th September 1916*
*'Battalion in reserve to 16th Brigade in attack on German lines between MORVAL and LESBOEUFS. Attack commenced at 12.35 pm and Battalion moved up to original front line when second objective had been taken about 2.35 pm. Casualties from enemy barrage very slight. Attack proved successful and many prisoners taken. At night Battalion furnished carrying parties to front line Battalion with ammunition and water. 6 Platoons were detached to 1/London Coy R.E. as working parties in captured trenches, 2 platoons from C coy suffered very heavily from shell fire'*

One of the casualties of this action was James Frederick Cutts Avis, who was probably killed by shell fire and his body was never recovered.

He is commemorated on the Thiepval Memorial on the Somme and on the West Mersea War Memorial.

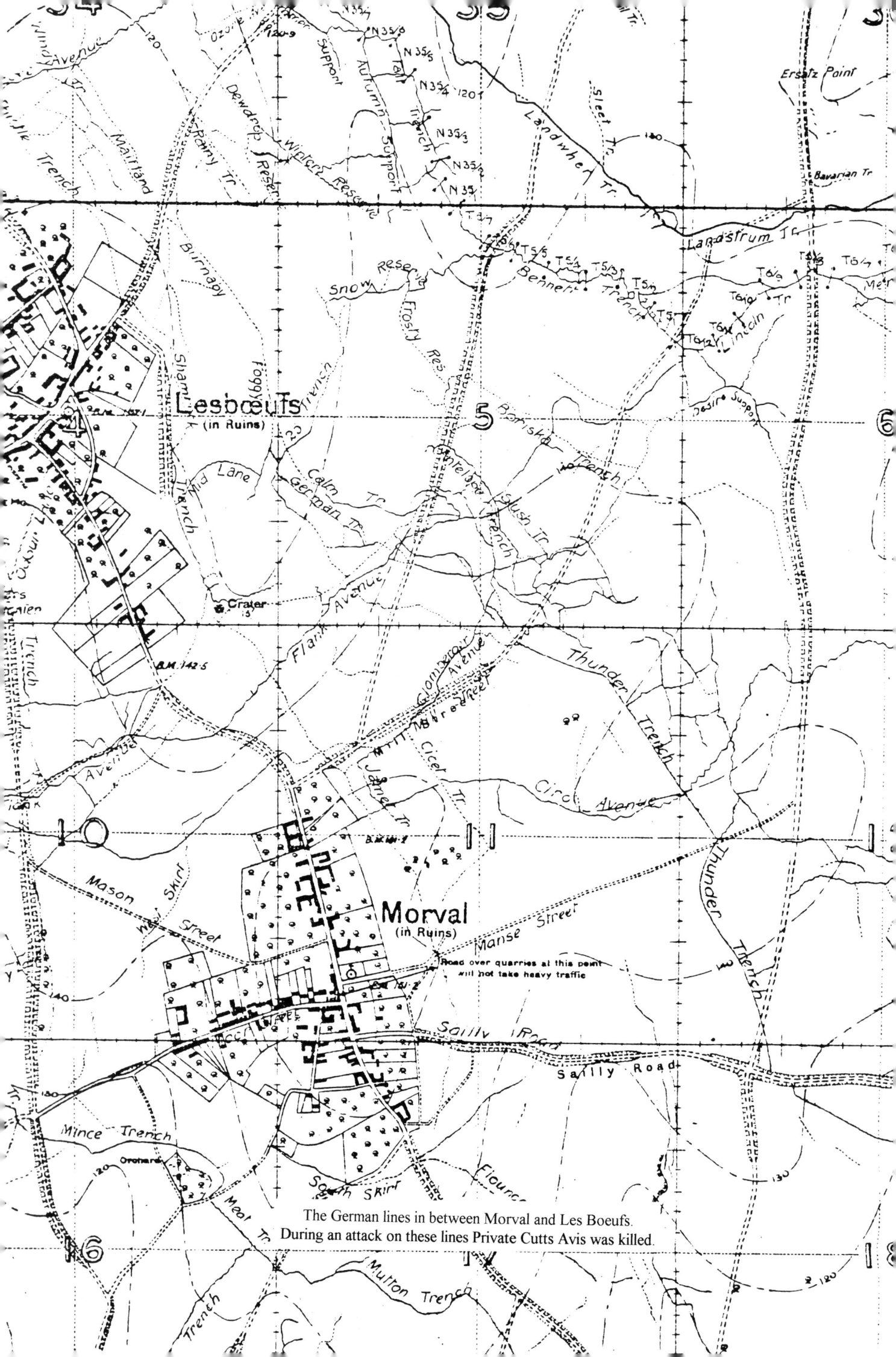

The German lines in between Morval and Les Boeufs. During an attack on these lines Private Cutts Avis was killed.

## Sources

*Commonwealth War Graves Commission*
*8th Battalion, Bedfordshire Regiment War Diary, PRO, Kew, Ref no: WO95/1611*
*Essex Regiment Museum*
*Bedfordshire Record Office*

Private James Frederick Cutts Avis's name inscribed on the Thiepval Memorial on the Somme.

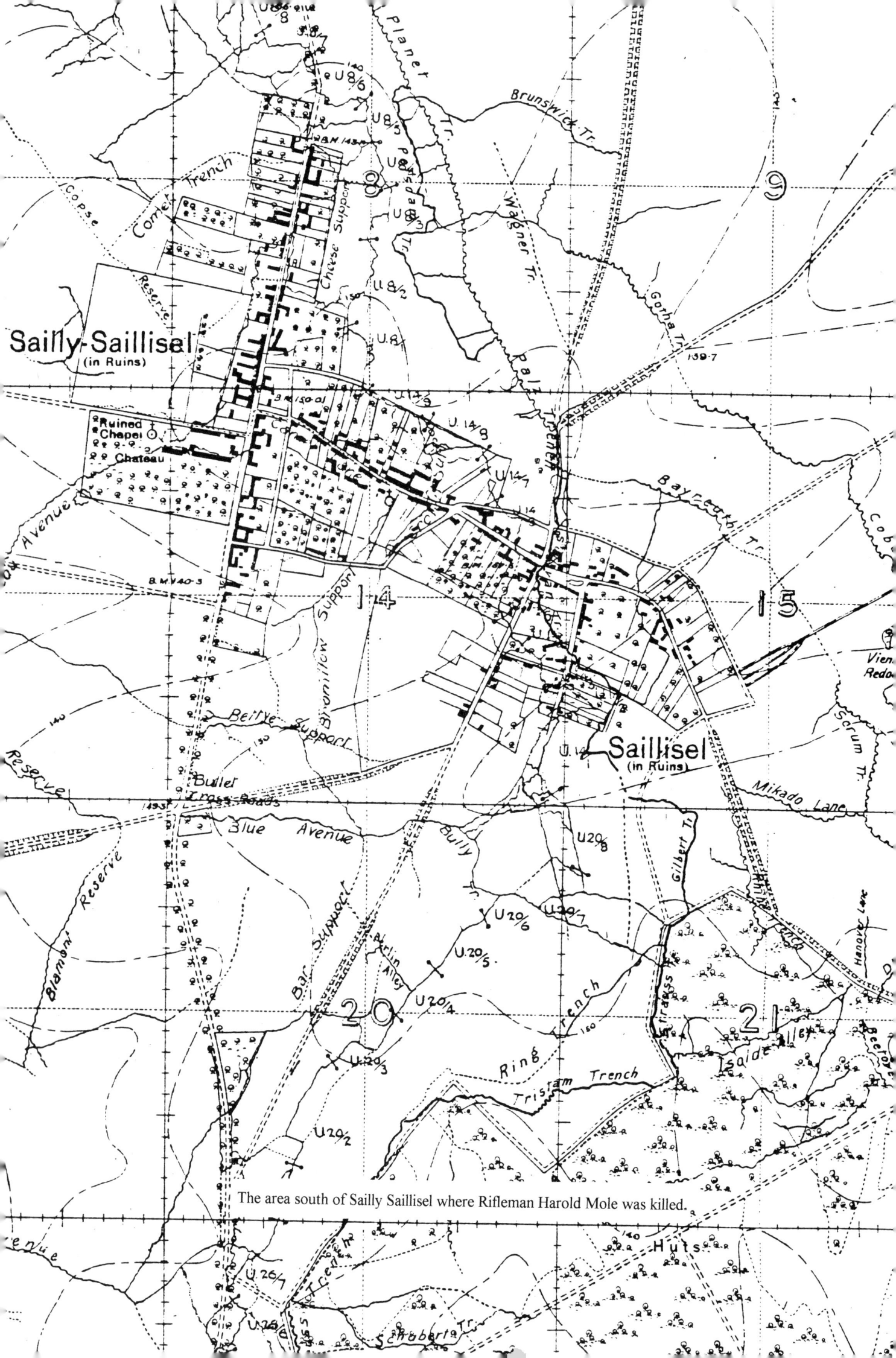

The area south of Sailly Saillisel where Rifleman Harold Mole was killed.

**SURNAME: Mole**

CHRISTIAN NAME(S): Harold

AGE: Unknown

RECRUITMENT OFFICE: Colchester

SERVICE NO: 1097          RANK: Rifleman

SERVICE/REGIMENT: 10th Battalion, Rifle Brigade (The Prince Consort's Own)

DECORATIONS EARNED: 1914 Star, War Medal, Victory Medal

DATE KILLED/DIED: 12th January, 1917     LOCATION: France

LOCATION OF GRAVE: Combles Communal Cemetery Extension, The Somme.

---

**BACKGROUND AND SERVICE HISTORY:**

Harold Mole was born on Mersea Island. Before the First World War he lived in South Hackney, Middlesex and served as a regular soldier. He had just left the army when war was declared and was mobilised with the Reserves, re-joining in Colchester and being posted to the 10th Battalion, Rifle Brigade (The Prince Consorts's Own). His Medal Record Card shows that he arrived in France on 10th September, 1914

On 3rd June, 1916, the following report appeared in the Essex County Standard.

*'WEST MERSEA HERO - Corporal Harold Mole, Rifle Brigade, has been recommended for the Distinguished Conduct Medal. Just before Easter, a German shell burst in the trench where he was fighting. Two of his comrades were completely buried under the earth cast up by the shell. He himself was wounded, but in spite of his wounds he succeeded in unearthing his comrades. He had been out of the army only a week or so when war was declared, and he with more of the Reserves were called up.'*

Early in 1917 the Battalion was on the Somme, and the following is an extract from the War Diary for 11th - 12th January, 1917.

*'Trenches S. of SAILLY SAILLISEL. The enemy were very quiet during this trip to the line, and this enabled a lot of work to be done. Unfortunately, just before the relieving Battalion arrived on the night of 12/13th, the enemy put two whizz bangs\* on the Reserve Line and killed two and wounded a third man.*
*The Battalion was relieved by the 7th Somerset Light Infantry, and on completion of the relief, proceeded back to COMBLES. 2/Lt URRY joined the Battalion for duty on the 12th'.*

\*This was the British soldier's name for shells fired by German 77 mm field guns, since their velocity was greater than the speed of sound so that the victim heard the 'whizz' of the shell before he heard the 'bang' of the gun and hence received no warning.

Harold Mole was one of the two men killed. He is buried in Combles Communal Cemetery Extension on the Somme, and is commemorated on the West Mersea War Memorial.

**Sources**

*Commonwealth War Graves Commission*
*Essex County Standard*
*The Royal Green Jackets Museum*
*10th Battalion Rifle Brigade War Diary, PRO, Kew, Ref no: WO95/2117*

The grave of Rifleman Harold Mole in Combles Communal Cemetery on the Somme

**SURNAME:** Hoy

CHRISTIAN NAME(S): Harris William

AGE: 22

RECRUITMENT OFFICE: Chelmsford

SERVICE NO: A/200880     RANK: Rifleman

SERVICE/REGIMENT: 21st Battalion, Kings Royal Rifle Corps
(Transferred from 3/8th Battalion, Essex Regiment, service no: 2967)

DECORATIONS EARNED: War Medal, Victory Medal

DATE KILLED/DIED: 17th February, 1917   LOCATION: Belgium

LOCATION OF GRAVE: Klein-Vierstraat British Cemetery, Belgium

---

## BACKGROUND AND SERVICE HISTORY:

Harris William Hoy was born in 1894 on Mersea Island, the fourth child of Henry and Ruth Hoy of Haycock's Farm, East Mersea. He was one of ten children born to the couple and was baptised on 14th September 1894.

Nothing is known of his early life and it is assumed that he attended East Mersea school.

He enlisted at Chelmsford and joined the 3/8th Battalion, Essex Regiment. After initial training he was transferred to the 21st Battalion, Kings Royal Rifle Corps.

In February 1917 the Corps were in the line south of Yypres. On 17th February they were in an area known as Ridge Wood. At 4.10 pm the enemy commenced a violent bombardment on the Corps reserve line and the redoubts in Bois Carre. At about 4.30 pm, this bombardment spread down Ghicory Lane, their right communications trench, to the right section of their front line, and the telephones were cut immediately afterwards. Owing to the mist and the heavy bombardment, communication with the parts of the line affected were impossible.

Soon after dusk, an enemy raiding party is believed to have entered the Corp's trench, capturing the crew of a Lewis gun, which was in an isolated position in a salient in this trench. Two trenches were completely blown in, being a series of Minenwerfer (mortar) craters, and the remainder of their front line, redoubts and reserve line around Bois Carre were severely damaged in places. Total casualties suffered by the Corps on that evening were 7 killed, 14 wounded, and 5 missing. There were no officer casualties.

One of the seven killed was William Hoy, who was buried, together with Rifleman E.H. Elson who was also killed that evening, in Klein-Vierstraat British Cemetery, Belgium. He is also commemorated on the West Mersea War Memorial.

Studio photograph of Rifleman Harris William Hoy.
Above are his notebook and Army Prayer Book, both exhibiting the ravages of battle.

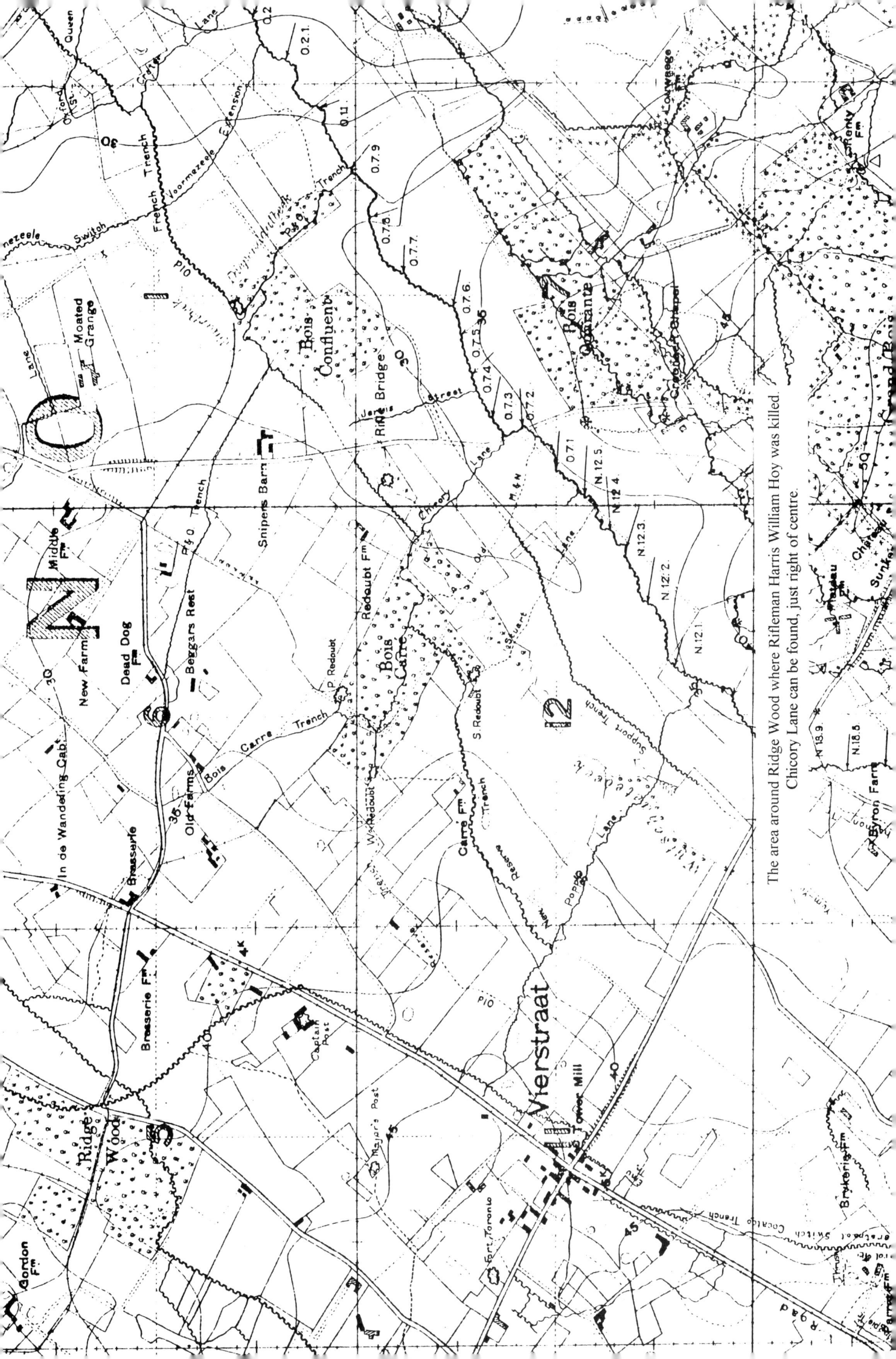

The area around Ridge Wood where Rifleman Harris William Hoy was killed. Chicory Lane can be found, just right of centre.

**Sources**

*Commonwealth War Graves Commission*
*Essex Regiment Museum*
*The Kings Royal Rifle Corps Chronicle - 21st Battalion War Records, The Royal Green Jackets Museum.*
*21st Battalion, Kings Royal Rifle Corps War Diary, PRO, Kew, Ref no: WO95/2643*
*Mrs Broad, Coggeshall.*
*Mrs Heather Hoy*
*The late Mrs Hoy*

The grave of Rifleman Harris William Hoy. Buried in the same grave is Rifleman E.H. Elson who was also killed on 17th February, 1917. Klein-Vierstraat British Cemetery, Belgium.

**SURNAME: Pullen**

CHRISTIAN NAME(S): Alfred Lewis

AGE: 27

RECRUITMENT OFFICE: Enlisted London

SERVICE NO: 18108        RANK: Private

SERVICE/REGIMENT: 3rd Battalion, Coldstream Guards

DECORATIONS EARNED: War Medal, Victory Medal

DATE KILLED/DIED: 24th February, 1917    LOCATION: France

LOCATION OF GRAVE: Grove Town Cemetery, The Somme

---

**BACKGROUND AND SERVICE HISTORY:**

Alfred Lewis Pullen was born in 1890, the son of Henry William and Julia Pullen of May Cottage, West Mersea. He was baptised on 20th May, 1894.

He enlisted in London, and joined the 3rd Battalion, Coldstream Guards.

In February, 1917, the Battalion was on the Somme, in the line south of Combles. Its War Diary for the month is very brief and is as follows:

*1.2.17 - Priez Farm - In close support.*
*2.2.17 -    "      - Relieved by 1st Battalion Irish Guards, marched to Billon Camp 107.*
*3-8.2.17 - Billon 107 - Rest and training.*
*9.2.17 -    "      - Marched to camp at Maurepas Ravine*
*10.2.17 - Relieved 2nd Battalion Scots Guards, left sector, Fregicourt U20c5-1-U20b3-2.5 Ref 57c SW 1/20,000.*
*10-14.2.17 - Trenches - Casualties 5 other ranks wounded.*
*14.2.17 - Relieved by 2 Coldstream Guards, marched to Maurepas Ravine.*
*14-18.2.17 - Brigade Reserve.*
*18.2.17 - Maurepas Ravine - Relieved 2nd Battalion Coldstream Guards - Left sector.*
*18-22.02.17 - Trenches - Casualties 3 officers wounded, 13 other ranks wounded, 4 other ranks killed.*
*22.02.17 -    "      - Relieved by 2nd Battalion Coldstream Guards, returned to Maurepas Ravine.*
*22-25.2.17 - Brigade Reserve.*
*25.02.17 - Maurepas Ravine - marched to Billon Camp 107*
*25-28.2.17 - Billon Camp - Divisional Ravine.*

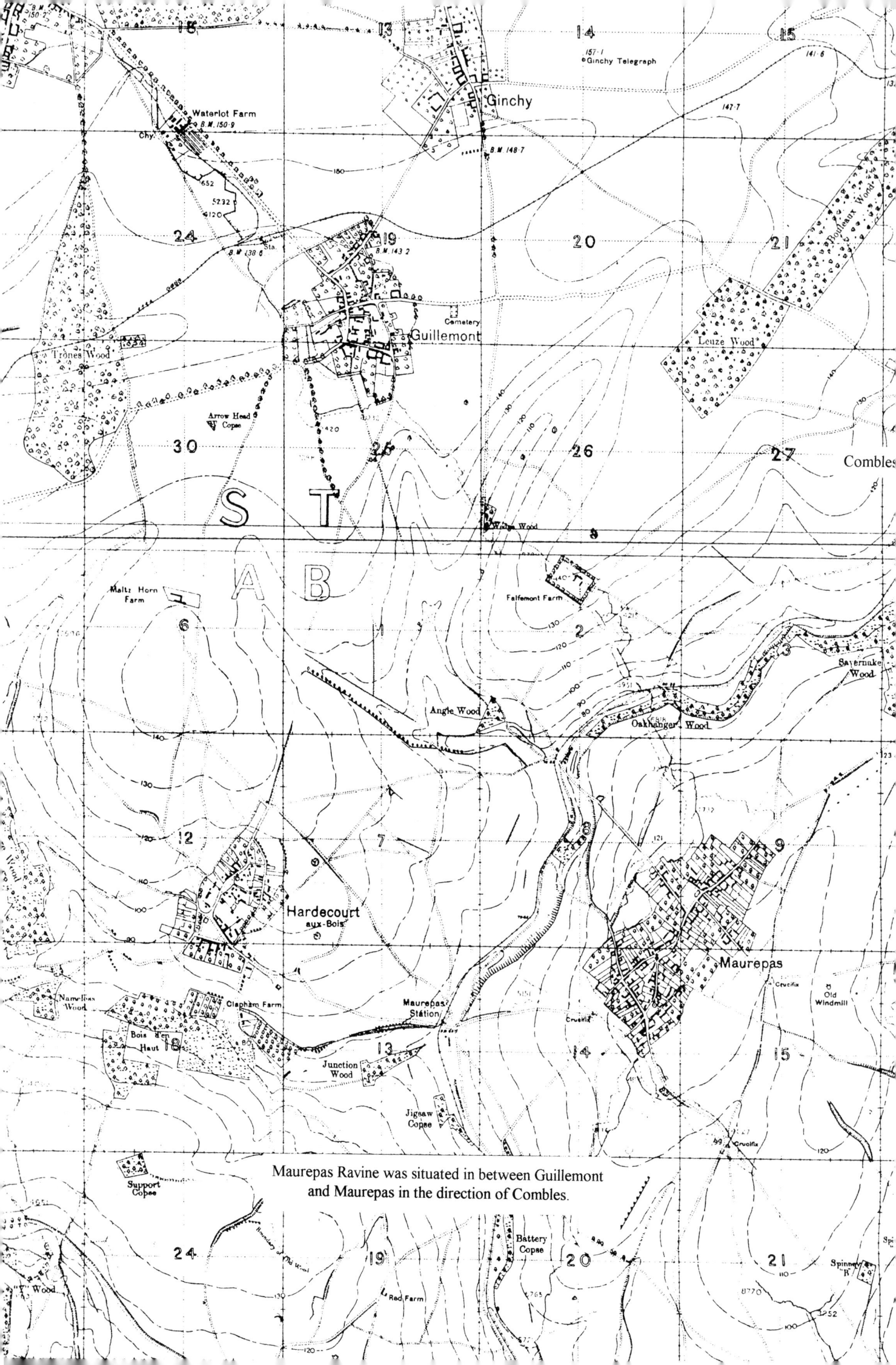

Maurepas Ravine was situated in between Guillemont and Maurepas in the direction of Combles.

Alfred was one of those wounded, and he was evacuated to the 34th and 2/2nd London Casualty Clearing Station near Meaulte, which was known locally as 'la demie-lieue' and by the British as 'Grove Town'.

Unfortunately, he died of his wounds on 24th February, 1917 and was buried in Grove Town Cemetery. He is commemorated on the West Mersea War Memorial.

**Sources**

*Commonwealth War Graves Commission*
*Essex Regiment Museum*
*3rd Battalion, Coldstream Guards War Diary, PRO, Kew, Ref no: WO95/1215*

The grave of Private Alfred Pullen in Grove Town Cemetery on the Somme

**SURNAME:** Gardner

CHRISTIAN NAME(S): Harry Victor

AGE: 22

RECRUITMENT OFFICE: Swansea

SERVICE NO: 202827   RANK: Private

SERVICE/REGIMENT: 1/7th Battalion Welsh Regiment (service no: 1333) attached to 2/4th Oxford and Buckinghamshire Light Infantry

DECORATIONS EARNED: Military Medal, War Medal, Victory Medal

DATE KILLED/DIED: 14th March, 1917   LOCATION: France

MEMORIAL IF NO KNOWN GRAVE: Thiepval Memorial, The Somme

---

**BACKGROUND AND SERVICE HISTORY:**

Harry Victor Gardner was born in 1895, in Hove, Sussex, the son of John Henry and Kate Gardner. The family later moved to Mersea Island.

He enlisted in Swansea and joined the 1/7th Battalion Welsh Regiment, but later became attached to the 2/4th Battalion, Oxford and Bucks Light Infantry.

On 28th June, 1916, the Battalion were in the Aubers Ridge area when an incident occurred which led to him being awarded the Military Medal. It is described in the Battalion War Diary as follows:

*Laventie 28/6/1916 - In trenches and front posts - Capt R.F. Cuthbert assumed the duties of acting adjutant, Capt W.D. Scott taking command of D Coy, 2/Lt Hopkinson to hospital (sick). Lt K.E. Brown and 2nd/Lt W.H. Moberly left our lines about 1.00 pm to make a reconnaissance of the enemy's line in view of a raid that evening. Lt Brown successfully accomplished his task, returning about 5.30 pm. 2nd/Lt Moberly was wounded in left shoulder by a sniper at about 2.30 pm and remained in NO MANS LAND till dark when he managed to get back to our trenches. A raid was carried out by B Coy at night. Casualties: missing believed killed 2nd/Lt Zelder, wounded Capt H.N. Davenport. Other ranks: killed 8, wounded 25, also 2nd Lt Moberly as mentioned above.*

On 13th July, 1916, the following Citation for a Military Medal for Private Harry Victor Gardner was issued:

*At Fauquissant on 28th June, 1916, showed conspicuous gallantry in that after returning unhurt from the raid, he subsequently went out four times under heavy fire and assisted to bring in one dead and three wounded comrades.*

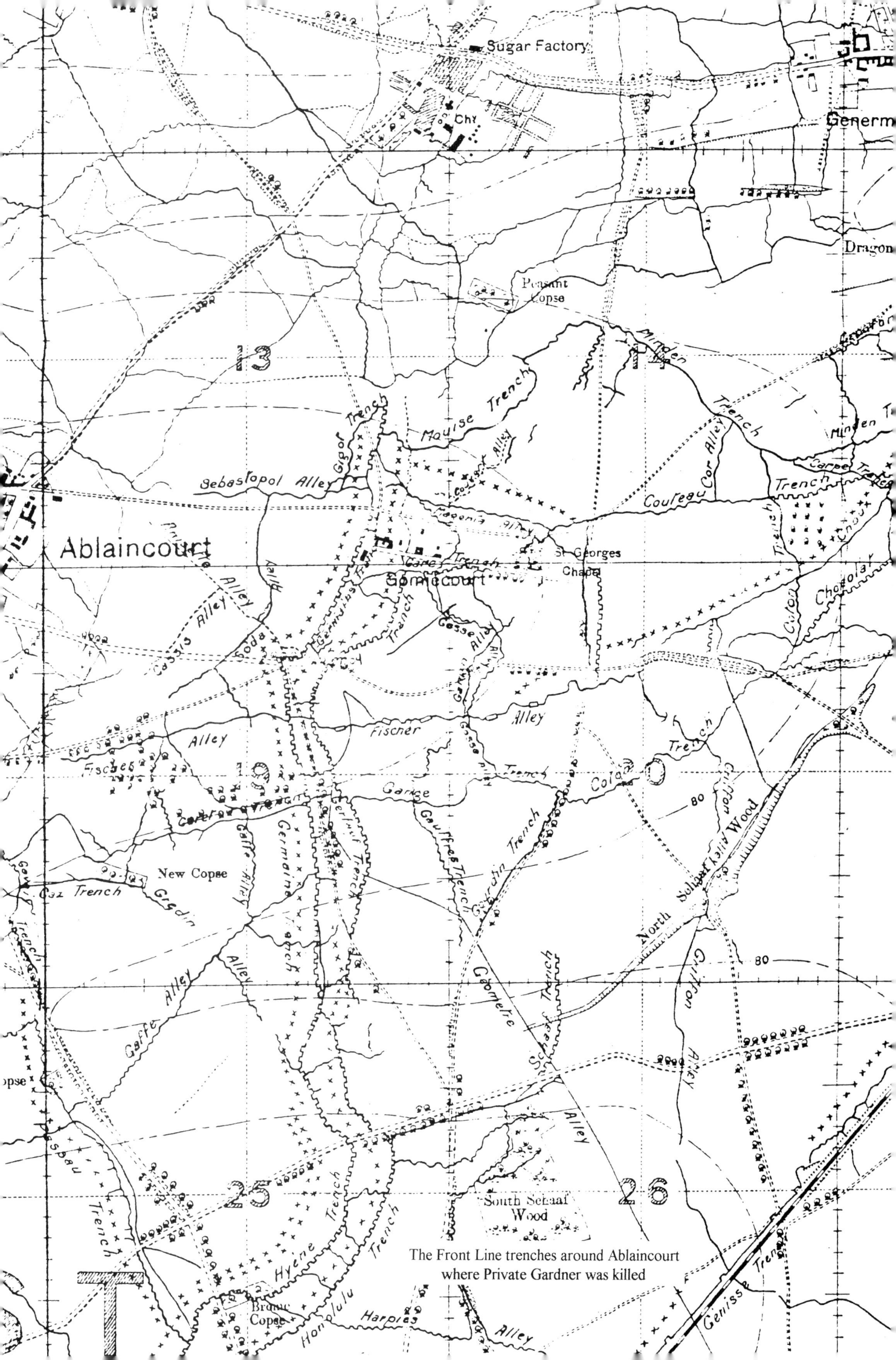

The Front Line trenches around Ablaincourt where Private Gardner was killed

In early March 1917, the Battalion relieved the Royal Berkshire Regiment in the front line trenches around Ablaincourt on the southern Sector of the Somme. For the next few days patrols went out to check and repair the wire. It was during one of these patrols on 14th March that Private Gardner was killed and his body never recovered.

He is commemorated on the Thiepval Memorial on the Somme and on the West Mersea War Memorial.

**Sources**

*Commonwealth War Graves Commission*
*Essex Regiment Museum*
*2/4th Oxford and Buckinghamshire Light Infantry War Diary, PRO, Kew,*
*Ref no: WO95/3067*

Private Harry Gardner's name inscribed on the Thiepval Memorial on the Somme

**SURNAME:** Cudmore

CHRISTIAN NAME(S): Nathan

AGE: 30

RECRUITMENT OFFICE: Greenwich

SERVICE NO: 94529    RANK: Gunner

SERVICE/REGIMENT: 'B' Battery, 70th BDE Royal Field Artillery

DECORATIONS EARNED: 1914/15 Star, War Medal, Victory Medal

DATE KILLED/DIED: 21st March, 1917    LOCATION: France

LOCATION OF GRAVE: Faubourg d'Amiens Cemetery, Arras

---

### BACKGROUND AND SERVICE HISTORY:

Nathan Cudmore was born in 1886, the second son of Nathan and Emma Cudmore of Home Farm Cottage, East Mersea, and the younger brother of George.

He enlisted at Greenwich, joining the 70th Brigade, Royal Artillery, and eventually 'B' Battery. The Battery embarked from Southampton on 7th July, 1915 arriving at Le Havre the next day.

In March 1917, the Battery was at Duisans near Arras. The Battery Diary describes the period in which Nathan Cudmore was wounded.

*March 19th - Enemy movement was fired on with good effect. Hostile artillery very active.*
*March 20th - Much enemy movement observed and fired upon. Hostile artillery very active.*
*March 21st - 'NF' targets engaged. Enemy aeroplanes very active, one flying over battery positions unmolested by anti-aircraft gun or our own machines.*

He died from his wounds on 21st March, 1917, and is buried in Faubourg d'Amiens Cemetery, on the outskirts of Arras. He is commemorated on the East Mersea War Memorial in the church.

His name also appears on his brother George's headstone in East Mersea churchyard.

### Sources

*Commonwealth War Graves Commission*
*Essex Regiment Museum*
*70th Brigade Royal Field Artillery War Diary, PRO, Kew, Ref no: WO95/1923*

Top: The grave of Gunner Nathan Cudmore in Faubourg d'Amiens Cemetery, Arras
Above: General view of the Faubourg d'Amiens Cemetery looking towards the Arras Memorial.

**SURNAME:** Cudmore

CHRISTIAN NAME(S): George

AGE: 34

RECRUITMENT OFFICE: Warley, Essex

SERVICE NO: 33212     RANK: Private

SERVICE/REGIMENT: 8th Battalion Bedfordshire Regiment

DECORATIONS EARNED: War Medal, Victory Medal

DATE KILLED/DIED: 9th April, 1917     LOCATION: France

LOCATION OF GRAVE: East Mersea Church Cemetery

---

**BACKGROUND AND SERVICE HISTORY:**

George Cudmore was born in 1882, the first son of Nathan and Emma Cudmore of Home Farm Cottage, East Mersea. He was baptised on 16th July, 1882.

He attended school at East Mersea and the school log reported that at the age of seven he was seriously punished for playing truant. In 1889 his parents announced their intention to leave the parish but later changed their mind, and George remained at the school. He featured in the school log again in 1893, when he was eleven. It was recorded that he had left school to go to work, although he was not eligible to do so. He was described as being somewhat backward.

He married Emma Louisa and they had a daughter, Alice Winifred, who was baptised on 13th September, 1914. They lived at Walnut Tree Cottage, East Mersea.

In July, 1916, he was working as a groom, employed by Mr E. G. Mears. He applied at the local Tribunal for exemption from military service, but he was refused.

He enlisted at Warley and joined the 8th Battalion, Bedfordshire Regiment.

In February, 1917, he was with the Battalion near Vermelles and the events of the first two weeks of that month, which represented a typical tour of duty in the front line trenches, are described in the Battalion War Diary.

*Noyelles - Vermelles*
*February 1st - Battalion in hutment camp in Brigade Reserve. Training and inspection of arms.*
*February 2nd - Battalion relieved 2nd Battalion, Yorks & Lancaster Regiment in left sub sector of 16 Infantry Brigade front opposite Hohenzollern Redoubt, 'A', 'B' & 'C' Coys. in front line and saps, 'D' Coy. in support.*

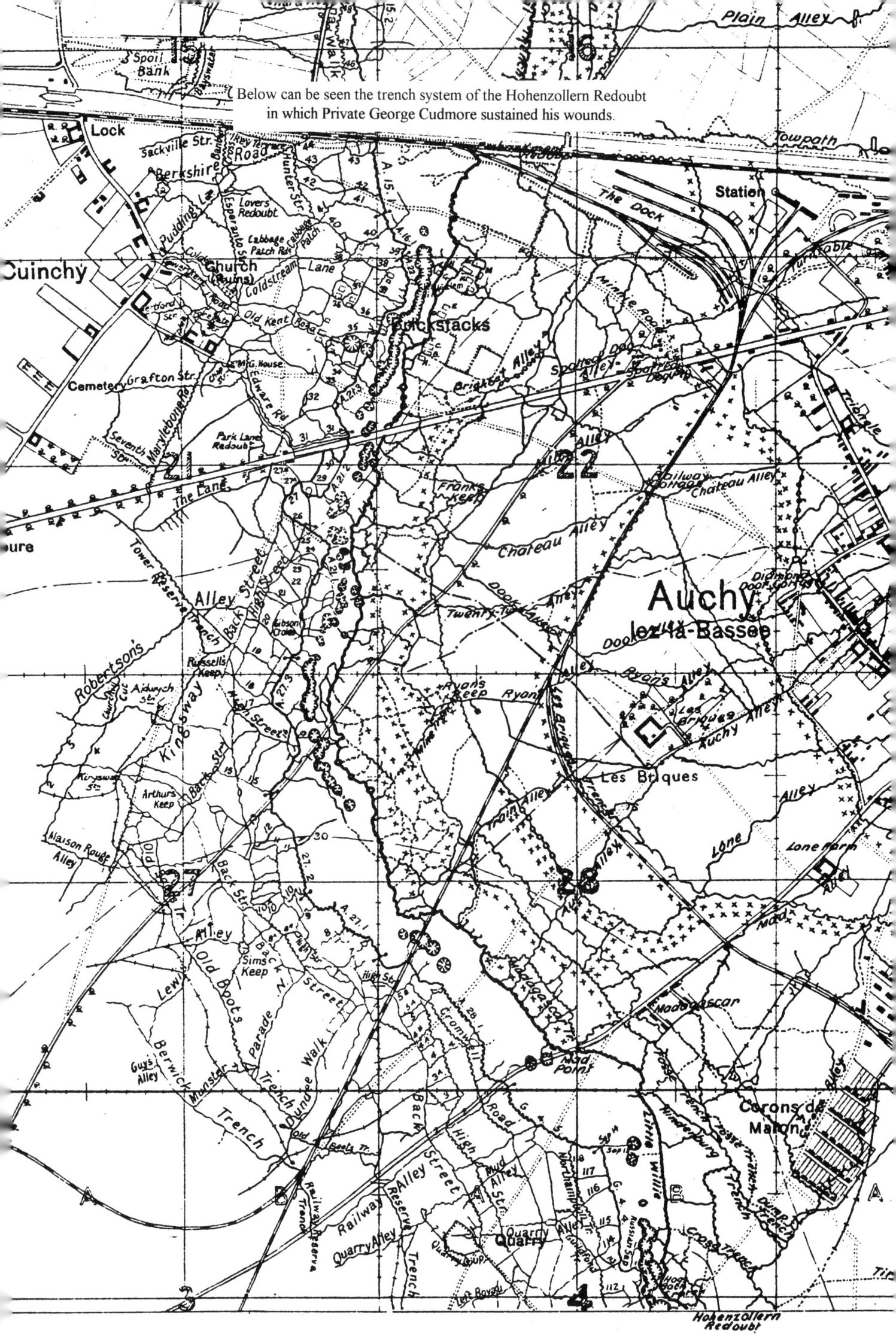

Below can be seen the trench system of the Hohenzollern Redoubt in which Private George Cudmore sustained his wounds.

*February 3rd - Battalion in line as above. Enemy snipers and machine guns very active. Casualties, 1 other ranks killed, 2 other ranks wounded. Our snipers claim 3 hits.*

*February 4th - Battalion in line as above. Enemy less aggressive except for trench mortars. Casualties, 1 other ranks killed.*

*February 5th - Battalion in line as above. Our retaliation with 4.5" howitzers appears to have caused hostile trench mortars to stop. Casualties, 1 other ranks killed, 4 other ranks wounded.*

*February 6th - Battalion relieved by 2nd Battalion, Yorks and Lancaster Regiment. Moved into Brigade Support, 'A' Coy., Railway Reserve, 'B' Coy., Junction Keep, 'C' Coy., Central Keep, 'D' Coy., Reserve Line.*

*February 7 - 9th - Furnished working parties during day and night for front line system.*

*February 10th - Battalion relieved 2nd Battalion, Yorks and Lancaster Regiment, in left sub sector Hohenzollen. 'B', 'C' and 'D' Coy. in front lines and saps. 'A' Coy. in support.*

*February 11th - Battalion in line as above, Enemy snipers active. Casualties, Lt Ball wounded, 3 other ranks killed, 4 other ranks wounded.*

*February 12th - Battalion in line as above. Hostile trench mortars active, snipers less so. Our snipers claim 2 hits.*

*February 13th - Battalion in line as above. Enemy quiet, though nervous. Our snipers claim 3 hits. Casualties, 2 other ranks wounded.*

*February 14th - Battalion in line as above. Enemy activity normal.*

*February 15th - Battalion relieved by 9th Battalion, Leicestershire Regiment, and marched to billets in Beuvry.*

George Cudmore was wounded during this period and was evacuated back to England. At the end of March he was recovering well but then suffered a relapse and died on 9th April, 1917.

He is buried in East Mersea churchyard and is commemorated on the War Memorial in the church. With George's death, the Cudmore family had lost both their sons within a period of a month. The epitaph on the headstone reads:

'Could we have raised their dying heads
and heard their last farewell
it would not have seemed so hard to part
with those we loved so well
                        Duty well done.'

**Sources**

*Commonwealth War Graves Commission*
*Essex Chronicle*
*8th Battalion Bedfordshire Regiment War Diary, PRO, Kew, Ref no: WO95/1611*
*East Mersea School Log (Essex Records Office, Colchester)*
*Essex Records Office (Colchester)*

The grave of Private George Cudmore in East Mersea churchyard
His brother Nathan's name is also inscribed on the gravestone.

**SURNAME: Green**

CHRISTIAN NAME(S): Ernest

AGE: 39

RECRUITMENT OFFICE: Colchester

SERVICE NO: 104987　　　　RANK: Gunner

SERVICE/REGIMENT: Royal Garrison Artillery (266 Siege Battery)

DECORATIONS EARNED: War Medal, Victory Medal

DATE KILLED/DIED: 20th April, 1917　　　LOCATION: France

MEMORIAL IF NO KNOWN GRAVE: Arras Memorial, Faubourg d'Amiens Cemetery

---

**BACKGROUND AND SERVICE HISTORY:**

Ernest Green was born in 1878 on Mersea Island, the son of Mr and Mrs C. Green of West Mersea.

He married Anne, and they lived at 19, Mersea Road, Colchester. There son was born in 1908. He was employed by F.G. Bloice, Builders, of Mersea Road.

He enlisted at Colchester, joining the Royal Garrison Artillery, his first unit being No. 406 2/2 Clyde, R.G.A. He transferred to No. 266 Siege Battery which was formed at Falmouth under the command of Lieutenant E.C.B. Bosanquet on 30th September, 1916.

After various moves around the south coast, the Battery embarked from Southampton to France, arriving at Le Havre on 17th February, 1917. Gunner Green was already in France having arrived there in December, 1916 with his first unit. It is not known on which date Gunner Green joined the Battery, but on March 9th, 1917, they took up position at Dainville, near the station, south west of Arras, where they fired their guns in anger for the first time. On 19th March, the guns moved to Agny, south of Arras, and there they remained in action until 11th April, the Battle of Arras having commenced on 9th April.

The Battery's next destination was Neuville-Vitasse, where it stayed until 17th April, when it left for St Martin sur Cojeul as described in the Battery's War Diary.

*St Martin sur Cojeul*
*April 18 - 8.00 am - Guns and stores begun arriving at St Martin, 4 wheel drives were used*
　　　*3.00 pm - Battery ready for action at Map ref N33.a.3.4.*
*April 20th - 10.15 am - Shelled by 5.9's, killed 7, wounded 5, shelling continued at rate of about 1 salvo every half an hour. Personnel of Battery has to clear to flank.*

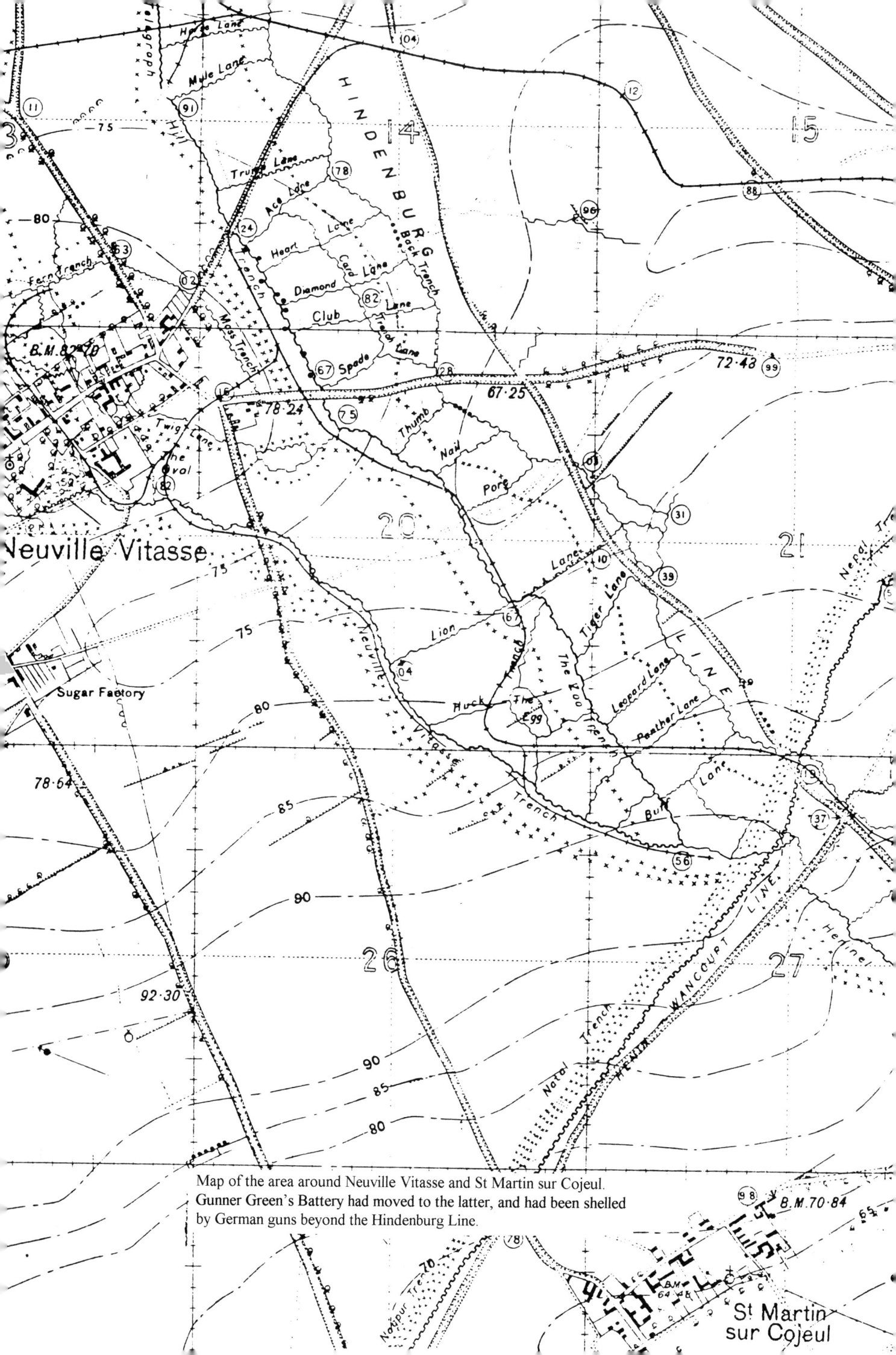

Map of the area around Neuville Vitasse and St Martin sur Cojeul. Gunner Green's Battery had moved to the latter, and had been shelled by German guns beyond the Hindenburg Line.

Gunner Ernest Green was one of those killed by the German shelling, and his funeral took place behind the lines. The location of his grave was lost, and therefore his body could not be exhumed for burial in a Military cemetery.

He is commemorated on the Arras Memorial (Bay 1), St Giles Memorial, Colchester, and on the West Mersea War Memorial.

**Sources**

*Commonwealth War Graves Commission*
*Essex Regiment Museum*
*Essex County Telegraph*
*Essex County Standard*
*Royal Garrison Artillery, 266 Siege Battery War Diary, PRO, Kew, Ref no: WO95/391*

Gunner Ernest Green's name inscribed on the Arras Memorial.

**SURNAME: White**

CHRISTIAN NAME(S): Frederick Samuel

AGE: 38

RECRUITMENT OFFICE: Darlington

SERVICE NO: 201033                    RANK: Private

SERVICE/REGIMENT: 1st/5th Battalion Durham Light Infantry

DECORATIONS EARNED: War Medal, Victory Medal

DATE KILLED/DIED: 23rd April 1917        LOCATION: France

MEMORIAL IF NO KNOWN GRAVE: Arras Memorial, Faubourg d'Amiens Cemetery

---

**BACKGROUND AND SERVICE HISTORY:**

Frederick Samuel White was born in Peldon, nr Colchester on 5th May 1879 to Samuel Cant and Martha White (nee Smith). He was their third child and first son, one of ten children, although one died in infancy.

His parents lived at West Mersea and his father had two grocery and millinery shops on the Island - one in Churchfields and the other on Mill Road. He also had grocery shops at Peldon and Tollesbury and was the representative for Barclays Bank on the Island.

Not much is known of Frederick's early life but it is presumed that he attended school at Mersea, and on leaving, he joined the family business, leading to him being manager of the shop in Mill Road. He married Elizabeth Anne, and they had two children, a son Norman, and a daughter Gladys.

At the outbreak of war, he was 35 years old and as the ceiling for joining up was 30 years, he was not required to enlist. However, as casualties grew and the need for more and more men to join the army, conscription was introduced at the beginning of 1916, with the proviso that single men would be called up first. Frederick was now 37 years old, and as a manager of a provisions shop, he could have applied for exemption, but there is no record of him having done so.

In early February, 1916, his elder sister Grace died: she had married Mr Dansie and had had one son, Leonard. They lived at the Stores, Peldon, presumably one of the shops owned by the White family.

Towards the end of 1916 or at the beginning of 1917, Frederick enlisted in Darlington, joining the 1st/5th Durham Light Infantry. After a period of basic training he was ready to be sent to France. Before leaving, he returned to Mersea to say his goodbyes and his young nephew Eric White recalls to this day waving to him as he walked down the path in his new uniform.

Above: Samuel Cant White's shop at the corner of Churchfields and Church Road, now part of the Blackwater Hotel.
Below: Samuel Cant White's other shop in Mill Road, West Mersea, which was managed by Frederick.

White family portrait - Frederick with his brothers and sisters:
*Standing from the left*: May, Frederick, Clifford, and Horace. *Sitting*: Grace, their father Samuel, and Kate. *Bottom*: Dorothy, Claud, and Elsie.

Frederick White with his wife Elizabeth Anne, daughter Gladys and his son Norman.

His Battalion was part of the forces involved in the allied offensive known as the Battle of Arras, which had begun on April 9th, 1917 with the Canadians successful attack on Vimy Ridge.

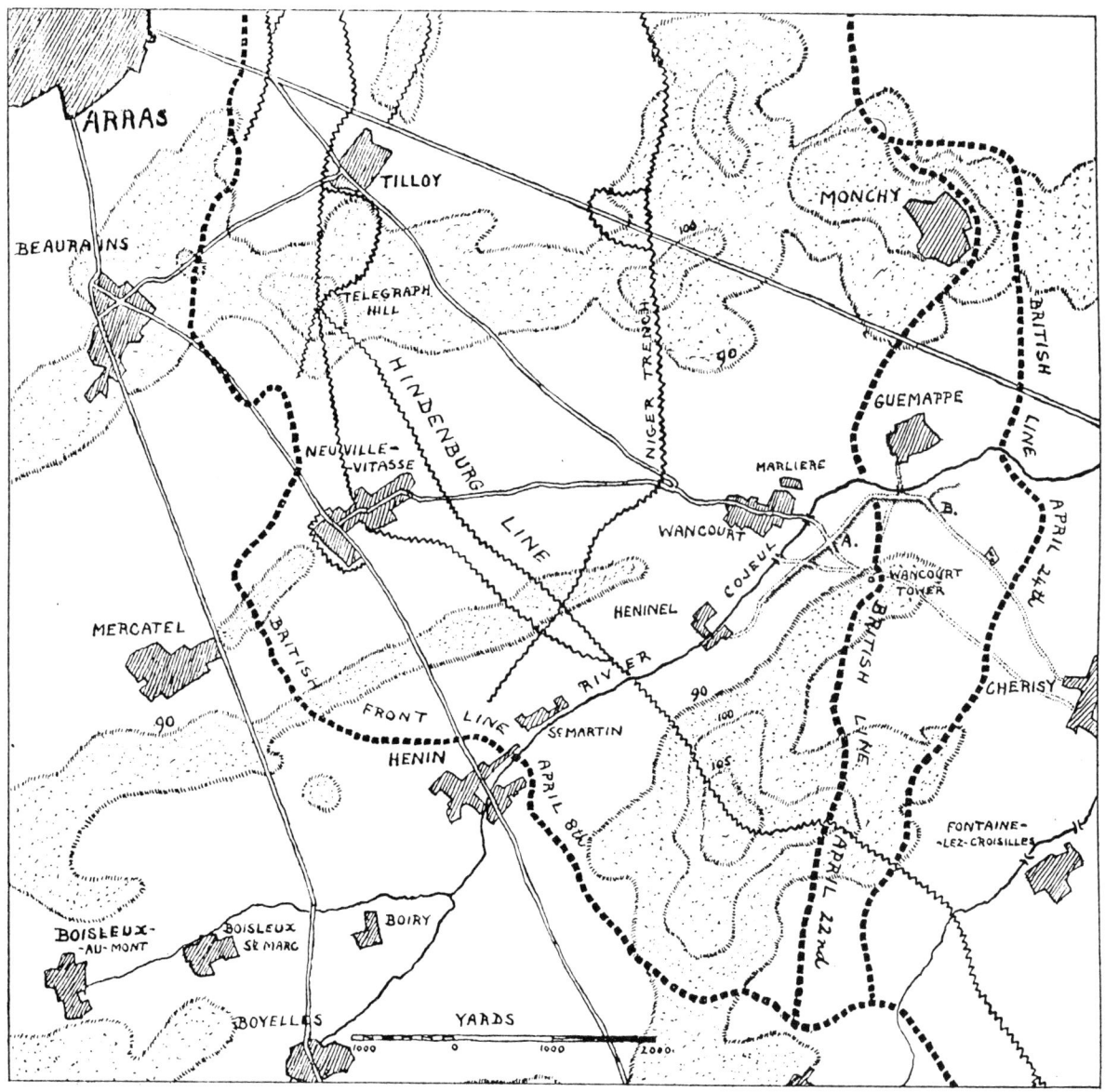

The Battle of Arras, April, 1917.

The principal German lines are indicated by wavy lines. Stippling indicates ridges.

A: Indicates the bank which was the assembly place of the 5th Durham Light Infantry and the 5th Yorkshire Regiment on April 23rd. Known as Albatross Bank.

B: Indicates the sunken road held by B Company during the morning of April 23rd, and occupied again in the evening by the remains of the Battalion.

On April 22nd, the 1st/5th Battalion Durham Light Infantry were busy completing arrangements for a big attack by the whole of the Third Army and part of the First Army which was to take place on April 23rd. The plan regarding the 50th Division was that the 4th Yorkshires and the 4th East Yorkshires, assisted by two tanks, should attack at dawn on a front of some 1,200 yards, and should advance to a depth of some 1,500 yards. Seven hours later the 5th Yorkshires and the 5th Durham Light Infantry were to advance through them and occupy a line commanding Cherisy and Vis-en-Artois. The 151st Brigade was in support and the 149th in reserve. The 30th Division was to attack on the Battalion's right and the 15th Division on the left.

April 23rd, St George's Day, was beautifully fine. The time for the attack to begin - zero hour - was 4.30 am. At 4.15 am, the Battalion lined up on the track running behind the Niger trench, and at 4.30 am every gun opened fire. It was reported that the noise was so great that it was impossible to hear an order even if shouted into one's ear. Lieutenant-Colonel G.O. Spence was in command, with Captain W.N.J. Moscrop as Adjutant, and the four companies were commanded by Major A.L. Raimes (A), Captain W. Marley (B), Lieutenant J.K.M. Hessler (C), and Lieutenant E.W. Coulson-Mayne (D). (It is not known which Company, Frederick was in). At 4.45 am, led by the Colonel, the men moved off in single file past Wancourt Cemetery, round by the south of the village and then across the shallow Cojeul valley, and lined up under cover of the bank at the far side, known later as Albatross Bank. There they dug in with the 5th Yorkshires on their right. As luck would have it the Cojeul valley, which the Germans had barraged so heavily on the 21st, was hardly shelled at all and they got across with only six or seven casualties. One of these however, was D Company commander, Lieutenant E.W. Coulson-Mayne, who fell fatally wounded. They were shelled intermittently as they lay along the bank but had very few casualties as it gave them excellent cover. Wancourt was being heavily bombarded and the bursting shells threw up clouds of smoke, red, grey, or black depending on the material of the house that was hit. Those who were on the extreme left had an uninterrupted view of the attack on Guemappe by the 15th Division.

Meanwhile, the two attacking battalions of the 150th Brigade had gone forward and had secured most of their objective. They were held up for a while by a small copse occupied by the Germans. By 8.30 am, however, it was surrounded and shortly afterwards, with the help of the tanks, it was captured. Both tanks unfortunately became over-heated, caught fire, and were stranded. The prisoners taken numbered 7 officers and 440 other ranks, in addition to a battery of 7.7 cm guns. As the prisoners were being sent behind the lines, the British field guns were being brought up through Wancourt to take up advanced positions in the Cojeul valley. However, it now became obvious that although the 4th Yorkshires and 4th East Yorkshires had reached their objective, it had been at a fearful cost. Hardly an officer remained unwounded, and the new line was held by a few scattered groups of men who were quite incapable of resisting the inevitable counter-attack. A Victoria Cross was won posthumously by Captain D.B. Hirsch, 4th Yorkshire Regiment for his gallant and brave leadership before he was killed.

Urgent messages came back for reinforcements, and at about 6.00 am, D Company (5th Durham Light Infantry) were sent up to reinforce the left of the line. They came under heavy machine gun fire and man after man fell, but the remainder pressed on, with a few finally being able to get into line with the 4th Yorkshires. One of those killed was Second Lieutenant F.W. Heap leading the Company. At about 7.00 am, B Company were ordered to occupy the sunken road leading from Guemappe to Cherisy, in order to protect the left flank against possible attack from the direction of Vis-en-Artois. Captain W. Marley led his men round the end of the ridge and they came under rifle and machine gun fire from the neighbourhood of Guemappe and suffered many casualties including the Captain, who was killed while he stood up to examine the position. The remainder of B Company took up their position in the sunken road. An hour or so later, 50 men of A Company led by Second-Lieutenant A.E.W. Pereira were sent forward with ammunition, but their task proved to be an impossible one, with many of them being killed or wounded by the German machine guns. Most of the remainder were captured in the counter attack which followed shortly afterwards. The 5th Yorkshires had also sent reinforcements forward, and they suffered the same fate.

The sunken road as it is today. Position 'B' on the map.

At about 11.00 am, a heavy counter-attack developed from the direction of Vis-en-Artois. After an artillery bombardment, a large force of German infantry advanced, sweeping right over the thin firing line and by noon the survivors were back in their original line. Very few of D Company got back, most of them were killed or captured. B Company found themselves enfiladed from both flanks by machine guns firing right down the sunken road and were attacked from three sides by the German infantry. The men were simply mown down, and among the casualties were Second-Lieutenant H.R. Herring, who was killed and Second-Lieutenant C.D. Marley, who was severely wounded. Only one officer, Lieutenant R.W.G. Robinson, and 27 men succeeded in getting back to the original front line. Sergeant F.W. Merryweather and Corporal J. Harper distinguished themselves by the way in which, hour after hour, they crawled out and brought in their wounded comrades. Corporal Harper, unfortunately, was wounded, and died as the result of his injuries soon after the end of the war. Sergeant Merryweather was awarded the Military Medal for his gallantry.

Guemappe on the Battalion's left had again fallen into enemy hands and the 30th Division on their right had also had to give up the ground they had captured and had even fallen back behind their original line. Although not known at the time, small parties of the enemy had got right through into Heninel and had captured four batteries of field guns that had been sent forward during the morning. However, the enemy was driven off and the guns recaptured. The position was now very serious, as there was real danger of the Germans following up their success by coming right over the Wancourt Tower ridge and down into the valley. Every available man, riflemen, Lewis gunners, Stokes gunners and machine gunners lined the bank and waited for the approach of the enemy over the brow of the hill. The Germans did not come, but contented themselves by occupying their old front line.

The position now was that both forces were back in their original lines. The British front line was held by the remains of the 4th Yorkshires and 4th East Yorkshires, together with a few men of the 5th Durham Light Infantry and 5th Yorkshires. Along Albatross Bank there still remained about one and a half companies of the 5th Durham Light Infantry and two companies of the 5th Yorkshires, in addition to machine gunners and trench mortar personnel. C Company was sent forward to occupy a bank further forward to support the front line while the remainder of the Brigade held Albatross Bank.

Wancourt Tower ridge today, with the village of Wancourt in the background, while in the foreground are the remains of the German strongpoint, Wancourt Tower.

Meanwhile, a further attack all along the line was being arranged and as part of this scheme the 9th Durham Light Infantry and the 5th Border Regiment from the 151st Brigade were brought up and lent to the 150th Brigade. The shelling died down during the afternoon and all was quiet until 6.00 pm when the barrage commenced and the attack began. The objective was again captured but due to the vulnerability of the flanks a position was taken up about 500 yards further back. During the action, German prisoners were taken, consisting of 10 officers and 200 men.

The two companies of the 5th Yorkshires advanced in support of the 5th Borderers. The remains of the 5th Battalion Durham Light Infantry had been collected together at short notice and went over in support of the 9th Durham Light Infantry. Their orders were to occupy the sunken road where B Company had suffered so severely earlier in the day and they arrived there with very few casualties to take up their position. The British barrage had been very successful, a trench that the Battalion crossed contained a great many dead Germans. The sunken road was shelled for a while and the Battalion took a few more casualties, but as the evening wore on the fighting died down entirely and it became perfectly quiet.

During the night the 151st Brigade, with the 4th Northumberland Fusiliers attached, took over the line from the 150th Brigade and shortly before dawn the 8th Durham Light Infantry relieved the 5th Battalion. Just as the day was breaking they again crossed Cojeul valley and marched wearily back to Telegraph Hill. Near Albatross Bank and in the valley were many signs of the previous day's battle, bodies of men and mules, equipment, and the smell of exploded shells.

The casualties were 4 officers killed or died of wounds, 2 wounded and 1 taken prisoner, while among the ranks, 83 had been killed, 124 wounded and 49 taken prisoner. One of those killed was Frederick White whose body was never found and has no known grave.

The new of his death was such a shock to his wife that she suffered a nervous breakdown, leaving his daughter Gladys, who was then about 12 years old, to cope with the upbringing of her younger brother.

Frederick is commemorated on the Arras Memorial, Faubourg d'Amiens Cemetery, (his name can be found on Bay 8), on his parents grave in Barfield Road Cemetery, West Mersea, and on the West Mersea War Memorial.

**Sources**

*Mrs Doreen Bryant, Mr David Buck, Mr Eric White, Mr John White, Ms Anita White.*
*The Essex Chronicle*
*The Durham Light Infantry Museum, Durham*
*Description of the battle quoted from 'The Fifth Battalion The Durham Light Infantry 1914-1918', by Major A.L. Raimes, D.S.O., T.D.*
*Commonwealth War Graves Commission*

Below: Frederick's name inscribed on the Arras Memorial, Faubourg d'Amiens Cemetery, Bay 8.

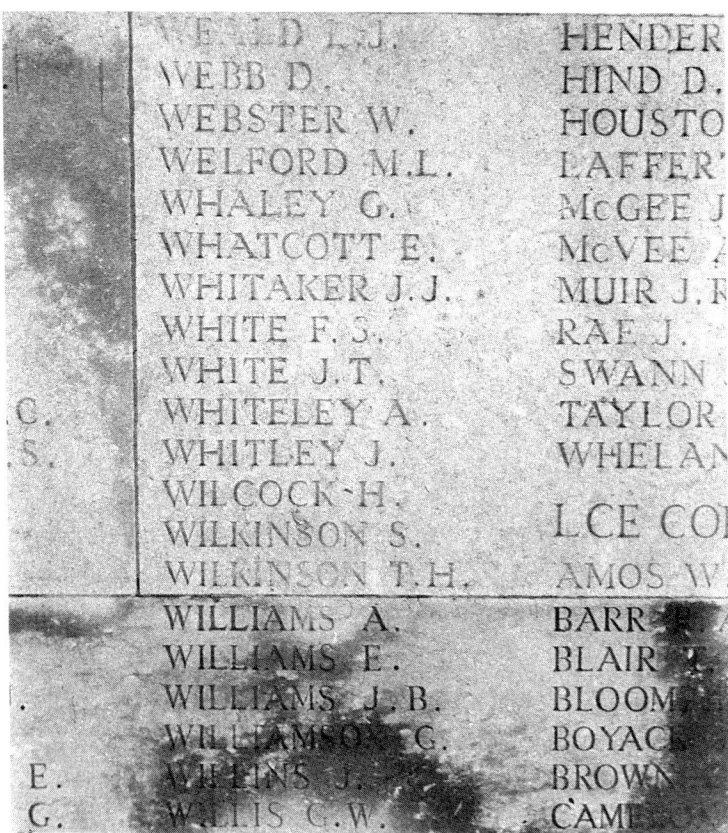

**SURNAME:** Howard

CHRISTIAN NAME(S): John D.

AGE: Unknown

RECRUITMENT OFFICE: Colchester

SERVICE NO: 31728     RANK: Private

SERVICE/REGIMENT: 13th Battalion, Essex Regiment

DECORATIONS EARNED: War Medal, Victory Medal

DATE KILLED/DIED: 28th April, 1917     LOCATION: France

MEMORIAL IF NO KNOWN GRAVE: Arras Memorial, Faubourg-d'Amiens Cemetery

---

**BACKGROUND AND SERVICE HISTORY:**

John D. Howard was born in Ipswich, Suffolk, the son of Edward and Agnes Finch Howard living at Bottom Lane, Ipswich. He had an elder brother and sister, Edward and Edith, and a younger sister, Mary. In 1907 the family moved to West Mersea to run The Stores in Church Road. However, tragedy was to strike the family when on 29 March, 1909 his brother died, followed in 1914 by his sister, aged 24, who was buried on 3rd July, 1914 in the Barfield Road cemetery.

Edward Howard's shop in Church Road, West Mersea, probably taken in 1914, looking down towards the church. *(Ron Green collection).*

John Howard enlisted at Colchester and joined the 13th Battalion, Essex Regiment, becoming a member of 'A' Company.

In April 1917, the Battalion was part of the British force involved in the Battle of Arras. On 23rd April, 1917, they returned to dug-outs around Roclincourt. They changed their positions once or twice during the next two or three days as heavy fighting was proceeding. On 27th April, the Battalion marched to assembly trenches beyond Bailleul in preparation to attack on the right of Oppy Village. The men were in excellent spirits, their army rations having been supplemented with chocolate and two cheese sandwiches, whilst a rum issue was also made before moving off. The fighting that followed on 28th April is described in the Battalion War Diary.

*2.00 am - The Battalion was formed up in their jumping off positions without any hitch occurring about 2.00 am in spite of heavy shelling. Companies were organised in three platoons, one platoon of each company representing 1st, 2nd & 3rd waves, each wave consisting of two lines - 1st Line: Bombers and Riflemen.*
*2nd Line: Lewis Gunners and Rifle Bombers.*
*Moppers up for each wave were formed up in the rear of the last wave. Close touch was gained with the Highland Light Infantry, the 17th Middlesex and Royal Marine Light Infantry.*

*4.25 am - At 4.25 am our own barrage came down and at 4.33 am, the 1st wave crossed the enemy's front line trench, with the exception of the extreme right of the Battalion, which was held up by uncut wire, and lost heavily from machine gun fire in endeavouring to get through it. At this period, touch was entirely lost with the Royal Marine Light Infantry on our right. It was maintained between the 13th Essex and 17th Middlesex, but was lost with the Highland Light Infantry, who were in the left of the 17th Middlesex.*

*The advance continued under the barrage to the line of the practice trenches in C.13.d, eastern end of Oppy Wood and trench in C.7.c. At this period, a party of German bombers attacked our right flank. Heavy machine gun fire and rifle fire took place from Oppy Village and large numbers of the enemy were advancing down the Sunken Road at the Crucifix.*

*5.50 am - At 5.50 am, I ordered one company of the King's Royal Rifle Corps (which company had been sent by 6th Infantry Brigade as support) to advance and form a defensive flank from B.18.d.3.5 to southern end of practice trenches. This company was unable to proceed further than the British front line owing to hostile barrage and machine gun fire.*

*About this time the Battalion on our left (17th Middlesex) was heavily attacked from the front and on the left flanks, and large numbers of the enemy advance through Oppy Wood, got in rear of the line and reoccupied parts of the German front line.*

*A senior officer was sent forward to clear up the situation about 7.30 am, but did not return, and no messages were received from him.*

*The heavy fighting continued and at 9.00 am, the troops were ordered to fall back, hold and consolidate the German front line. Small detached parties only succeeded in doing this and were unable to cope with the enemy who were then holding the trench. All the officers of this Battalion (13th Battalion, Essex Regiment) had become casualties and the majority of the non-commissioned officers and what was left of the Battalion were quite disorganised and exhausted. Small parties held out, but eventually retired to the old British line, running from shell hole to shell hole at dusk.*

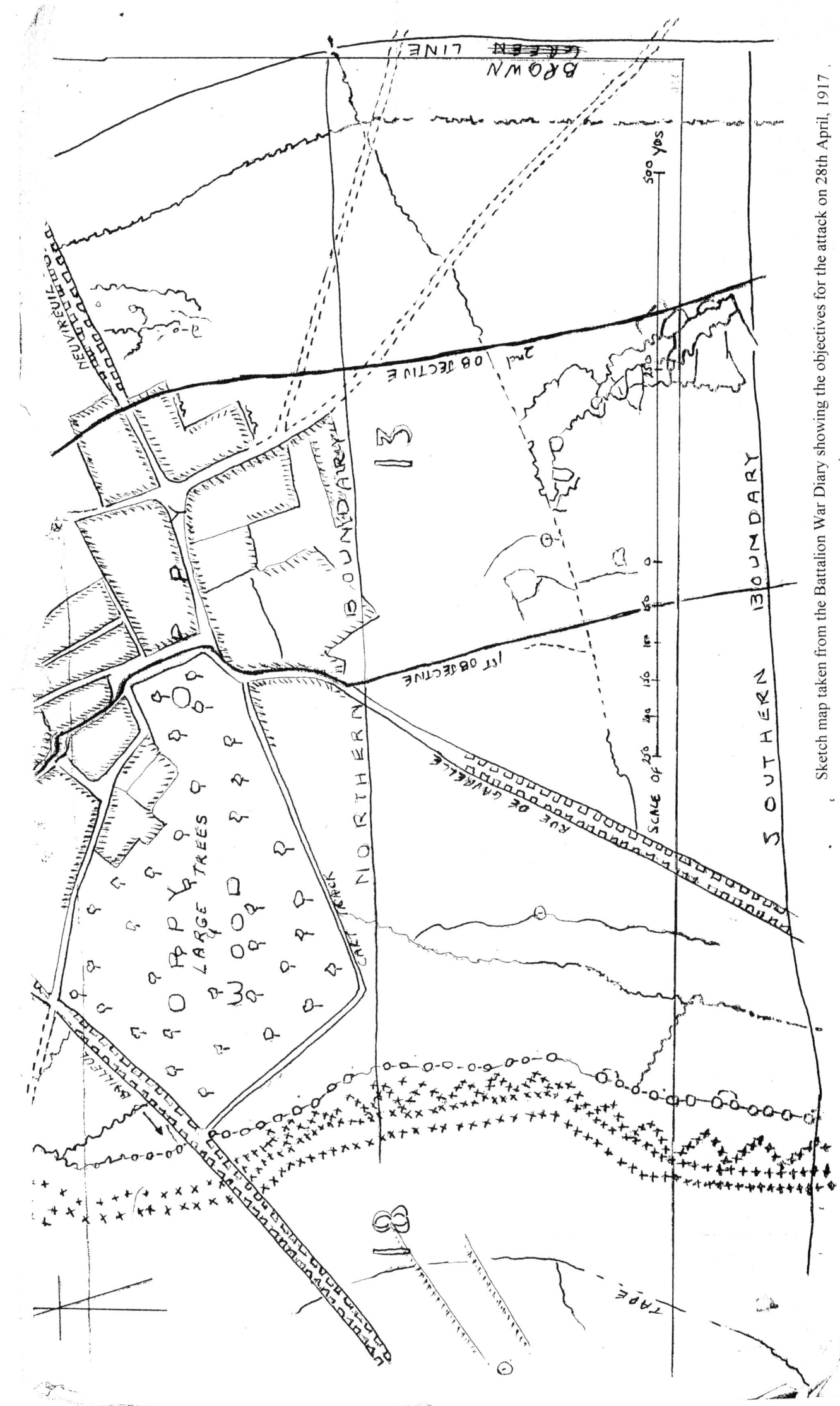

Sketch map taken from the Battalion War Diary showing the objectives for the attack on 28th April, 1917.

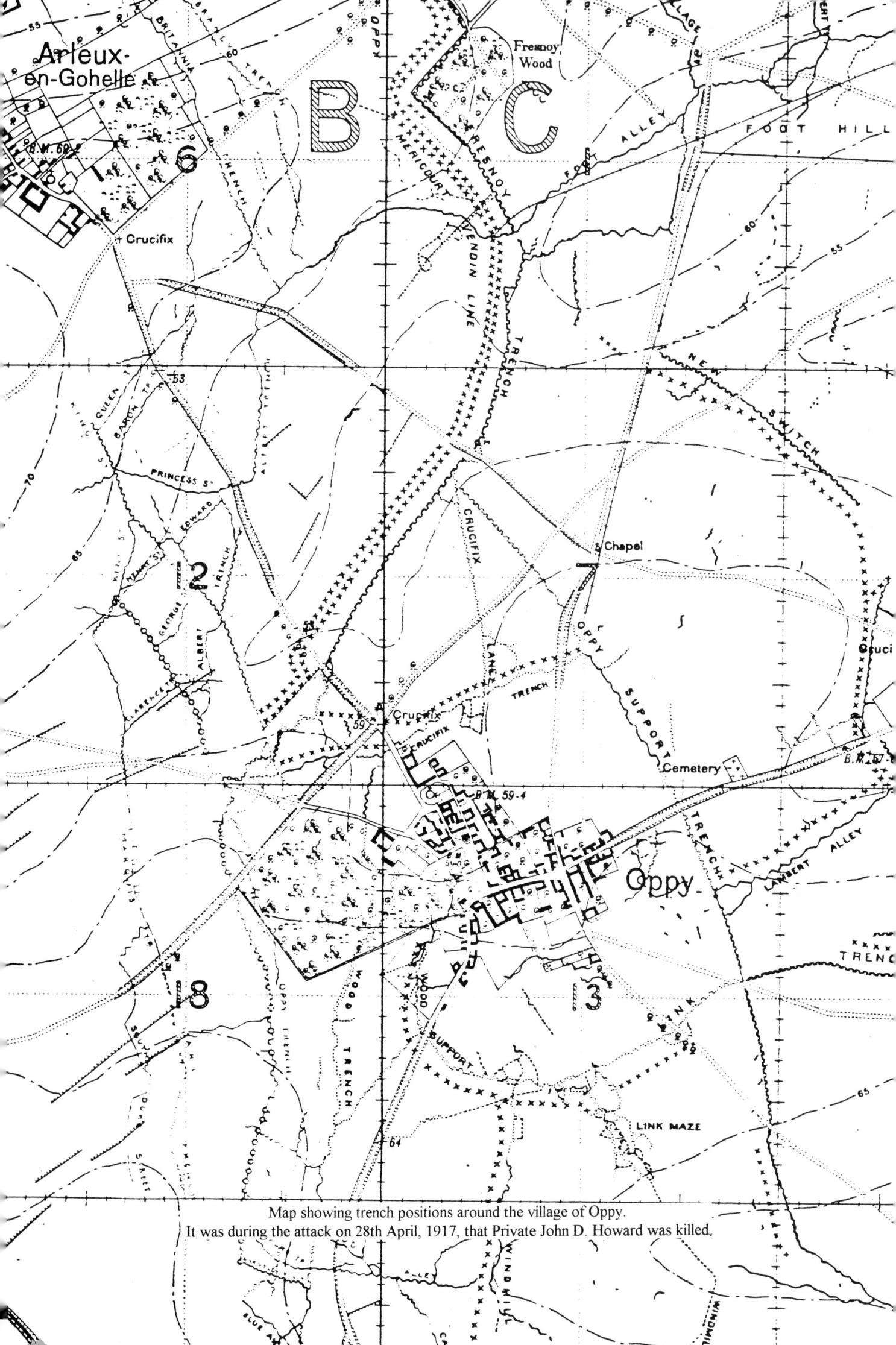

Map showing trench positions around the village of Oppy.
It was during the attack on 28th April, 1917, that Private John D. Howard was killed.

*The remainder of the Battalion and various troops holding the British line, were relieved on the night of the 28th by the 22nd Royal Fusiliers in the front line and a company of the 23rd Royal Fusiliers in the support line. The Battalion returned to dugouts near Roclincourt arriving there about 5.00 am on 29th April.*

Casualties were heavy, with seven officers killed, four wounded, three other ranks killed, 79 wounded and 240 missing. Of the missing, the great proportion were afterwards returned as killed. One of those missing was Private John Howard and his body was never found.

It was not until 6th June, 1917, that the news arrived back home, with these few words in the *Essex County Standard*, *'Pte Howard, Essex Regt., only son of Mr Howard, grocer, etc, West Mersea is also reported missing'*. In a period of eight years, the Howards had lost three of their children, leaving them with one remaining daughter, Mary.

John Howard is commemorated on the Arras Memorial and on the West Mersea War Memorial.

**Sources**

*Commonwealth War Graves Commission*
*Essex Regiment Museum*
*Essex Units in the War 1914-1919 by J. W. Burrows*
*Essex County Standard*
*13th Battalion, Essex Regiment War Diary, PRO, Kew, Ref no: WO95/1358*

Private John Howard's name inscribed on the Arras Memorial.

**SURNAME: Wright**

CHRISTIAN NAME(S): Sidney Elijah

AGE: 27

RECRUITMENT OFFICE: Warley, Essex

SERVICE NO: G/52286          RANK: Private

SERVICE/REGIMENT: 24th Battalion, Royal Fusiliers (City of London Regiment)

DECORATIONS EARNED: War Medal, Victory Medal

DATE KILLED/DIED: 28th April, 1917          LOCATION: France

MEMORIAL IF NO KNOWN GRAVE: Arras Memorial, Faubourg d'Amiens Cemetery

---

**BACKGROUND AND SERVICE HISTORY:**

Sidney Elijah Wright was born in Great Wigborough, the son of Elijah and Elizabeth Mary Wright. He had two younger brothers, Clifford and Travis.

Sidney's father was a farm labourer and during the early 1900s the family moved to West Mersea, first lodging in West Hall near the church and then moving to live in a cottage fronting Colchester High Street North, near Brick House. He was an expert ploughman, winning competitions in 1907 and 1910.

Sidney was conscripted in 1916, enlisting at Warley and joining the 24th Battalion, Royal Fusiliers (City of London Regiment). His brothers also enlisted, Clifford joining the Royal Fusiliers and Travis the 1/4th Battalion, Essex Regiment. Both survived the war.

On 28th April, 1917, the Battalion was in an area north east of Oppy Village when it was ordered to move in response to the enemy breakthrough south of Oppy Wood. This occurred during the attack by 13th Battalion, Essex Regiment which had resulted in the death of Private John Howard earlier in the day. The Battalion War Diary recounts the events of the day.

*April 28th - At 4.25 am an attack on a wide front was carried out. The Battalion was in Brigade Reserve and at 11.00 am it moved forward to occupy the old British support trenches opposite the front ARLEUX-OPPY WOOD. At 8.00 pm reports were received through Brigade that the enemy had broken through south of OPPY WOOD and the Battalion were consequently ordered to form a defensive flank facing S.E. from the northern outskirts of BAILLEUL to their former right flank in the old British support line. Posts were dug on this new alignment and work was still in progress when orders were received that at dawn 2 Coys were to co-operate on the left flank of an attack by the 99th Brigade against OPPY WOOD. A and B Coys were detailed for this attack, C and D Coys following them and mopping up and holding the German front line immediately north of OPPY WOOD.*

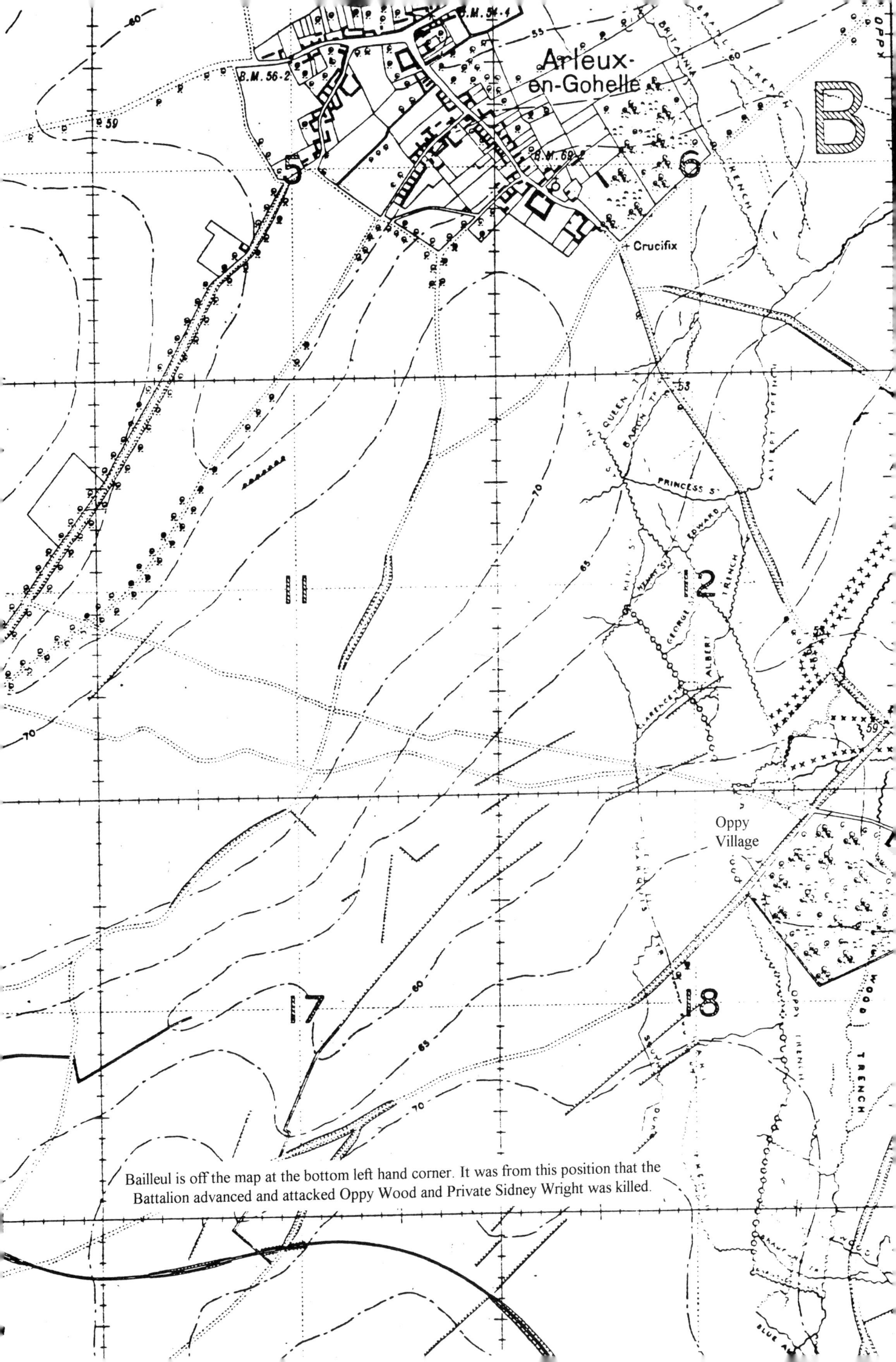

Bailleul is off the map at the bottom left hand corner. It was from this position that the Battalion advanced and attacked Oppy Wood and Private Sidney Wright was killed.

During the events of 28th April, Private Sidney Wright was killed, the second Mersea man that day to lose his life in the fighting around Oppy Wood.

His body was never found and he is commemorated on the Arras Memorial (Bay 3) in the Faubourg d'Amiens Cemetery and the West Mersea War Memorial

**Sources**

*1891 Census*
*Commonwealth War Graves Commission*
*Soldiers Died CD Rom*
*Essex Record Office*
*Mr H. Cock, Mersea*
*Essex Chronicle*
*The Royal Fusiliers Museum and Archives*
*24th Battalion, Royal Fusiliers War Diary, PRO, Kew, Ref No: WO95/1349*

Private Sidney Wright's name inscribed on the Arras Memorial

**SURNAME:** Farthing

CHRISTIAN NAME(S): Clifford

AGE: 20

RECRUITMENT OFFICE: Colchester

SERVICE NO: 12806   RANK: Acting Sergeant

SERVICE/REGIMENT: 2nd Battalion Essex Regiment

DECORATIONS EARNED: 1914/1915 Star, War Medal, Victory Medal

DATE KILLED/DIED: 3rd May, 1917   LOCATION: France

MEMORIAL IF NO KNOWN GRAVE: Arras Memorial, Faubourg d'Amiens Cemetery

---

**BACKGROUND AND SERVICE HISTORY:**

Clifford Farthing was born on Mersea Island, on 16th May, 1897, the son of Horace Lewis and Rosina Farthing. He was baptised on 11th June, 1899.

He was one of those who answered the call of duty when war was declared. He enlisted in Colchester, and like many of his contemporaries, he first joined the 1st Battalion, Essex Regiment. He then transferred to the 2nd Battalion, Essex Regiment, which was part of 4th Divison of the Regular army.

He disembarked for overseas service in France on 27th July, 1915, serving with the Battalion on the Somme and the Ypres Salient.

In the late Spring of 1917, the Battalion took part in the last great push in the Arras offensive, known later as the Third Battle of the Scarpe. The following account is taken from the Regimental history by Burrows.

On 1st May, 1917, the Battalion found itself once again near to the Roeux Chemical Works on the Arras front, with heavy artillery active on both sides. There was a good deal of sniping, which caused severe casualties, seven being killed and 18 wounded. Preparations were to continue the following day for a strenuous attack, with the men in outlying posts having been brought in on the nights of April 30th and May 1st.

The 4th Division had on its left the 9th Division, with the 17th Division in reserve. In planning a combined operation, the greatest problem was to arrange a creeping barrage to suit the conflicting objectives of the two latter Divisions. The northern part of Roeux was a formidable obstacle. The group of houses called the Chemical Works lay on either side of the Gavrelle-Roeux road, the principal being the chateau, which had thick stone walls and extensive cellars. East of the buildings were two large factories and a quarry, the latter being the site of two dug-outs. Behind the chateau, the Germans had constructed a strong point,

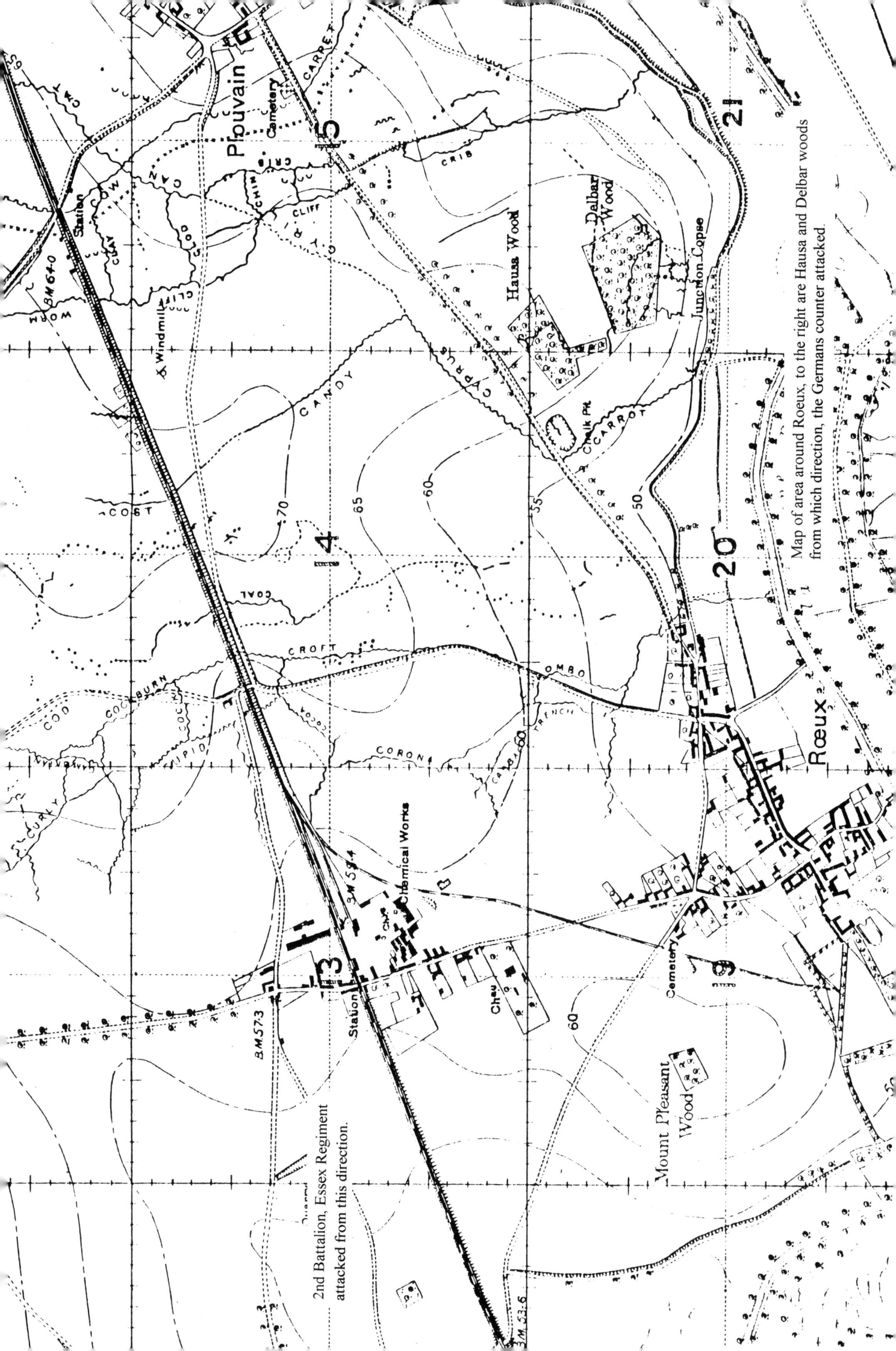

protected by a wall of concrete 7ft thick and served by four machine guns, which swept all the country behind the chateau up to the railway on the north and the cemetery on the south. This part of the village had been attacked on previous occasions, but so far the British troops had been unable to hold it.

Movement over the forward slope of the Point du Jour-Fampoux spur or along the Scarpe valley was in full view of the enemy on Windmill Hill and the British assembly trenches could therefore not be occupied during daylight hours. The high ground which constituted the second objective sloped very steeply to the Scarpe, so that all ground behind the ridge was invisible. The difficulties to be overcome in taking the second and third lines were intensified by the railway running diagonally across the line of advance of the 4th Division, the rails being carried for several hundred yards east of the station on an embankment with machine gun emplacements, whilst further on was a deep cutting. Troops who started north of the railway had therefore to remain north of it. The 4th Division had to conform to the movements of the 9th Division, who were north of the railway line, and the instructions were that the portion of the Division on the north of the railway should form a defensive flank facing south along the railway cutting until the troops advancing south of the railway at a slower rate had got level with them.

The bombardment of Roeux was not as effective as was hoped and this fact had considerable influence upon the subsequent operations. The 2nd Battalion, Essex Regiment, were on the left, north of the railway line, with the 9th Division on their left flank. On 3rd May, at 3.45 am, under a heavy barrage, the men advanced to secure the ground to the left of the chemical works. 'A' Company was on the left and 'C' on the right, with 'B' in support and 'D' in reserve. The two leading companies were caught by a devastating machine gun fire which mowed them down in scores, and the same fate met 'B' Company when it strove gallantly to fill their places. The men made some progress in Crook and Crow trenches and possibly went farther in the smoke and darkness, but the confusion of conflict was increased by the right flank of the 9th Division coming across the front of the Battalion. After fighting for some time, it was realised at 5.00 am that the attack on this part of the line had failed, with the enemy still holding the Chemical Works on the right and the 9th Division being unable to make way on the left. Lieut. St. G. Showers at this juncture organised the Battalion front line for resistance to a possible counter-attack with two platoons of 'D' Company and details of the 2nd Lancashire Fusiliers and the 1st Kings Own, 1st Rifle Brigade, being brought up in close support during the afternoon.

At 10.30 am and 2.20 pm, the enemy counter-attacked from the direction of Delbar and Hausa Woods. The latter made some ground, first sweeping past the north of Roeux, then east of the Chateau, crossing the railway line near the station, reaching Crook and Crow trench and occupying Clover trench until they were bombed out of it. The remainder of the first wave took cover in the trenches north of the railway and in the railway cutting whilst the second succumbed to the artillery fire directed at it. An attack was ordered at 11 pm, the purpose of which was to extricate any surviving men at the chateau and beyond it.

Thus the 4th Division did not achieve its planned objectives that day, and it was not until 11th May that it captured Roeux cemetery and chemical works, the 51st Division completing the good work on the night of 13th-14th May by securing possession of Roeux.

The 2nd Battalion, Essex Regiment's losses were heavy, totalling 207 non commissioned officers and men, of whom 106 were given as missing, most of whom were later reported as killed. One of those was Clifford Farthing, whose body was never recovered.

He is commemorated on the Arras Memorial (Bay 7) and on the West Mersea War Memorial.

**Sources**

*Commonwealth War Graves Commission*
*Essex Regiment Museum*
*Essex Units in the War 1914-1919 by J.W. Burrows*
*2nd Battalion, Essex Regiment War Diary, PRO, Kew, Ref no: WO95/1505*

Acting Sergeant Clifford Farthing's name inscribed on the Arras Memorial

**SURNAME: Marriage**

CHRISTIAN NAME(S): Thomas

AGE: 20

RECRUITMENT OFFICE: Colchester

SERVICE NO: 27963          RANK: Private

SERVICE/REGIMENT: 2nd Battalion, Suffolk Regiment

DECORATIONS EARNED: War Medal, Victory Medal

DATE KILLED/DIED: 5th May, 1917     LOCATION: France

LOCATION OF GRAVE: Etaples Military Cemetery

---

**BACKGROUND AND SERVICE HISTORY:**

Thomas Marriage was born on 26th June, 1896, the youngest child of George and Annie Marriage of Weir Farm, East Mersea. He was baptised on 16th August, 1896.

He had two sisters, Grace, born on 21st April, 1889, and Kate, born on 4th March, 1894. His elder brothers were Frank, born on 17th May, 1891, and John Bolton, born on 13th July, 1892.

Class photograph taken at East Mersea School, Thomas Marriage is one of those kneeling in the front row.

Thomas attended East Mersea school. It is not known what he did on leaving school, but it is possible he may have worked on his father's farm.

In the Spring of 1916, he enlisted at Colchester, and joined the Suffolk Regiment. During his training, he was in 'G' Company of the 10th Battalion and was billeted at Dovercourt. In April he was isolated with fifty of his fellow recruits when they all caught measles. Thomas describes this event, and his experiences in the training camp before he left for France, in letters to his family.

*April 13th, 1916*
*Dear Frank,*
*Am just writing a few lines in answer to your letter. I suppose you will be surprised to hear we are isolated with measles in this room about 50 of us, there has been 3 cases this last week, this means we are shut up in our room except when we all go out to drill or for a walk or the beach. Its not much better than being a prisoner and of course we are not learning anything, this lasts for about 16 days after the last illness. I am quite alright as yet. I had a letter from home yesterday, they are alright, Linda has got a bicycle from Colchester for 50 shillings (£2 50p). I don't think there's any chance of getting home for Easter and 24 hours does not seem much good, I want 48. Hope you will be able to go as I suppose they will be pleased to see you. There's bunches of recruits come here every afternoon and some get discharged. I wrote to A. Wopling yesterday as we do not get much to do now and mother said he asked her to tell me to write. He does not seem to get his papers yet, as just going to close this now as we have been out for 2 hours drill since I wrote the other part, so hoping you are quite well and will write soon.*
*I remain your loving brother, T. Marriage*
*P.S. any old fag ends you have to spare you might send on.*


*Dear Mother & all*
*Just a few lines in answer to your letter and to let you know I am quite well. I am sending a few of my things home out of the way, them brushes I bought off a chap for 6d (2.5p) as he was broke, I expect we are going out to the base in a day or two* (France) *and finish our training out there most likely for 2 or 3 months before we go any further. I expect we shall get plenty of drill as them that have been out say its harder work at the base then it is here. I had some photos taken on Saturday, but I don't think they will be up to much so if I get them sent home when they are finished don't swing them all over the Parish as I know what you are. Fancy them Mersea chaps copping out after being out so long, there are several chaps back with us who have been out there. My neck is better now as I have put that ointment on it every day, it was a bit sore one day just after I came back. I was going sick the next day but it was nearly better and you cannot see anything of it now but I still use the ointment on it, in case it breaks out again. It seems to be all up with Mr Wopling, you seem to come in for all the lovely jobs there is to be had. I don't think its much good you writing until I write again as we are most sure to be gone away before it gets here, and I shall write again first chance I get. I haven't any more news so must now close with best love to all.*
*From your loving son, T. Marriage*

The photograph of Private Thomas Marriage, referred to by him in his letter to his mother.

*Dear Frank,*
*Just a few lines in answer to your letter and to let you know that I am quite well. We are going to make a start in the morning at 3 o'clock, we have heard from the last lot that went away from here last Wednesday, but they cannot tell you anything about where they are, I expect we shall be at the base for another 2 or 3 months finishing our training at the least as of course you know they are sending every active serviceman there is in the country nearly out there now as soon as they have done their firing. I expect the idea is so as they have plenty of reinforcements out there in case of accidents now that they are advancing. One thing we can expect some hard training now I think as they don't have any nonsense out there. There's one thing we shall see about a little even if we come home with our head under our arm, but I think it will soon be over now most likely before we ever get to the firing line, although of course you never know as we might go right up there. I am writing this in the YMCA as we are having a tea and concert there for the last evening. There are about 280 of us here tonight, we have got everything to eat we could wish for. Haven't any more news so must close with love.*
*From your loving brother, Tom.*

The next letter Frank was to receive was postmark dated '27 July 1916' with Thomas addressing his correspondence from 'Suffolk Regt, 15th I.B.D., A.P.O., Sec 17 B.E.F., France.' He was now 'somewhere in France' continuing his basic training.

*Dear Frank,*

*Just a few lines to let you know I am quite well but of course cannot tell you where abouts we are. We are a long way from the firing line where we are now but I don't expect we shall be here many more days. We get plenty of food where we are now, better than we did in England and not a lot of work. Its alright to be here for a week or two just to have a look round as things seem quite different to England, tobacco and cigarettes are cheaper here than at home. There are dozens of French women about here with baskets selling different things, chocolates, etc, everyday. Things seem to be a bit rough up the other end according to all accounts, it will be a good job when its over as I expect we shall be quite ready to come home, when we get the chance, if we have luck enough to pull through, must close now, so hoping you are quite well.*
*I remain your loving brother, Tom.*

By early August, he had been assigned to Z Company, 14 Platoon, of the 2nd Battalion, Suffolk Regiment, a development which he passed on to his brother, Frank.

*August 8th, 1916*
*Dear Frank,*
*Just a few lines in answer to your letter and to let you know I am quite well. Was glad to hear about Maud's brother being found, I suppose he will get to England for a little while now if he's lucky. I noticed your address the other week but kept on forgetting about it when I wrote to you. If you don't mind you might send me a little tooth paste and one of them little pocket mirrors and comb in leather cases if you can get them, if not, don't send any big ones. My address is Pte T. Marriage, No. 27963, 2nd Suffolks, Z Company, 14 Platoon, B.E.F., France, take care of this as I shall not put it in every time. I suppose you will soon be going home now as mother said she was expecting you on the 26th of this month (hope it keeps fine for you) and Kit on the 12th. I suppose you will take your new bike home with you, expect they are cheap now as there is not so many at home to want them. Well Frank haven't any news, so hoping you are quite well.*
*I remain your loving brother, Tom.*
*P.S. you might send some envelopes and writing paper as we don't seem able to get any here.*

*September 4th, 1916*
*Dear Mother and all,*
*Just a few lines in answer to Grace's letter* (his eldest sister) *and to let you know I am quite well. It has been very wet out here this last day or two, quite different to what it has been. I'm afraid it isn't very nice for the holiday makers. I had a letter from Frank Bolton today, he is out here somewhere and got my address from his home. I suppose there are four of them out here now altogether. I shall write back to him soon. Kit tells me that George Pudney is wounded, I expect it is rather bad as he has got to England with it* (Lance Corporal George Pudney of Shop Lane, East Mersea recovered sufficiently from his wounds to transfer to a Labour Corps). *I have not had any letters from Walter, I don't suppose if he wrote to Dovercourt, I should get them now. Well mother I haven't much news so hoping you are all well at home, I will now close.*
*With best love, from your loving son Tom.*

So far, Thomas Marriage was the only son from the Marriage family to enlist, his two brothers, Frank and John Bolton had not joined up. Frank was serving in the Police Force in London, and a report on the sitting of a local Tribunal in the *Essex County Telegraph* dated 7th October, 1916, gives us a clue regarding John Bolton. *'J.B. Marriage (23), married,*

*seedgrower, East Mersea, appealed for exemption as the cultivator of 13 acres of land; in his spare time he assisted Mr Trim as horseman and threshing machine feeder,- Mr O. Thompson Smith supported the appellant and called Mr William Trim, who said he did all the threshing on the Island, and he could not get on without the assistance of the appellant,- The Tribunal recommended the military not to call up the man until Nov. 30th, and dismissed their appeal.'*
This appeal from the military was a follow up to a previous hearing in July when he was given exemption until 15th October, 1916. It is assumed that he appeared at further Tribunals and gained exemptions to the end of the war.

By October, 1916, it is probable that Thomas would have now joined his Battalion which was on the Somme at Serre. On 13th November, 1916, the Battle of the Ancre commenced and the Battalion were part of the attacking force. Due to the muddy conditions, the attack ended in a shambles with some men reaching the German support line while others lost direction completely. Early in the morning, attempts were made to collect the exhausted men, while further attacks were planned during the day. But by 4.30 pm, all operations were cancelled. Thomas's Company was part of the reserve force and although he did not take part he must have experienced the waist deep mud and the German artillery barrage.

He next wrote home at the beginning of December, when in his billets at Bus-les-Artois, making no mention of the attack of the previous month. If he had, the censor would have made sure that the news did not reach home.

*December 9th, 1916.*
*Dear Frank,*
*Just a few lines in answer to your letter and to thank you for the parcel. I have been a long time writing but have been busy, missed the post, or something every day when there's been a collection. The cake was very nice, the socks also were very handy. So Jack will be home for Christmas after all. I had a letter from home also one from Kit, they were all well excepting Dada has a bad cold. I got a Sunday Pictorial yesterday dated Dec 3rd, this makes the third one. I am sending Maud and Kit a French card as I thought they were rather pretty if they get them alright. Well Frank I don't think I've anymore news now so hoping you are quite well, as this leaves me at present. I must now close.*
*With best wishes, from your loving brother, Tom.*

At the beginning of January he was in the front line trenches around Serre. On 12th January, 1917, he was at Pernois, where the Battalion War Diary noted that re-organisation, general cleaning up and re-equipping was taking place. Platoons were organised into 3 rifle and 1 bombing section. Amongst all this activity, time was found to send another letter.

*January 12th, 1917.*
*Dear Frank,*
*Just a few lines in answer to your letter, and to let you know I am alright. I had a letter from home, they are all well, also one from Kit. Do you think you could send me a bottle of cough mixture as I have got rather a bad cold, also a bottle of blood mixture, hope I am not troubling you too much. So E. Woods and several others have got their papers, mother tells me. It is very wet here now, but I suppose it is anywhere. What kind of Xmas did you spend this year, we done fairly well considering, hope you enjoyed yourself. Well Frank, haven't much news so hoping you are quite well and will write soon. I must now close with best wishes.*
*From your loving brother, Tom.*

On 16th February, 1917, the Battalion moved to Arras, marching via Wanquetin and Warlus, a distance of 9 miles. Billets were reached at 7.30 pm that evening and here he found time to write to his mother.

*16th February, 1917*
*Dear Mother & all,*
*Just a few lines in answer to your letter and to let you know I received the parcel quite safely and enjoyed it all very much, it was a good while coming as I didn't get it until yesterday 15/2/17, everything was quite fresh and very nice, was glad to hear you are all well. I had a letter from Grace yesterday also one from Frank, they are both well. The weather here is much milder here now and not quite so fine. Was glad to hear Jack is still at home and that he has done pretty well this year. I suppose Mr Wopling isn't any better yet. Well mother, I haven't any news, so hoping you are all quite well. I must now close with best love.*
*From your loving son, Tom.*

Towards the end of February, preparations for the coming Battle of Arras were put in hand, and on 25th February, 1917, the Battalion supplied 580 men to work on dugouts and tunnels.

*25th February, 1917*
*Dear Maud,*
*Just a few lines to thank you for the nice things you sent and to let you know I am quite well, was glad to hear you are all well at home, I received the parcel on the 24th, so it was 10 days coming. It is much warmer here now than it has been, but not quite so fine. Haven't much news now so hoping you are quite well and thanking you again for the parcel. I must now close, with best wishes.*
*From Yours Sincerely Tom.*

By 13th March, 1917, the Battalion were in training and involved in construction work in preparation for the attack.

*13th March, 1917*
*Dear Mother & all*
*Just a few lines in answer to your letter, 5/3/17, to let you know I am quite well, was glad to hear you are all well, was sorry to hear about George Cudmore* (see page 73), *you had never told me Mr Wopling was dead, until I asked you if he was any better. Frank sends me a Sunday Pictorial nearly every week and we also get some English papers, so I don't think it is worth while you sending any. It was good of Mr Trim to give you that money for me, I think you had better keep it to help pay for sending them parcels out. I don't think it is worth while sending any underclothes out as we can only dump them when we get more clean ones. I am expecting a letter from Kit and Frank any day now. Well Mother I haven't any news so hoping you are all well, I must now close with best love.*
*From your loving son, Tom.*

More training for the attack took place on 19th March, this time at Denier.

*19th March, 1917*
*Dear Mother & all*
*Just a few lines in answer to your letter 12/3/17, which I received yesterday, was glad to hear you are all well. I expect you have received another letter from me since you wrote that, as I wrote one a few days ago and sent a field card before that. I had a letter from Kit yesterday,*

*she is quite well. We are getting some nice weather here now and there are a lot of snowdrops out I see, I expect we have nearly finished with the winter now, haven't any more news now so hoping you are all well. I must now close with best love to all.*
*From your loving son, Tom.*
*P.S. Remember me to Ward and Bunks, I hope Ward is feeling better now.*

With the Battle of Arras now only a few days away, the Battalion took part in further training in attack practice on 28th March.

*28th March, 1917*
*Just a few lines in answer to your letter, and to let you know I am quite well, and received your parcel on the 26th, everything was alright and very nice. I had a letter from Grace yesterday, she is quite well, also a paper from Maud and Frank. It still keeps trying to snow here every little while and raining. I had a letter from Kit a few days ago, she was quite well and tells me George Cudmore is getting on nicely now. Don't you think the papers have had some good news in lately. Well mother I haven't anything interesting to tell you so must now close with best love, and thanking you very much for the parcel.*
*From your loving son Tom.*

On 9th April, 1917, the Battle of Arras commenced, and as Private Thomas Marriage and the 2nd Battalion, Suffolk Regiment took part in the first days fighting.. In East Mersea his mother was posting him a letter.

*9th April, 1917*
*My dear Tom*
*We were very pleased to get your letter on the 2nd, also your Field Card on 8th, and to hear you are well. We are all well, Kit tells me she has had a letter from you dated March 30th. We are having awful weather, snow squalls every few minutes. Mr Hunter and Allen are at Wivenhoe training some recruits, so Allen came over on Sunday, he is looking better then when he was at Mersea. George Pudney was at church last night, he came over from Brightlingsea, Mrs Wopling asked him to stay at hers until today. I am sorry to tell you poor Nackie Cudmore was killed on the 21 of March, (see page 71), George is getting on nicely. I see America has come into the war now and as they have plenty of money, I hope you will soon settle the Huns. Arthur Hoy's young lady is here, she is as big as Kit. All our hens are ill, I think it is the cold weather. We cannot get any early seed potatoes, we have got plenty of late ones. I had a letter from Uncle Job, his boys are alright. I think I have told you all. With love from Dada and myself.*
*Your loving mother, A. Marriage*

The events of the first three days of the Battle are described in the Battalion War Diary.

<u>APRIL 9th</u>
*12.45 am. Battalion left WELLINGTON CAVES* (these were part of the caves and sewer system under Arras and sheltered the troops before the attack began) *to take up position in Assembly trenches as detailed in operation orders where it was joined by one section of the 9th Machine Gun Company under Lieut. W. Willingate.*

*4.45 am. Reported to Brigade 'In position'.*

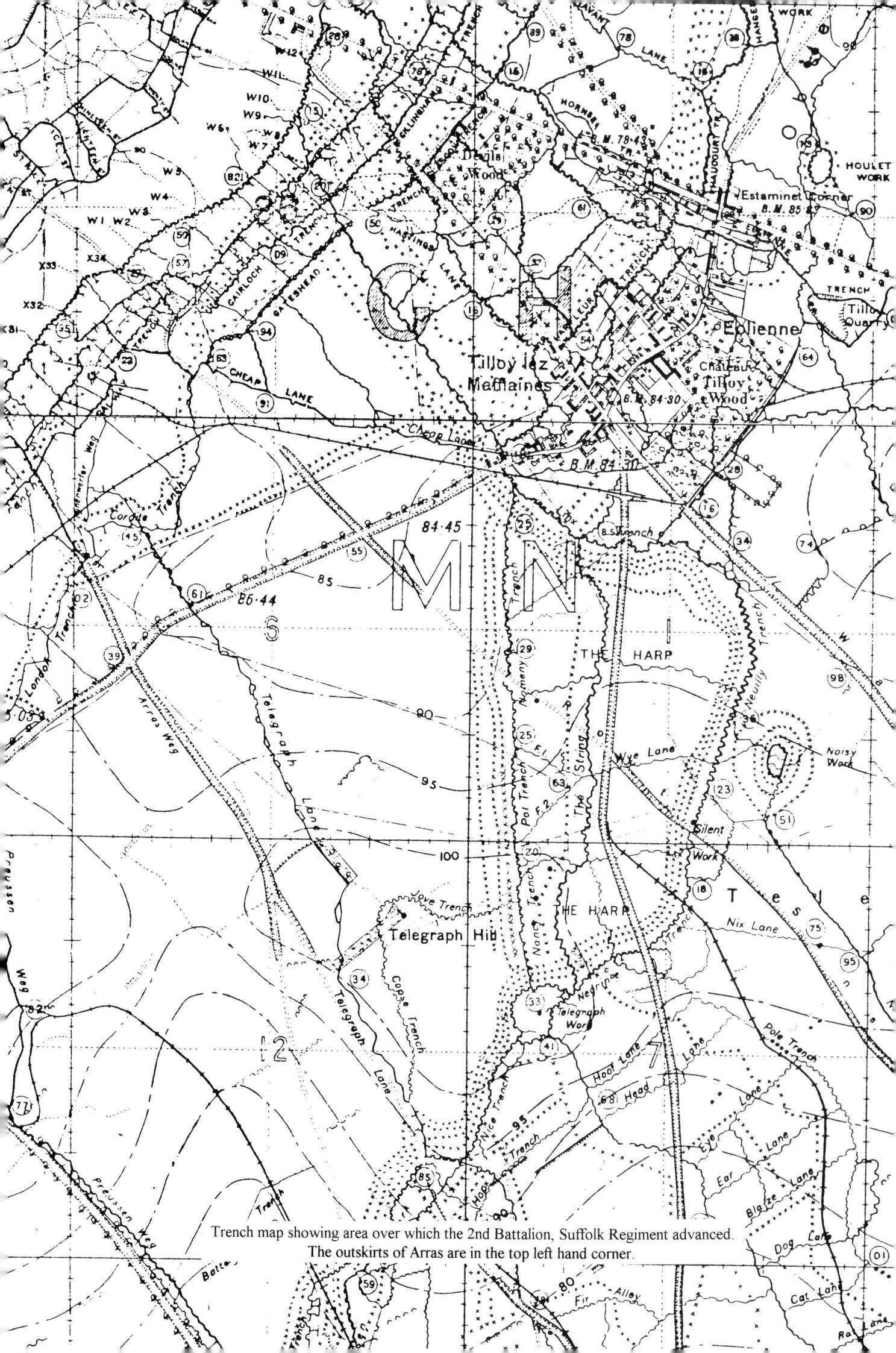

Trench map showing area over which the 2nd Battalion, Suffolk Regiment advanced. The outskirts of Arras are in the top left hand corner.

*5.30 am.* Zero hour. Black Line was assaulted and captured. Retaliation by the German Artillery was shrapnel on our front line and 5.9" barrage on 'no man's land.

*7.15 am.* 4th Royal Fusiliers crossed old German front line system and came under our barrage.

*7.50 am.* The Battalion crossed old German Front Line system and passed through the German 5.9" barrage in M6.b Central in Section Columns keeping good direction and intervals with apparently few, if any casualties. From the Observation Post, the British troops were observed to be on the ridge and over the String of the HARP (a German strong point) and numbers of Germans of 76th R.I. Regt and a few of the 9th Pioneers began to come in. The German Signal of white lights was sent up and his barrage brought back to the HARP along the String.

*9.15 am.* Verbal reports from two reliable N.C.O.'s wounded were received that the objective had been taken and this was confirmed from another source by the Adjutant who had gone forward to the HARP.

*9.30 am.* Artillery report at 8.40 am red flares burning on E. side of HARP. 2nd Lieut. Pryke, L/Cpl. Ashworth and Pte Garrett went forward with telephone wire to find and establish a new Battalion H.Q. in the HARP.

*11.00 am.* Written reports were received from the right and left company commanders (Capt. C.B. Nichols and 2nd Lieut. Francis) timed 8.55 am that the objective was taken and that the 12th West Yorks Regt. was through TILLOY but were not yet in touch.

*12 noon.* Battalion H.Q. moved to the String of the HARP and the line was visited, and consolidation found to be in an advanced stage. Prisoners were not counted, but the Battalion captured 1 Field Gun and 4 Machine Guns. The HARP was subjected to heavy shelling about 1 pm. The 8th Infantry Brigade passed through the 9th Infantry Brigade. Tank No. 777 did useful work along the Eastern face of the HARP.

*6.00 pm* The battalion was relieved in the HARP by the 1st Northumberland Fusiliers and withdrew to the German 1st System south of DEVILS WOOD returning to the 76th Infantry Brigade. Owing to the lack of dug out accommodation rest and reorganisation was very difficult.

<u>APRIL 10th</u>

*3.30 am.* Battalion H.Q. moved to the St Sauveur Tunnel next 10 Street and the Battalion commenced consolidation of GAIRLOCH TRENCH and strong point at C.36d.09.

*1.00 pm.* Warning order received to be ready to move to take over an outpost line and consolidate a defensive position along Southern portion of the GUEMAPPE N.E. to the CAMBRAI ROAD joining up with the 112th Infantry Brigade of 37th DIVISION.

*3.45 pm.* Battalion assembled ready to move.

*5.30 pm.* Order cancelled but Battalion to remain in readiness to move tomorrow.

*12.00 midnight. Brigade ordered to move in one hour's time.*

*<u>APRIL 11th</u>*

*Companies ordered to stand by for move, starting point as before, in German 4th Line.*

*2.00 am. Battalion moved, but movement was very slow owing to thick wire between 4th Line and TILLOY.*

*4.00 am. Battalion left TILLOY with Captain Vinden as guide.*

*5.15 am. Reached Brown line where battalion assembled in Artillery formation and was very heavily shelled by 5.9" and 'Woolly Bears' directed at Cavalry Bivouacs.*

*5.45 am. Proceeded to Brigade H.Q. for orders and reached there 6 am. Order to attack at 6.30 am postponed to 7 am. The 8th Kings Own were informed of change of time only just in time. Company Commanders received verbal orders:- 'X' Coy on left directed by 8th Kings Own with 'Y' Coy on the right. 'W' Coy supported by 'X' Coy and 'Z' Coy supported 'Y' Coy. One section of 76th machine Gun Company under 2nd Lieut. PASKYN co-operated on the right flank. The advance was made under a considerable amount of shelling but on coming into view of GUEMAPPE down the convex slope of the ridge, the lines met heavy Machine Gun fire from WANCOURT on their right flank as well as from GUEMAPPE. The attack was held up and a line of shell holes consolidated in N.11.d. Central.*

*10.30 am. Order to reorganise for further attack.*

*2.00 pm. Gordons attacked and the disjointed units in shell holes were ordered to support them. Heavy shelling at dusk of the line held by units of the 76th Infantry Brigade.*

During this period, Thomas Marriage was wounded and evacuated to Ward B21, No. 7 Canadian General Hospital, at Etaples, near Le Touquet. At the end of April he wrote home to say that he was recovering.

*28th April, 1917*
*Dear Mother & all,*
*I haven't had any letters in answer to my last one yet, but I thought I would let you know I am getting on nicely and feel better every day. I am still in the same hospital and very comfortable as we get everything we could wish for, but I expect, I might be marked for England any day now. Well mother, I haven't any news much now so hoping you are all well and that you are not worrying about me. I must now close, with best love.*
*From your loving son, Tom.*

But this was followed quickly by another letter from him telling his family that he had had his left leg amputated below the knee.

*Dear Mother & all*
*Just a few lines in answer to your letter which I received quite safely. I have been under an operation, they have had to take my left leg off at the knee as they said it was very bad. I believe I have been very bad but I begin to feel a lot better now. I shall be a mate for Ward if I get home again, but still it might have been a lot worse. I don't mind if I can but get well*

*and get home again. I think I can mess about and content myself alright as I suppose they will have to keep me. I never got Frank's parcel, I suppose it went to the Battalion after I got wounded. I expect I shall be sent to blighty as soon as they think I am strong enough to travel. I have had a letter from Kit also one from Grace. Well mother, I haven't any more news now so hoping you are all well at home.*
*I remain your loving son, Tom.*

This was the last they were to hear from him as he died on 5th May, 1917, and was buried the next day in Etaples Military Cemetery. The Ward Sister in the hospital wrote the following letter to the family.

*No 7 Canadian General Hospital*
*B.E.F. France*
*May 6th, 1917*

*Dear Mrs Marriage,*
*I regret very much to inform you that your son, Pte Thomas Marriage 27963, 2 Suffolk Reg. passed quietly away last evening at 5.30 pm, May 5/1917. All that medical skill could do, was to no avail, he was given every care and attention and made comfortable. For a time after his left leg was amputated, he was very ill, but lately had picked up and was quite cheerful and happy. I had hoped that he would pull through. But he seemed to take a weak spell yesterday and never rallied gradually sank and passed away, he was unconscious all afternoon, so did not suffer. I myself was talking to him in the morning and he said he was much better and I asked him if he wanted anything, and he said no. I have been in the habit of getting anything special for him, that he was allowed to have. He will be laid to rest today, Sunday in the Etaples Military Cemetery.*
*Assuring you of our sincere sympathy in your great sorrow*

*I remain*
   *Sincerely Yours*
     *Frances E. Ellwood, Sister*
       *for*
     *Matron Willoughly RRC*

By the middle of May the family were slowly coming to terms with Thomas's death as is shown in this letter from his mother to his brother Frank.

*16th May, 1917*
*My Dear Frank,*
*Just a line to wish you many happy returns of the day. It was a comfort to us having Kit for a few days. I am looking forward to seeing you again in June. I had a nice letter from Mrs George Cudmore this morning, also Mrs Rose and Aunt Ruth, she has got Stanley's boy and hopes Toms getting better, she heard from Laura he was wounded, she didn't say where Stan was. Gertie died the 3rd of April, the day Tom was wounded* (There seems confusion when Tom was wounded. The Battalion were in camp on 3rd April, with all training cancelled due to heavy snow, therefore we can only assume that his mother was confused over the date and that he was wounded between 9th - 11th April). *Mr Sam White had a message this morning to say his eldest son was killed in action* (see page 80). *Please give my love to Maud and tell I got her letters but have not had time to write. We got Tom's insurance money today. Dada and I both wished they had kept the money and we had our boy, but we must be thankful he'd*

*died so peaceful and had everything he wanted. That was better than been taken prisoner. Have you had anything to do with these strikers. I have got some wool to foot your socks, but have not had time. Several children have got measles at Mersea. Poor Ward has been laid on a bed in our garden the last two days. He says its the best rest he has had for months. I must close now.*
*With best love from your loving mother.*
*The lord bless and keep you.*

Thomas Marriage is commemorated on the East Mersea War Memorial in the church.

**Sources**

*Commonwealth War Graves Commission*
*Suffolk Record Office*
*2nd Battalion, Suffolk Regiment War Diary*
*Mrs Marriage, East Mersea Road*
*Mr R.J. Marriage, Layer de la Haye*
*Mrs Clifton*
*Essex Regiment Museum*
*Essex County Telegraph*

The grave of Private Thomas Marriage in Etaples Military Cemetery

**SURNAME: Woods**

CHRISTIAN NAME(S): Bertie

AGE: 26

RECRUITMENT OFFICE: Colchester

SERVICE NO: 32434          RANK: Acting Bombardier

SERVICE/REGIMENT: Royal Garrison Artillery

DECORATIONS EARNED: 1914 Star, War Medal, Victory Medal

DATE KILLED/DIED: 11th August, 1917   LOCATION: France

LOCATION OF GRAVE: Maroc British Cemetery, Nord

---

## BACKGROUND AND SERVICE HISTORY:

Bertie Woods was born on Mersea Island in 1891, the son of Mark and Emma Amelia Woods of East Road, East Mersea. He was baptised on 6th November, 1891. He was the middle child of the family with an elder sister, Alice Mary, and a younger sister, Emma.

He attended East Mersea School.

He enlisted at Colchester and joined the Royal Garrison Artillery, eventually being posted to 24th Heavy Battery. The Battery embarked from Southampton, sailing for France on 9th September, 1914.

On 11th August, 1917, he was killed in action. (Location and circumstances are unknown)

He is buried in Maroc British Cemetery, near Loos, and is commemorated on the East Mersea War Memorial in the church.

**Sources**

*Commonwealth War Graves Commission*
*Essex Regiment Museum.*
*Essex Record Office (Colchester)*

The grave of Acting Bombardier Bertie Woods in Maroc British Cemetery, near Loos.

**SURNAME: Cudmore**

CHRISTIAN NAME(S): Albert Victor Juba

AGE: 20

SHORE BASE: Chatham

SERVICE NO: 12866          RANK: Deckhand/Sea Gunner

SERVICE/REGIMENT: Royal Naval Reserve

DECORATIONS EARNED: Not Known

DATE KILLED/DIED: 11th October 1917          LOCATION: Not known

MEMORIAL IF NO KNOWN GRAVE: Chatham Naval Memorial

---

**BACKGROUND AND SERVICE HISTORY:**

Albert Victor Juba Cudmore was born on 22nd June, 1897, the youngest son of Mr Robert and Mary Ann Cudmore of Fairlight Villa, Kingsland Road, West Mersea. It was said that his third name 'Juba' was derived from his having been born in the year of Queen Victoria's Diamond Jubilee.

On 1st November, 1916, he joined the Royal Naval Reserve, enlisting at HMS *Pembroke*, the shore station at Chatham, transferring to the strength of HMS *Thalia* another shore station at the Dunskaith Naval Depot, Invergordon. Here he served on HM Trawler *Aster\** as a deckhand and sea gunner. On 28th October 1917, it was reported that she was overdue whilst on a North Sea patrol, having last been seen on 11th October A note on Albert Cudmore's Naval record states:

*28.10.17 - Telegram from A.G.C., Fishing trawler Aster overdue, last seen 11.10.17, feared lost with all hands. Cudmore regarded as having lost his life*

He is commemorated on the Chatham Naval Memorial, Kent, on his parents' grave in the Barfield Road, Cemetery and on the West Mersea War Memorial.

**Sources**

*Commonwealth War Graves Commission*
*Essex Regiment Museum*
*Essex County Standard*
*Ministry of Defence, DR2A - Navy*

---

\* On the family grave the trawler's name is given as HMT *Astor* which is incorrect.

The family grave in the cemetery in Barfield Road, West Mersea. Albert Cudmore's name is inscribed on the gravestone.

Albert Cudmore's name inscribed on the Chatham Naval Memorial.

**SURNAME:** Cutts Avis

CHRISTIAN NAME(S): Frederick Joseph

AGE: 20

SHORE BASE: Chatham

SERVICE NO: 14636DA   RANK: Deckhand

SERVICE/REGIMENT: Royal Naval Reserve

DECORATIONS EARNED: Unknown

DATE KILLED/DIED: 27th October, 1917   LOCATION: North Sea

MEMORIAL IF NO KNOWN GRAVE: Chatham Naval Memorial

---

## BACKGROUND AND SERVICE HISTORY:

Joseph Frederick Cutts Avis was born on Mersea Island on 28th June, 1897, the son of Frederick and Emily Jane Cutts Avis of Clarence Villa, Captains Road, West Mersea.

On 7th February, 1917, he joined the Royal Naval Reserve, enlisting at HMS *Pembroke*, the shore station at Chatham, transferring to the strength of HMS *Ganges* another shore station near Shotley in Suffolk on 28th February, 1917. This was the administrative centre for mine sweeping operations in this sector of the North Sea and he became a deckhand on HM Trawler *Strymon*. She was a Grimsby trawler, no GY912, of 198 tons, and was hired by the Royal Navy (Navy No: 1842) in August 1915. After being converted for mine sweeping duties and given a 12 pounder gun for protection, she became one of the many trawlers that patrolled the North Sea on mine sweeping operations.

On 27th October, 1917, she left harbour at 6.00 am in the company of HMT *Neree* and HMT *Victorian II* with orders to make an exploratory sweep from Sunk light vessel, a channel midway between War Channel and Shipwash Shoal, as far as a point X.1. Sweep, and then return down the Shipway. It was reported that the weather was fine, with a moderate sea and a south west wind. The sweep commenced at 8.15 am in a 'D' formation with *Strymon* and *Victorian II* being the leading pair of sweepers. As the formation reached 51.57.30.N. 1.48.E, the *Strymon* struck a mine amidships and went down in about one minute. The formation immediately slipped their sweeps and rushed to the scene. Boats were lowered to pick up survivors, of which two were rescued, while three bodies were picked up. No trace could be found of the remainder of the crew including Frederick Joseph Cutts Avis.

On 30th October, 1917, a Court of Enquiry was held at HMS *Ganges*.

One of the witnesses was Leading Seaman Edward Albert Walters, one of the survivors who recalled the moment when the mine struck.

*'We were sweeping as ordered by the Divisional Leader. We were first pair, inside ship, sweeping with HM Trawler 'Victorian II'. At 9.10 am I was standing on the fore deck, the three Reserve men had been cleaning the gun, we had just finished, and I had gone down to the forecastle to get some potatoes, and brought them on deck. The next thing I knew was that I was blown into the water. I came up from amongst the wreckage, and saw some wreckage and a part of the mast, to which I clung. I saw Ackroyd the other survivor, and whistled to him. I then saw 'Victorian's' Boat coming towards us. The boat first picked up me, and then Ackroyd'.*

One of the findings of the Court of Enquiry was the suspicion that some of the crew had ignored a Navy standing order that once out of port, life belts (jackets) should be worn. Apparently they were rather cumbersome things when working with heavy equipment on deck. This led to the following statement being issued.

*17th November, 1917*
*The Rear Admiral,*
*Harwich.*
*With reference to your submission of the 31st ultimo, No 745/H7, forwarding the minutes of the proceedings of a Court of Enquiry held to investigate the circumstances attending the loss of HM Trawler 'Strymon' on 27th ultimo, I am to acquaint you that Their Lordships are of the opinion that disciplinary steps should be taken when the order to put on life belts is contravened.*
*By Command of Their Lordships.*
*Charles Walker*

The bodies of the eight missing crewmen including Frederick Joseph Cutts Avis were never found. He is commemorated on the Chatham Naval Memorial and the West Mersea War Memorial.

**Sources**

*Commonwealth War Graves Commission*
*Court of Enquiry in the sinking of HMT Strymon, PRO, Kew, Ref. no: ADM137/3323*
*Ministry of Defence, DR2A - Navy*

Frederick Joseph Cutts Avis's name inscribed on the Chatham Naval Memorial, Kent.

H. M. S. "GANGES".
Harwich.
30th October. 1917.

Sir,

In accordance with your instructions, we have this day held a careful enquiry into the circumstances attending the loss of H. M. Trawler "STRYMON" No. 1842, of the 27th October 1917.

We find that the loss of H. M. Trawler "STRYMON" No. 1842, and resulting loss of life was caused by that ship striking an enemy moored mine, this mine being one of the group probably laid on the night of the 24th.

We further find that no blame can be attributed to anyone concerned.

The work of rescue appears to have been well carried out under the conditions.

We consider, that to emphasize the carrying out of A.M.O. 2340/17, Leaders of Minesweeping Divisions, should be instructed that when their Divisions are proceeding out of Harbour, they are to make a general signal to their Division to put on lifebelts.

We have the honour to be, Sir,
Your obedient servants

COMMANDER. R. N. R.
(President of Court).

LIEUTENANT. R. N. R.

Letter to the Rear Admiral, Harwich, from the Court of Enquiry, confirming their findings.

**SURNAME: Green**

CHRISTIAN NAME(S): Edward Oscar

AGE: 24

RECRUITMENT OFFICE: Colchester

SERVICE NO: 2899 Essex Territorials                    RANK: Rifleman
            392922 2/9th Battalion, London Regiment (Queen Victoria's Rifles)

SERVICE/REGIMENT: Essex Territorials. Transferred to 2/9th Battalion London Regiment (Queen Victoria's Rifles)

DECORATIONS EARNED: War Medal, Victory Medal

DATE KILLED/DIED: 24th December, 1917   LOCATION: France

MEMORIAL IF NO KNOWN GRAVE: Tyne Cot Memorial, Tyne Cot Cemetery, near Ypres

---

**BACKGROUND AND SERVICE HISTORY:**

Edward Oscar Green was born in 1893, the son of Oscar and Ellen Kate Green of Moss Cottage, Queen Corner, West Mersea. He was baptised on 27th September, 1896.

He enlisted at Colchester and initially joined the Essex Territorial Force. He was then transferred to the 2/9th Battalion, London Regiment, known as Queen Victoria's Rifles. The Battalion spent some time at Bromeswell Camp, Melton, near Ipswich. On 4th February 1917, it arrived in France, disembarking from the *La Marguerite* at Le Havre.

In the summer and autumn of 1917, the Battalion took part in the campaign known as the 'Third Ypres' and even better known as the 'Battle of Passchendaele'. The battle began on 31st July, 1917, under a tremendous creeping barrage and in good weather. There were early successes, but the attacking forces came up against German strong points and pill boxes in a well organised defence line. Coupled with the effects of the enemy artillery barrage and counter attacks by specially trained units, the advance came to a halt. The weather then broke, and Belgium suffered the worst rainfall in the preceding seventy five years, which turned the battlefield into a swamp. Movement up on to the battlefield was restricted to walking on duckboards in between the water-filled shell holes, where it was known for men and even pack mules to lose their footing, fall into the shell holes and drown. The campaign finally ended on the 10th November, after a number of hard fought battles, with Passchendaele in allied hands.

On Christmas Eve, 24th December, 1917, the Battalion were still in the area in support in an area known as Kempton Park and at Pheasants Trench. This trench had been captured from the Germans after a number of hard-fought assaults. On that night Rifleman Edward Oscar Green was killed, probably by an enemy shell. His body was never recovered.

Map showing the area where Rifleman Green was serving when he was killed. Pheasant Trench is in the centre of the map.

He is commemorated on the Tyne Cot Memorial near Ypres, and on the West Mersea War Memorial.

**Sources**

*Commonwealth War Graves Commission*
*Essex Regiment Museum*
*9th Battalion, London Regiment (Queen Victoria's Rifles) War Diary, PRO, Kew,*
*Ref no: WO95/3009*
*Passchendaele, The Day-by-Day Account by Chris McCarthy, published by*
*Arms & Armour*

Rifleman Edward Oscar Green and his wife.

Rifleman Edward Oscar Green's name inscribed on the Tyne Cot Memorial, Tyne Cot Cemetery.

**SURNAME:** Roberts

CHRISTIAN NAME(S): Edmund Percy

AGE: 24

RECRUITMENT OFFICE: Colchester

SERVICE NO: 22889        RANK: Lieutenant

SERVICE/REGIMENT: 11th Battalion, Essex Regiment

DECORATIONS EARNED: 1914/15 Star, War Medal, Victory Medal

DATE KILLED/DIED: March 21st, 1918     LOCATION: France

MEMORIAL IF NO KNOWN GRAVE: Arras Memorial, Faubourg d'Amiens Cemetery,

---

### BACKGROUND AND SERVICE HISTORY:

Edmund Percy Roberts was born on 21st December, 1894 in the London area, the son of George Edgar and Elizabeth Ann Roberts. He had an elder brother named John Corfield Roberts who was killed in an accident in Los Angeles on 4th July, 1912. There was a sister, Margerita and a younger brother, Edgar.

Edmund was educated at All Saints School, Blosham. On leaving school, he went to Aspatria Agricultural College. In 1913, he took up farming on his father's land at East Mersea; the family were now living at 'Rosebank', Coast Road, West Mersea.

After the outbreak of war, he gave up farming and on 10th September, 1914, enlisted with his friend, Harry Pearl Cross, at Colchester, both joining the 11th Hussars, part of the 12th Reserve Cavalry Regiment. Harry's recollections of the period have been recorded by his relative, Mr R.G. Weldon.

*Percy Roberts, a great friend of mine,* ( It seems that Edmund preferred his second name and was known in adult life as E. Percy Roberts) *was also waiting to enlist and, as we both had motorcycles, we decided to enlist together. As soon as the harvest was gathered in we reported to the Albert Hall in Colchester, where we passed our medicals. We then signed up, asking to be posted to the 11th Hussars, who were then based in Colchester, as we were keen on riding and thought it would be great fun to join the cavalry. It was a fortuitous request to have made, because had I gone into the infantry my name would quite probably have been on the fatality lists beginning to come back from the Front.*

*We received our call-up papers after four long days and were instructed to report to the depot in Scarborough. We left Waldegraves on our motorcycles one morning and headed north, stopping overnight at Grantham. Riding off to the war on that wet morning will always remain a vivid memory, as no sooner had we set off down the muddy Waldegraves Lane than my bike skidded and I came down a real purler. No damage was done, though I was in a terrible mess and had to go back to the house rather sheepishly to clean up. In hindsight it seems silly but by the time we finally left I was angry with myself for losing a precious hour in this way, as it seemed to be yet another delay to us joining up. As we finally rode off together a second time, we were both genuinely worried that we were going to be too late for the war.*

'Rosebank', Coast Road, West Mersea, the home of the Robert's family. Now demolished and replaced by flats named after the original house. *(Brian Jay Collection).*

*At Scarborough, Percy and I reported to the depot at midday, where our details were taken down and we were given numbers. We were told we could do what we liked for the next few days, but that we should report each morning to the same place until we received further instructions. The barracks were full so we had to find cheap lodgings in town, where we stayed for three restless nights, wondering what lay ahead for us. Then came the day when, on reporting as usual, we were told to remain in the barracks as we were due to be moved. It proved impossible to discover our destination, so we were obliged to leave our motorcycles at the station, with instructions that we would send forwarding orders later.*

*Later, that day, as excitement and tension mounted, we were all marshalled in the barrack square from where we marched proudly down through the town. It was about six o'clock, a balmy late summer's evening, and the streets were full of people waving animatedly and cheering as we entrained at Scarborough station. Still nobody would tell us where we were going, though probably very few people actually knew.*

*As the flags and cheers grew distant, it became apparent that this was a long slow train, crammed with men packed uncomfortably together. The train rattled on through the night, while some of the men managed to sleep fitfully and all became desperately hungry. We had been instructed to stay on board until told to get off, but when we stopped briefly at one dimly-lit station I dashed across the platform to see if the refreshment room was open. At this point I had my first taste of military discipline and I cannot repeat what the N.C.O. bawled across the station.*

*Early the next morning, the train creaked to a halt, and we disembarked stiffly to find ourselves in Aldershot. We were marched straightaway to the parade ground at the East Cavalry Barracks, then situated on the edge of the town, where we were to be allocated to units. In order to encourage volunteers, the 1914 recruiting campaign had made a great feature of the fact that friends joining up as a group could stay together in whichever unit they were posted to. Accordingly, as Percy and I had struck up a lively friendship on the train with four fellows from Lancaster, we all decided to keep together.*

*We were told to get into a single line and number from the right. The Sergeant ordered numbers 1-60 to march off in one direction, and 61 and above to march off in another. As my luck would have it I was number 61, while my friend were numbers 56-60 in the other group. Naturally, I asked to change places with somebody so as to be with my companions, whereupon I received my second dose of army discipline. Did I realise I was in the Army? That I had left my mother? Was I weaned......? Despite several attempts, I never did get a transfer to rejoin Percy and my friends.*

*We were stationed in the married quarters, eight to a room, and our first breakfast consisted of bread and cheese, washed down with tea drunk from grimy mess tins. Everything was still very disorganised as this was about six weeks after the outbreak of war and, although we were issued with rather dirty blankets, we were not given any proper uniform for some time. Such training as we did was done initially in our civilian clothes until, little by little, we began to receive uniforms. I was issued with some blue breeches with a yellow stripe up the side, khaki puttees, boots, a coarse army shirt and a red jacket, one of the old kind, which looked as though it might well have seen action at Waterloo. These uniforms, such as they were, were generally badly fitting and extremely uncomfortable and it was weeks before I was equipped with a hat.*

*On arrival of our motorcycles, we managed to get weekend leave to London. These trips were enormous fun, and Percy and I would drive up to London for the Saturday night in the little three-wheeled two-seater motorcar he had acquired. This was dreadfully unreliable and kept breaking down, but somehow we always managed to get there and back in time.*

Percy and Harry were soon to go their separate ways, when on 10th October, 1914, Percy requested permission from his Commanding Officer to apply for a commission. Lieutenant Colonel Ronald Brooke recommended him for a commission in the infantry, although his application showed that he wished to remain with the 11th Hussars.

Officers of the 11th Battalion, Essex Regiment at date of embarkation for France.
Second Lieutenant Edmund Percy Roberts is in the front row, second in from the left.

On 15th November, 1914, he was commissioned as a 2nd Lieutenant with the 11th Battalion, Essex Regiment, and joined them during their training at Shoreham, where they were billeted in tents on Shoreham golf course. The weather became very wet and huts were ordered to be built. However their erection was slow and for a time the Division was billeted in Brighton. In January, 1915, he became unfit due to an unerupted upper wisdom tooth which he had to have extracted, and he did not return to the Battalion until mid-February. Training continued, and while practising trench warfare on Chobham Common on 21st August, 1915, the Battalion was notified that it would probably be ordered to France within a week. The advance party left on 28th August, followed by the main body of men on 30th August, landing at Boulogne and immediately moving to Ostrohove rest camp situated on a hill overlooking the town.

The Battalion undertook a further period of training, until orders came on 21st September to march to the front line near Bethune, to be in place for the planned offensive to be known as the Battle of Loos. The offensive commenced on 25th September, and lasted until 8th October, although the Battalion only saw action in the first two days, before being relieved by the Guards.

On 20th October, 1915, the Battalion moved to the Ypres Salient. During this tour of duty Percy was taken ill and diagnosed as having tonsillitis and jaundice, the jaundice possibly having been caused by contaminated needles, as he had had an injection prior to the jaundice appearing. He was evacuated from the Salient and admitted to the St John Hospital at Etaples from where his family received the following telegram.

*2/12/15*
*TO: Roberts, Rosebank, West Mersea, Essex.*
*2n Lieut P. Roberts Essex Regiment admitted St John Hospital, Etaple 23rd Nov. Case not then diagnosed. Particulars will be wired on receipt.*

On 30th December, 1915, he returned to England to recover at home in West Mersea. Recovery was slow, and there followed a number of appearances at Medical Boards until he was pronounced fit for duty on the Home Front. He reported for duty with the 12th (Reserve) Battalion, Essex Regiment at Harwich on 11th March, 1916. On 1st April, while on Home Service, he represented his father with regard to one of his employees, a Mr Waterman, at the local Tribunal. These proceedings are described in the biography of Charles Thomas Powell.

On 22nd April, 1916, a Medical Board at Harwich pronounced him fit for General Service, and it is assumed that soon afterwards he rejoined his Battalion in France which was still on the Ypres Salient. In July, they were involved in the Battle of the Somme, and later again in the Loos area. On July 29th, 1916, Percy left the Battalion and transferred to the Royal Flying Corps to train as either a pilot or an observer. However, Percy's experiences on the battlefield must have had a profound effect on him, as in the following November he was home again suffering from the effects of shell shock.

On 16th March, 1917, a Medical Board decided that he was permanently unfit to serve as a pilot or observer, and he was ordered to join the 3rd Battalion, Essex Regiment at Felixstowe for a further period of service on the Home Front while he recovered fully. Another five months passed before he was deemed fit for service overseas, and on 10th August, 1917, he once again embarked for France, arriving at Boulogne, and rejoined the 11th Battalion, Essex Regiment which was again in action in the Loos area. On 11th November, 1917, he was promoted to the rank of Lieutenant and he took part in the Battle of Cambrai. The new year saw Percy taking command of 'A' Company on 3rd January, 1918.

In March 1918, Intelligence sources received reports of a German build up along the Hindenburg Line and it was felt that a German offensive was imminent. The Battalion was at the front near Bapaume on the Somme and its War Diary describes events prior to the German attack.

*March 8 -12th*
*The whole energies of the Battalion were directed towards preparing the sector for defence. Firebays were increased, parapets adjusted and thickened and some thousands of yards of double apron wire were put out. A German attack was expected on the morning of the 10th, but did not materialise. Our artillery was extremely active throughout the tour - must have caused considerable loss to the enemy. A large number of hostile dumps were exploded. An inter-company relief was projected for the 11th, but this had to be abandoned on account of the working and carrying parties required for the laying of two minefields on the battalions front which were intended as a defence against tanks. These fields were constructed by burying 200 2" trench mortar bombs fuse upwards, the fuse fixing of a special type calculated to explode the bombs when an unusually heavy object passed over them. The work of leaving these fields occupied the night of 11/12th-12/13th. There were strong indications of an attack on the morning of the 13th, every possible precaution was taken, but once more the attack was not delivered. The patrolling during the past few nights had been most arduous, but after the 13th, the situation eased down somewhat although precautions were not relaxed appreciably as it was quite certain that the hostile offensive was imminent.*

*March 13th*
*An inter-company relief was carried out in accordance with Operational Orders.*

*March 14 - 19th*
*Work on the defences of the sector was vigorously carried out for the remainder of the tour. The weather throughout was excellent. On the night of the 19/20th, the Battalion was relieved by the 2nd Battalion, Durham Light Infantry.*

*March 20th*
*The Battalion arrived in Camp at Beugnatre at 3 am and bathed at Bapaume and Favreuil during the morning. At 5 pm practically the whole Battalion except 'A' Coy and two Platoons of 'B' who had been left at Morchies, paraded for a working party under Major Stockdale, the 2nd in command. This party, 300 strong, moved by light railway from Favreuil to Maricourt Wood and was employed on digging a trench called the Lagnicourt Switch under the 71st Infantry Brigade. The two forward platoons of 'B' Company who were billeted in the sunken road nearby were also employed on this work.*

On 21st March, 1918, the Germans launched their planned Spring offensive, code named 'Michael' in an attempt to break the Allied lines. On the morning of 21st March, at 2 am, the command was given to the Battalion to put into action the order issued on 13th March, giving detailed precautions in the event of a German attack as it was felt that the German attack was now imminent. The action of that day is vividly described in an Appendix in the Battalion War Diary.

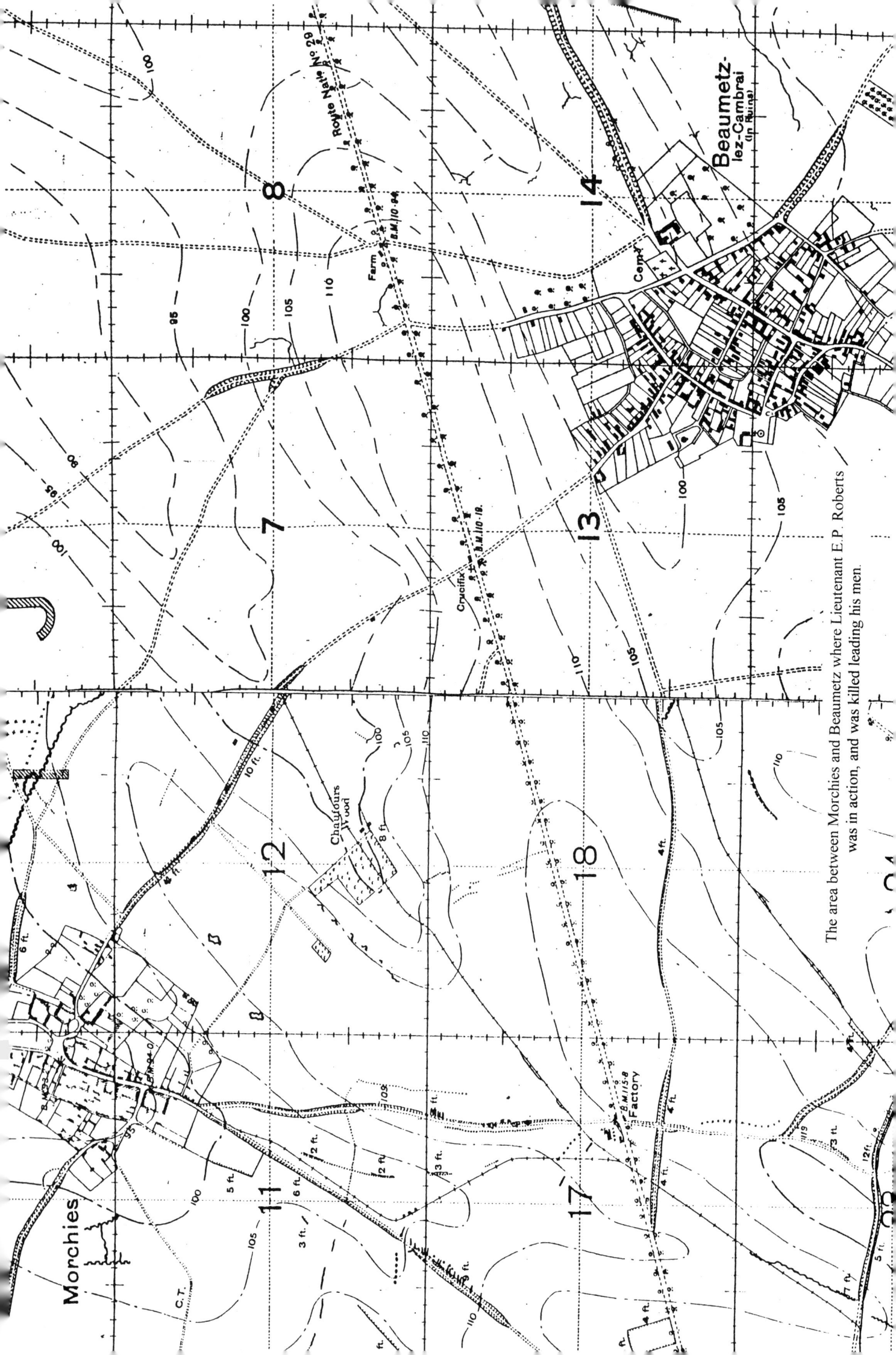

The area between Morchies and Beaumetz where Lieutenant E.P. Roberts was in action, and was killed leading his men.

*March 21st*

*The roll of the reserve Battalion was to proceed, less one Coy., to a pre-determined assembly point, and to be in position by 5.30 am. The working party of the previous day had not yet begun to return, but in a few minutes a wire was received saying that it was on the way.*

*It transpired later that the arrangements made for the train were defective and the party had to march back. It began to arrive at about 3 am in a very exhausted condition. Tea and rum had been prepared and the first Coy 'C' was on its way back to the assembly position by 4.15 am.*

*The greater part of the Battalion had left Camp once more by 4.45 am with the exception of a few men of the working party who had not yet returned.*

*At 5 am just after the Commanding Officer had left Camp in the rear of the Battalion, a heavy shell fell into it, and the hostile bombardment began.*

*The personnel moved along roads via Vaux while Echelon A of the transport moved by cross country tracks.*

*The enemy was using a considerable number of gas shells especially in the Maricourt Wood and Morchies valleys and Box Respirators had to be put on. A gas shell fell near a man who had not done so and he died in a few moments.*

*By 6.30 am the Battalion Headquarters personnel began arriving in the sunken road at map ref I.5.c. followed at intervals by 'D', 'C' & 'B' Coys. The road was being shelled steadily with 5.9s and a few gas shells, and some casualties were sustained. Lt A. Nethercott, M.C. and 2nd Lt W.B. Stoner were wounded, the latter severely.*

*The Medical Officer, Captain F.P. Freeman, M.C. was also wounded slightly in five places but declined to leave the Battalion and remained with it throughout the battle, working in considerable discomfort towards the later stages.*

*Echelon 'A' of the transport had arrived in the road, but after one limber had been hit by a shell and rendered useless, the limbers were unloaded and sent back to the transport lines.*

*At about 11 am a message was received from Brigade Headquarters that Lt-Colonel Dumbell was to take charge of troops in the Brigade Sector Beaumetz-Morchies Line, and shortly afterwards 'C' Coy (Captain W.F. Martinson) and 'D' Coy (Captain J.S. Marks) moved off under Major G.N. Stockdale, M.C. to reinforce the 1st West Yorkshire Regiment in the right sub-sector of the Brigade Front.*

*Immediately these Coys had left the sunken road, the rest of the troops in the road, consisting of half 'B' Coy and Battalion Headquarters moved onto the Beaumetz- Morchies or 'Corps' line. This portion of trench was already occupied by 'A' Coy* (under the command of Lt Percy Roberts) *and half of 'B' Coy 11th Essex, the 12th Field Coy, Royal Engineers, and its attached infantry and one Coy of the 11th Battalion, Leicestershire Regiment (Pioneer Battalion). Very fortunately the German barrage ceased while the manoeuvre was being carried out and there were no casualties between the assembly position and the Corps Line.*

*At 12.30 pm, the following message was sent to the O.C. 'A' Coy. (Lt E.P. Roberts) 'You will move your Coy, forward and reinforce the 2nd Durham Light Infantry at once. You will take forward all ammunition you possibly can.'*

*Lt Col. Dumbell then re-organised the troops in the Brigade Sector of the Corps Line so that it was held as follows from right to left, 'B' Coy, 11th Essex, 87 O.R's, 12th Coy. R.E. and attached infantry, 120 O.R.'s, 11th Leicestershire (Pioneer Battalion) 60 O.R.'s. 'B' Coy. 11th Essex was in touch with a Battalion of Gordon Highlanders on its right. Shortly afterwards, Battalion Headquarters was moved to what was formerly the 18th Light Trench Mortar Battery H.Q. Here the O.C. the Battery, Captain Pearl was of great assistance in arranging accommodation and providing refreshment for the headquarters officers, some of whom had had nothing to eat or drink for twelve hours.*

*The hostile artillery and machine gun fire now increased considerably and was maintained until dusk.*

*The following message which was sent to the Quartermaster at 1.45 pm summarises the situation at the time. 'D' & 'C' Coys are up with the West Yorks. 'A' Coy. is with the 2nd Durham Light Infantry. The line has been driven in on the Yorks front but the German success does not appear to be considerable. Send rations for Battalion H.Q. and 'B' Coy. here. Rations for the others can go up with anything going to the respective battalions in the line. Casualties fairly light.*

*This comparatively satisfactory state of affairs unfortunately was not maintained. Machine gun bullets began to whistle straight down the road in which Battalion H.Q. was situated showing that the enemy must have penetrated deeply on our left flank and a message was received stating that our troops had been seen retiring along the Lagnicourt Spur.*

*Towards the end of the afternoon the following spirited message was received from Lieutenant E.P. Roberts O.C. 'A' Coy. 'Half of my company are at the disposal of the C.O. 2nd D.L.I. The other half are forming a defensive flank facing north, also aided by the stragglers of 'C' Company, under C.S.M. Grant. We suffered several casualties getting here and the situation is far from bonne. West Yorks have fallen back and the C.O. of the 2nd D.L.I. expects to withdraw at dusk, I have to act as covering party for them. Otherwise all O.K. P.S. - 'A' Company has had great sport at sniping the Boche.*

An appendix in the War Diary of the 2nd Battalion, Durham Light Infantry written by Lieutenant Colonel D.L. Brereton gives a vivid account of the final events of the day.

*Two Companies of the 11th Essex had previously reinforced the 1st West Yorkshires and one Company came about this time (3.00 pm) to reinforce me* (this was 'A' Coy. under Lieutenant Roberts). *In view of the intended retirement. I arranged for this Company to take up position in the open in D25 a & c to cover it.*
*Lieutenant Colonel Boyell D.S.O. and Major Stockdale M.C., with remnants of their Battalions, reached my sector about 04.30 pm and arrangements were made for covering the right flank. The enemy up 'Leech Avenue' continued to press on and were with great difficulty checked. It was decided between the C.Os that a retirement by daylight would be impossible, owing to the enemy's machine guns which were now on three sides of us, the only thing to be done was to hang on until dusk and then attempt to get back. The enemy were easily prevented from coming over the open from our front, but they were quickly getting round the right flank, and a series of blocks were made down 'Autumn' and 'Winter' reserve trenches to check the enemy. About 6.50 pm all the bombs* (grenades) *had been used and it was decided that the only thing to do was to fight it out, as dusk was not expected for an hour and the position seemed hopeless. About 7.15 pm, a thick mist appeared and the opportunity was seized and the order was given for everyone to get back to the Corps Line on his own. The order was given only just in time, as 5 minutes later the whole of the reserve line would have been surrounded. I estimated that about 300 all ranks attempted to leave and that probably about 250 reached the Corps Line. These numbers were made up of the different units. Directly the move was made, heavy machine gun fire opened up on three sides and the Germans followed in great numbers at about 300 yds. There was no chance for anyone who was hit. The majority reached the Corps Line by the copse in front of Morchies.*

Nothing was ever seen or heard of Lieutenant Percy Roberts again, and his body was never recovered. It was not until 2nd April, 1918, that his family in West Mersea were informed by telegram, shown opposite, that Percy had been killed.

**TO:** Roberts Rosebank West Mersea Essex

Deeply Regret Lieut E P Roberts Essex Regt Killed in Action March Twenty first The Army Council express sympathy

**FROM:** SECRETARY WAR OFFICE

His colonel wrote 'Your son's sad death will cause a sad gap in the battalion. He was a capable, hard working officer, and much beloved by his men, with whom he was always closely in touch. He died gallantly, as an officer should, leading his men, and gave his life for his country and our dear ones at home.'

He is commemorated on the Arras Memorial in the Faubourg d'Amiens Cemetery and on the West Mersea War Memorial. His name also appears on the family grave in the West Mersea Cemetery, Barfield Road.

**Sources**

*Commonwealth War Graves Commission*
*Essex Regiment Museum*
*Essex Units in the War 1914-1919 by J.W. Burrows*
*11th Battalion, Essex Regiment War Diary, PRO, Kew, Ref no: WO95/1616*
*Essex County Standard*
*Officers Records, PRO, Kew, Ref no: WO339/23423*
*2nd Battalion, Durham Light Infantry War Diary, PRO, Kew*

Lieutenant Edmund Percy Roberts's name inscribed on the Arras Memorial.

The Arras Memorial, Faubourg d'Amiens Cemetery, Arras.

**SURNAME: Stacey**

CHRISTIAN NAME(S): Joseph

AGE: 28

RECRUITMENT OFFICE: Colchester

SERVICE NO: 6345     RANK: Gunner

SERVICE/REGIMENT: 107th Brigade, H.Q. Royal Field Artillery

DECORATIONS EARNED: 1914/15 Star, War Medal, Victory Medal

DATE KILLED/DIED: 21st March, 1918     LOCATION: France

LOCATION OF GRAVE: Vermand Communal Cemetery, Plot A Grave 3

---

**BACKGROUND AND SERVICE HISTORY:**

Joseph Stacey was born in 1890, the youngest son of Harry and Mary Ann Stacey who resided at No 49, High Street, West Mersea. He was baptised on 12th October, 1890.

He enlisted at Colchester, joining the Royal Field Artillery. He arrived with his Battery in France on 29th August, 1915.

On 21st March, 1918, the Battery were in the village of Maissemy, north east of Vermand, when it was overrun by the Germans on the first day of their Spring offensive. The Battery War Diary describes the events.

*Vermand 21/3/1918*
*Enemy opened a heavy bombardment at 4.30 am during a thick mist which did not clear until midday. He used a large quantity of gas shells as well as some smoke shells. The enemy attacked at 10.30 am and advancing rapidly forced B & C batteries in Maissemy to leave their guns. They brought away breech blocks and dial sights. The barrages on the approaches to Maissemy were especially heavy. The Officer Commanding of 'B' battery (Major W.S.N. Curle MC) was reported missing and 18 other ranks captured at the battery position, the enemy surrounding them from the right flank. A number of men of 'C' battery took up a position with the infantry in a trench in rear of their battery position and used their Lewis and rifles with good effect.*

*'A' battery lost its two forward guns, 2nd Lieut Sheffield who was in charge of them, being wounded, and two howitzers of 'D' battery were destroyed by shell fire. Batteries were withdrawn to new positions in the afternoon.*
*Casualties - 1 officer missing, 4 wounded.*
     *Other ranks, 8 killed, 4 wounded, 18 missing, 3 gassed.*

One of those killed was Joseph Stacey. He is buried in Vermand Communal Cemetery, west of St Quentin, and is commemorated on the West Mersea War Memorial.

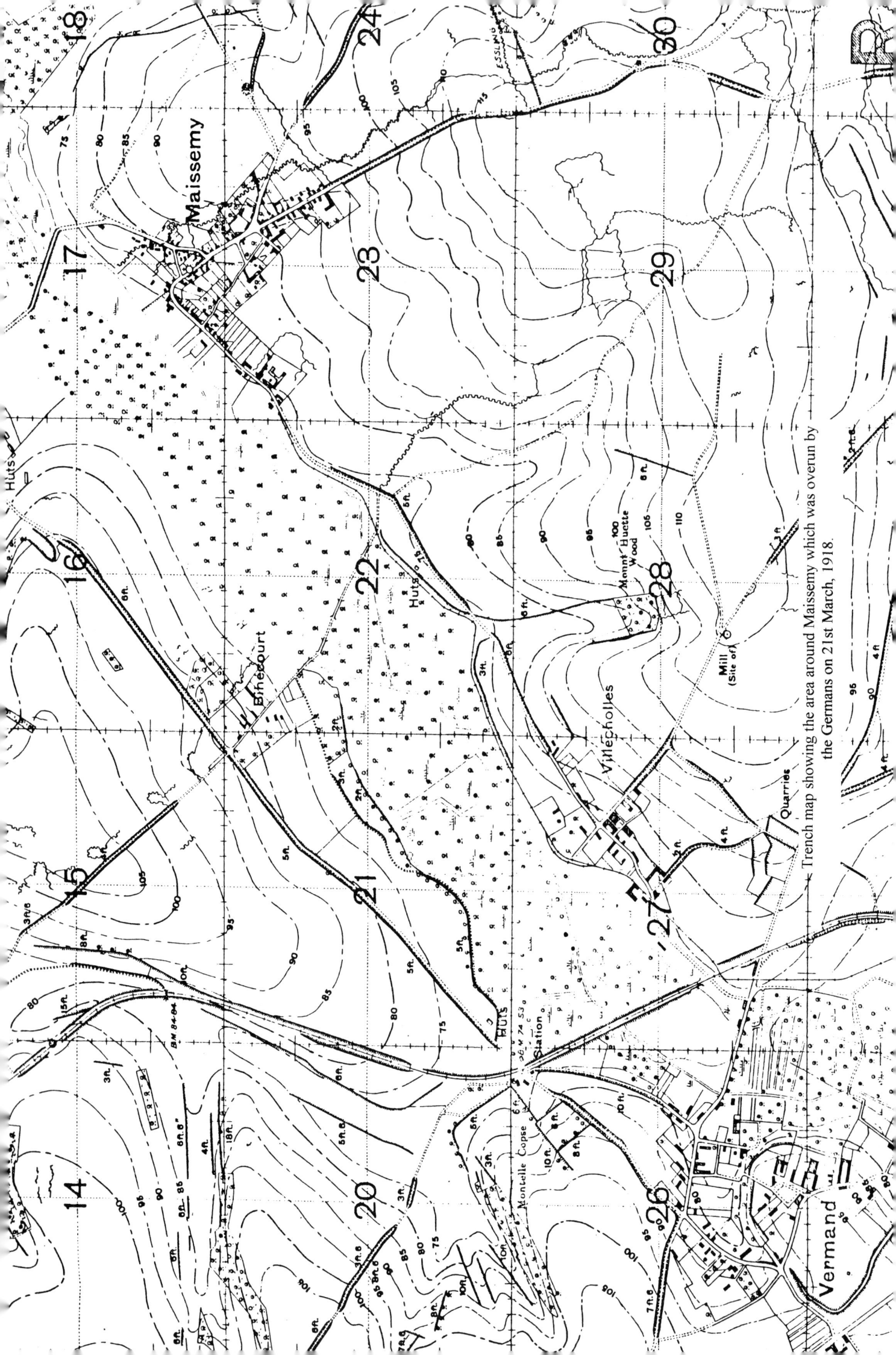

Trench map showing the area around Maissemy which was overrun by the Germans on 21st March, 1918.

**Sources**

*Commonwealth War Graves Commission*
*Essex Regiment Museum*
*Essex Record Office (Colchester)*
*107th Brigade, H.Q., Royal Field Artillery War Diary, PRO, Kew, Ref no: WO95/2197*

The grave of Gunner Joseph Stacey in Vermand Communal Cemetery.

**SURNAME:** Brand

CHRISTIAN NAME(S): Christopher Pullen

AGE: 31

RECRUITMENT OFFICE: Southend

SERVICE NO: 253185 (formerly 6393 & G/29880)     RANK: Private

SERVICE/REGIMENT: 1st/7th The Argyll and Sutherland Highlanders

DECORATIONS EARNED: War Medal, Victory Medal

DATE KILLED/DIED: Died of wounds 27th May, 1918     LOCATION: Germany

LOCATION OF GRAVE: Niederzwehren Cemetery, near Kassel, northern Germany

---

**BACKGROUND AND SERVICE HISTORY:**

Christopher Pullen Brand was born on 18th July, 1887, the son of George and Katherine Brand who lived at York Cottage, West Mersea. He was one of four sons and he had five sisters.

It is thought that he attended the school at West Mersea. The family and the Island had connections with Paglesham, near Rochford, both being oyster producing areas. It was here that he met his wife, Alice Dora Popplewell and they were married on 24th July, 1910 at Paglesham Parish Church. They made their home in Waterside Cottage, Paglesham, where he worked as an oyster dredgerman. Their only son, George was born on 2nd December, 1910.

On 9th December, 1915, he enlisted at Southend, joining the Middlesex Regiment on a short service engagement. The next day he was released to the Reserve and returned home. He was not mobilised until 31st May, 1916, when he joined the 6th Battalion, Middlesex Regiment, on 2nd June, 1916. After spending a short time with the Battalion, he was transferred to the 2/6th Battalion, Argyle and Sutherland Highlanders on 22nd June, 1916. After a period of training, he embarked for France from Folkestone on 15th March, 1917, landing at Boulogne. From here he was posted to the 19th Infantry Base Depot at Etaples, where he stayed until 30th April, 1917, when after further training he was posted to the 1/7th Battalion, Argyll and Sutherland Highlanders.

The Battalion saw action in the Plouvain-Fampoux area, south of Arras, throughout May and on 28th May he was admitted to the 1/2nd Field Ambulance Unit with shell shock, from which he recovered by 9th July, when he was posted to the Officer Command Battalion of the 1/7th Battalion, Argyll and Sutherland Highlanders.

On 15th July, 1917, the Battalion were in the Ypres Salient, near the canal, when Private Brand was wounded and admitted to No 47 Casualty Clearing Station. The events of the day are described in the Battalion War Diary.

*15/7/17 - Crome-Straete*
*At 2.25 am our heavy Trench mortars bombarded enemy's support line, Below and Hurst Farms with gas shells. Gas shells had again used by enemy at 1.00 am on our battery positions west of the canal. Incendiary shells were also freely used by the enemy west of canal. A German wearing a green cap with badge on left side was seen. Our officers patrol again examined the enemy wire.*

Having recovered from his wounds he returned to his Battalion, but on 4th August, he reported sick and was admitted to No 62 Casualty Station, from where he was sent to the 6th General Hospital at Rouen, and then on to No 2 Convalescence Depot, but returned to the 6th General Hospital with tonsillitis in 12th December, 1917.

On 17th January, 1918, he was posted to the Scottish Base Depot at Calais, before re-joining the Battalion a week later. A period of leave followed from 10th February to 24th February, when he probably returned home to Paglesham unaware it was for the last time.

On 21st March, 1918, he was with his Battalion when it took the full brunt of the German offensive. An appendix to the Battalion War Diary written by the Officer Commanding describes the Battalion's experiences as it came under heavy attack, leading up to Private Brand being wounded.

*21st March*
*4.50 am - Heavy barrage of the whole Battalion sector of both High Explosive and gas began.*
*6.30 am - High Explosive barrage continued but the gas slackened off and enabled Companies to clear dugouts and shelters. The gas precautions were very good indeed, and no casualties occurred.*
*8.30 am - Barrage ceased.*
*10.00 am - No enemy action took place in Battalion sector until this time when the enemy had driven the 6th Gordon Highlanders on our left back from Boursies, and they were holding a flank defence along Sturgeon Avenue, and the enemy were attempting to bomb along our front and support lines with the aid of Flamenwerfer* (Flamethrower). *It became obvious at this time that the enemy had broken through north of us, and that we should have to form a defensive flank facing north. I, therefore, ordered up the two platoons of 'D' Coy. from Bruno Mill to Roach Avenue.*
*11.30 am - Enemy had driven us out of the front line as far as Aldgate where a block was made, and he was held there. The block at the junction of Sturgeon Avenue and Sturgeon Support still held.*
*1.00 pm - The enemy had driven us out of the front line as far as Trout Avenue where a block had been established and out of the support line as far as Aldgate where another block had been established. Enemy was seen advancing from Boursies towards Crucifix. I therefore decided to reinforce the platoon at the Crucifix by two platoons of 'D' Coy. from Roach Avenue.*
*3.00 pm - The party of 6th Gordon Highlanders, who had been badly attacked by Flamenwerfer and were in a state of panic rushed across Grayling Support and created a panic amongst the troops there who retired until they were rallied by the Company Commander in Sunken Road.*
*3.30 pm - Situation was as follows:*
*'B' Company on the right holding same positions as before.*
*'C' Company on the left holding Trout Avenue with blocks in front line and Grayling Support, remainder in the Sunken Road.*

'D' Company - 3 Platoons Crucifix and reserve line.
'A' Company - 3 Platoons in the Intermediate line, one platoon, Roach Avenue.
4.30 pm - I ordered the Platoon of 'D' Company in the Sunken Road to man the reserve lines across the valley from Aldgate in touch with the rest of the Company nearby. These dispositions were maintained up to the time of the withdrawal.

<u>Remarks</u>

Owing to the haze, the anti-tank gun was of no value until about mid-day, and then after firing a few rounds broke. The machine guns at Demicourt Cemetery and my troops in Roach Avenue beside Demicourt had to evacuate their positions, owing to one of our howitzers shelling Demicourt in the vicinity of the Cemetery steadily in the whole afternoon.

22nd March
1.10 am - Received orders to withdraw to the B.M. Line. Companies withdrew with out incident and at 05.00 am, the dispositions were as follows:
'A' Coy. in B.M. Line on right of 4th Seaforths
'D' Coy. in Sunken Road, in support of 4th Seaforths.
'C' and 'B' Coys and Battalion H.Q. in Sunken Road.
At dawn and onwards throughout the day, the enemy kept up an intermittent and heavy barrage on the B.M. Line, but no infantry action developed as far as this Battalion was concerned.
9.00 am - 'C' Coy. were ordered up to take up a position on the road in order to thicken up Jargon Trench or the Hermies defences if necessary.
8.00 pm - Two platoons of 'D' Coy. were sent forward into the B.M. Line to thicken up as the 4th Seaforths had suffered pretty heavily through the barrage.

23rd March, action of 'A'. 'D' and 'C' Coys.
At dawn, heavy barrage started on the B.L. Line and continued intermittently until 12.00 pm, when a heavy attack developed on the 4th Seaforths' front and they were driven back to form a defensive flank facing north together with 'D' Coy. and elements of the 19th Division, who had retired from east of Beaumetz, the left flank of this position was completely in the air. The enemy attacked continuously from this time onwards, and at 03.00 pm, had completely turned the left flank, and the line had to be withdrawn to the railway embankment. Two platoons of 'D' Coy. that remained behind to cover withdrawal were all killed or taken prisoners. At this time 'C' Coy., who were still holding the line of the Sunken Road, were informed by an officer of the 17th Division, that the whole of his Division was going to be withdrawn from the Hermies defences to form a defensive flank facing east on the ridges south of the canal. This left both the right and left flanks of the position in the air. However, the remnants of my three Companies and of the 4th Seaforths fought on until 03.30 pm, when they were almost completely surrounded and had to withdraw with heavy losses. The intention was to withdraw as far as the high ground, and link up with the 17th Division, but on arrival, it was found that the 17th Division had not stayed here, but had retired through the Bertincourt Line, consequently these three Coys. withdrew to the Bertincourt Lines, and took up a position astride the Bertincourt-Ytres road with the 63rd Division. They were afterwards directed to rejoin their Division by an Officer of the 63rd Division, and at 05.30 pm, they withdrew, and 'C' Coy. went to Villers-au-Flos and continued to le Transloy for the night. 'A' and 'D' Coys. went through to Guedecourt for the night.

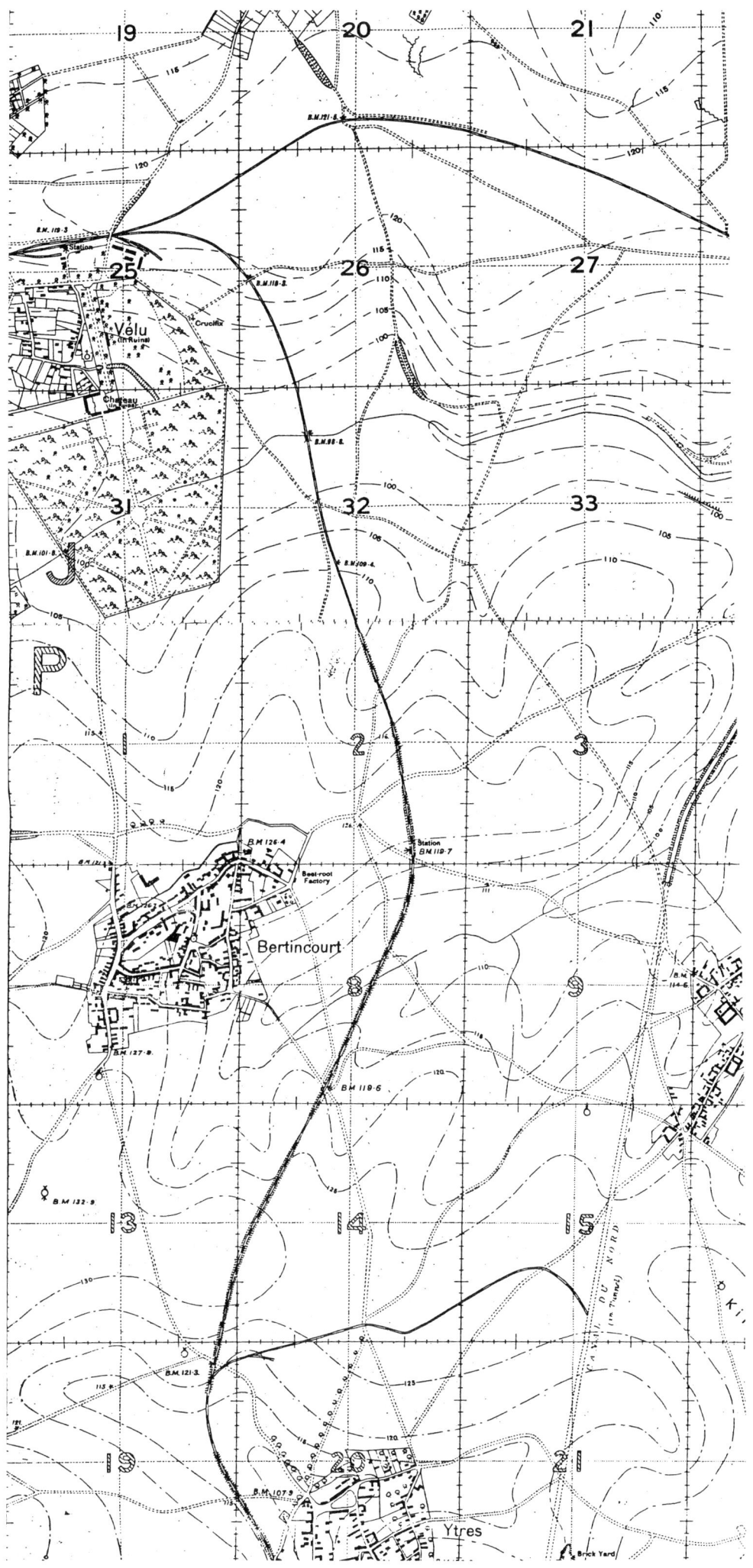

A combination of trench maps showing the area in which Private Brand's Battalion was in action, and he was wounded. Beaumetz is just off the map at the top, and Hermies is on the right opposite Velu.

*23rd March, action of Battalion H.Q. and 'B' Coy.*

*The shelling had been continuous on the dugouts and very heavy on the Sunken Road, and by 7.00 am, 'B' Coy. had lost fairly heavily. The enemy were reported to be massing north of Beaumetz, and to be moving up on the main road towards Beugny. 'B' Coy. was ordered to man the sleeper track from map ref. west as far as possible, and the 19th Division was supposed to be on their right along the railway, and the 5th and 6th Seaforths who were withdrawing from Beautmetz were supposed to come in on their left flank between Velu and Lebucquiere. However, the Warwicks withdrew early in the day without giving 'B' Coy. any warning, and the 5th and 6th Seaforths never manned this position at all, but withdrew right through beyond Velu to the Corps Line.*

*10.30 am - Enemy attack developed on the north and west, and the shelling and machine gun fire at Battalion H.Q. became so intense that it was decided to evacuate it, consequently Battalion H.Q. personnel were sent to thicken up 'B' Coy., and Battalion H.Q. staff withdrew to the Warwicks' Headquaters in the Quarry. 'B' Coy hung on and fought magnificently with both flanks completely turned until 11.45 am, when they withdrew with heavy losses to the position held by some of the 54th Machine Gun Coy. along the Sunken Road. As the enemy had already reached Velu Wood and was enfilading this position, it was decided at 12.15 pm to withdraw again to the line of the railway, thus forming a defensive flank facing west in order to allow any other troops still remaining in the B.M. Line, and to the east of it to withdraw without being cut off. This position was maintained until 03.30 pm, at which time, 'C' Coy. posted a Lewis gun on the high ground to keep the enemy from advancing from Velu Wood, while the remnants of the Coy. withdrew to the Corps Line. From here they were ordered to Ytres and then to le Transloy for the night. Battalion H.Q. had by this time lost all touch with the Coys., and putting up a fight with straggles from all different units in the Division on the outskirts of Velu Wood had withdrawn via Bertincourt to Rocquigny where they were directed to Reincourt for the night.*

Private Christopher Pullen Brand was wounded during the fighting on 23rd March while in 'D' Company. Because of the confused situation, arrangements for the evacuation of the wounded were in disarray: it was reported that 90 per cent of the Battalion's wounded had to be left behind and were taken prisoner by the Germans, including Private Brand.

He was transported to the Langenslza Prisoner of War Camp at Thuringen in Germany, and was subsequently transferred to Lazarett Camp at Ohrdruf, near Kassel in northern Germany. Conditions in the camps were not ideal and he died from blood poisoning as a result of gun shot wounds at 12.30 am on 27th May, 1918.

He is buried in Niederzwehren Cemetery, near Kassel in Germany, and is commemorated on the West Mersea War Memorial and on the Paglesham War Memorial in the Parish church.

**Sources**

*Commonwealth War Graves Commission*
*Regimental Headquarters, The Argyll and Sutherland Highlanders*
*1/7th Argyle and Sutherland Highlanders War Diary, PRO, Kew, Ref no: WO95/2886*
*Herr Beiderbeck, Friedhofsverwaltung, Kassel - photograph of grave.*

Private Christopher Pullen Brand's name inscribed on the Paglesham War Memorial inside Paglesham Parish church.

The grave of Private Christopher Pullen Brand in Niederzwehren Cemetery, northern Germany.

**SURNAME:** Thursby

CHRISTIAN NAME(S): Alfred Bertie

AGE: 20

RECRUITMENT OFFICE: Maldon

SERVICE NO: 44841 (Formerly 31680)     RANK: Private

SERVICE/REGIMENT: Essex Regiment transferred to 18th Battalion, Durham Light Infantry

DECORATIONS EARNED: War Medal, Victory Medal

DATE KILLED/DIED: 19th July, 1918     LOCATION: France

MEMORIAL IF NO KNOWN GRAVE: Ploegsteert Memorial, Belgium

---

**BACKGROUND AND SERVICE HISTORY:**

Alfred Bertie Thursby was born in 1898 at Brightlingsea, the son of Isaac and Lucy Thursby. The family later moved to Orleans Cottage, West Mersea.

He enlisted at Maldon, and joined the Essex Regiment, later transferring to 18th Battalion, Durham Light Infantry.

In July 1918, the Battalion were near the Foret de Nieppe, to the west of a stream known as the Becque. On 18th July, the line south of la Becque was taken over and an operation designed to bring the whole brigade front up to the Plate Becque was fixed for the following morning. There was no time for reconnaissance, but the outgoing troops reported that the German line was weakly held so a barrage was deemed unnecessary. South of the farm building known as la Becque, 'A' and 'B' companies of the 18th Battalion were to advance with the West Yorkshires on their right.

At 7.00 am, on 19th July, the attack was launched, small columns with scouts in front, creeping through the corn. 'B' company on the extreme left were soon met with machine gun fire. North of the road was an enemy occupied ruined building enclosed by hedges, and a Lewis gun team advancing along the north hedge were all killed or wounded. Second Lieutenant Turnbull attempted to rush the place with a section of riflemen, but all his men were hit. This officer made another attempt from the rear, but the accuracy of the machine gun fire proved it impossible. Lance Corporal Adams had tried to co-operate from the west side. He got his Lewis gunners through the hedge and engaged the machine gun firing on Lieutenant Turnbull's party, but a platoon of Germans at once evacuated the building, and bombed this section out. Second Lieutenant Langley reached the south west corner of the enclosure, and shot a German machine gunner, but every attempt to get further forward failed.

The men on the extreme right of 'B' company had got beyond the enclosure along the road to the south. Attacked in the rear by machine gun fire, they then had to retreat into line with the rest of the company now digging in about forty yards west of this enclosure, with the idea of trying again at dusk. Snipers in the trees were now active and bursts of machine gun fire were a constant threat.

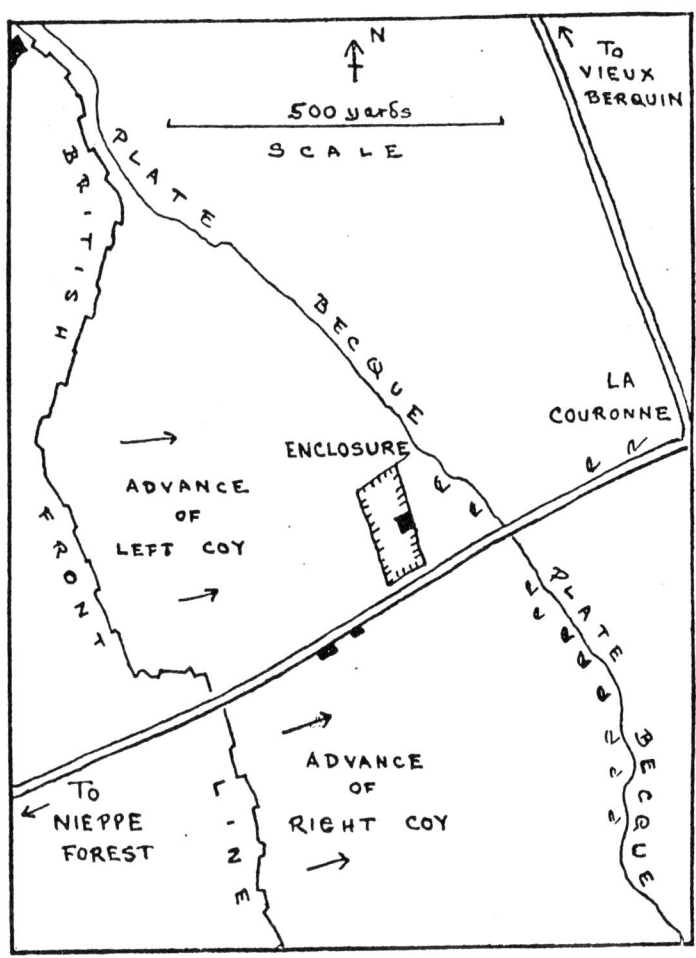

Diagram showing the plan of attack on 19th July, 1918.

Second Lieutenant W.L. Henderson, on the left of 'A' company, went forward until the stream was visible only 80 yards away, when his platoon suffered heavily from the German machine guns and snipers. The officer, with Sergeant W. Barker, of Darlington, occupied a shell hole into which they had drawn several wounded men. Suddenly, about sixteen Germans rushed up and Lieutenant Henderson shot two with his revolver. The remainder fell back and threw bombs, but Sergeant Barker threw one bomb back before it exploded, and killed two more of the enemy the remainder of whom then fled. This platoon was isolated, but hung on until ordered to retire later in the morning.

The platoon following Second Lieutenant Henderson's men were stopped further back by enfilade fire, though some on the right managed to get forward. Second Lieutenant W. Brown, who led the right of the Battalion, made good progress at first but eventually his platoon suffered heavy casualties. In attempting to deal single-handed with an enemy post, this officer collapsed badly wounded and was not seen again. Sergeant Whitfield led up the rear platoon with plans to thicken the line here, but he was afterwards killed. The confused fighting on the right led to acts of bravery, where the German machine guns maintained accurate fire from the willows along the stream. Private W. Harper, of Spennymoor, and Private R. Cowling of Doncaster advanced successfully against two enemy posts scoring seven hits,

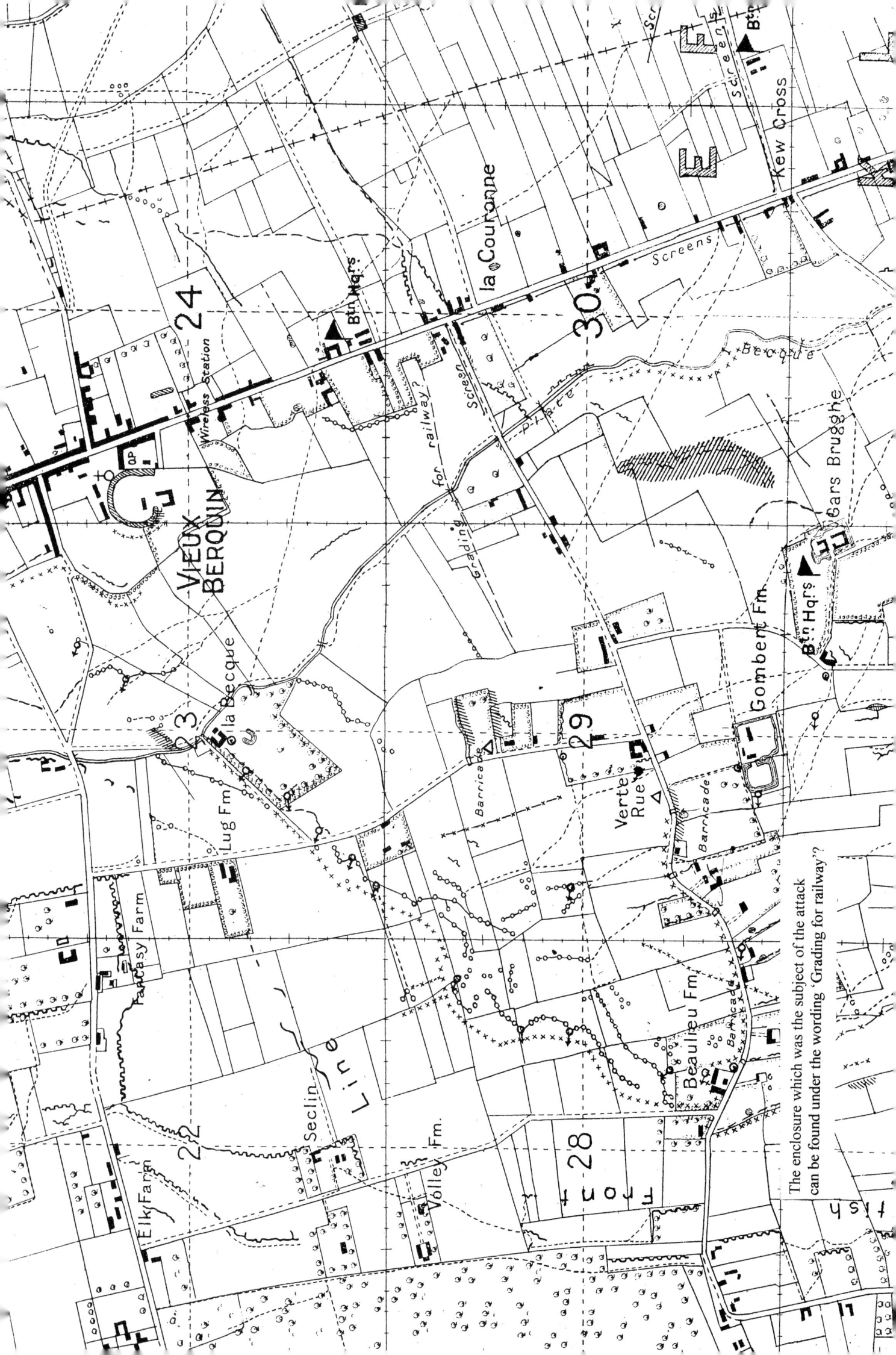

The enclosure which was the subject of the attack can be found under the wording 'Grading for railway?'

including a German officer. Corporal C. Lloyd, of Houghton-le-Spring, went forward alone, shot two Germans and silenced a machine gun though he was wounded in doing so. Sergeant Barker and these three men received the Distinguished Conduct Medal. Lieutenant Henderson was awarded the Military Cross.

The troops on the right of the Battalion had returned to their trenches after suffering heavy losses and the position of 'A' company, who were on that flank, became critical. It was difficult to convey orders for a withdrawal and in some cases small groups of men elected to stay and protect the wounded. The only way to retire was by creeping backwards carefully through the corn, and some of the Battalion did not get back until ten o'clock at night when 'C' and 'D' companies took over the line. Lieutenant C.L. Welford and Second Lieutenant R.W. Langley were wounded and losses in the ranks amounted to 100 killed, wounded and missing.

Albert Thursby was one of those missing, and his body was never found. He is commemorated on the Ploegsteert Memorial in Belgium, and on the West Mersea War Memorial.

**Sources**

*Commonwealth War Graves Commission*
*Essex Regiment Museum*
*The Durham Forces in the Field 1914-1918 by Captain Wilfrid Miles published by Cassell*
*18th Battalion, Durham Light Infantry War Diary, PRO, Kew, Ref no: WO95/2361.*

Private Alfred Thursby's name inscribed on the Ploegsteert Memorial, Belguim.

**SURNAME: Pullen**

CHRISTIAN NAME(S): Arthur David

AGE: 24

RECRUITMENT OFFICE: Colchester

SERVICE NO: 12866    RANK: Private

SERVICE/REGIMENT: 10th Battalion, Essex Regiment transferred to 14th Battalion Royal Welch Fusiliers (55876)

DECORATIONS EARNED: 1914/15 Star, Military Medal, War Medal, Victory Medal

DATE KILLED/DIED: 23rd August, 1918    LOCATION: France

LOCATION OF GRAVE: Bapaume Post Military Cemetery

---

**BACKGROUND AND SERVICE HISTORY:**

Arthur David Pullen was born in 1894, the son of Mr and Mrs W.J. Pullen of the High Street, West Mersea.

A fisherman in civilian life, he was always known by his second name, David, and earned the nickname 'Dash'.

He was one of the many Mersea men who answered Kitchener's call for volunteers and in Autumn 1914 he enlisted at Colchester, joining the 10th Battalion, Essex Regiment.

On 24th July 1915, the transport and machine guns of the Battalion under Major C.M. Wheatley left Codford St Mary and proceeded to Le Havre via Southampton. The next day, the main body of the Battalion also entrained and embarked at Folkestone at midnight, arriving in drizzling rain at Boulogne camp at 3.00 am on 26th July.

On 1st July, 1916, he was with them on the first day of the Battle of the Somme. They were part of 54 Brigade (18th Division), and were in the sector north of Carnoy, held in reserve.

After the initial attack by the Norfolks and Berkshires, a trench known as Pommiers Trench was captured but an adjacent trench known as The Loop was still held by the Germans. A Company from the 10th Battalion, Essex Regiment was sent up as reinforcements, but the trench leading to The Loop was blocked.

At 8.30 am, the Battalion, with the 7th Battalion, Bedfordshire Regiment and the 11th Battalion, Royal Fusiliers, carried out an attack against the Pommiers Redoubt. Lewis gunners from the Royal Fusiliers were sent to Maple Trench to enfilade the Redoubt. The Germans were taken by surprise, and the Redoubt was taken after heavy hand to hand fighting when it was rushed by the Royal Fusiliers and the Berkshires. Maple Trench was also captured. They

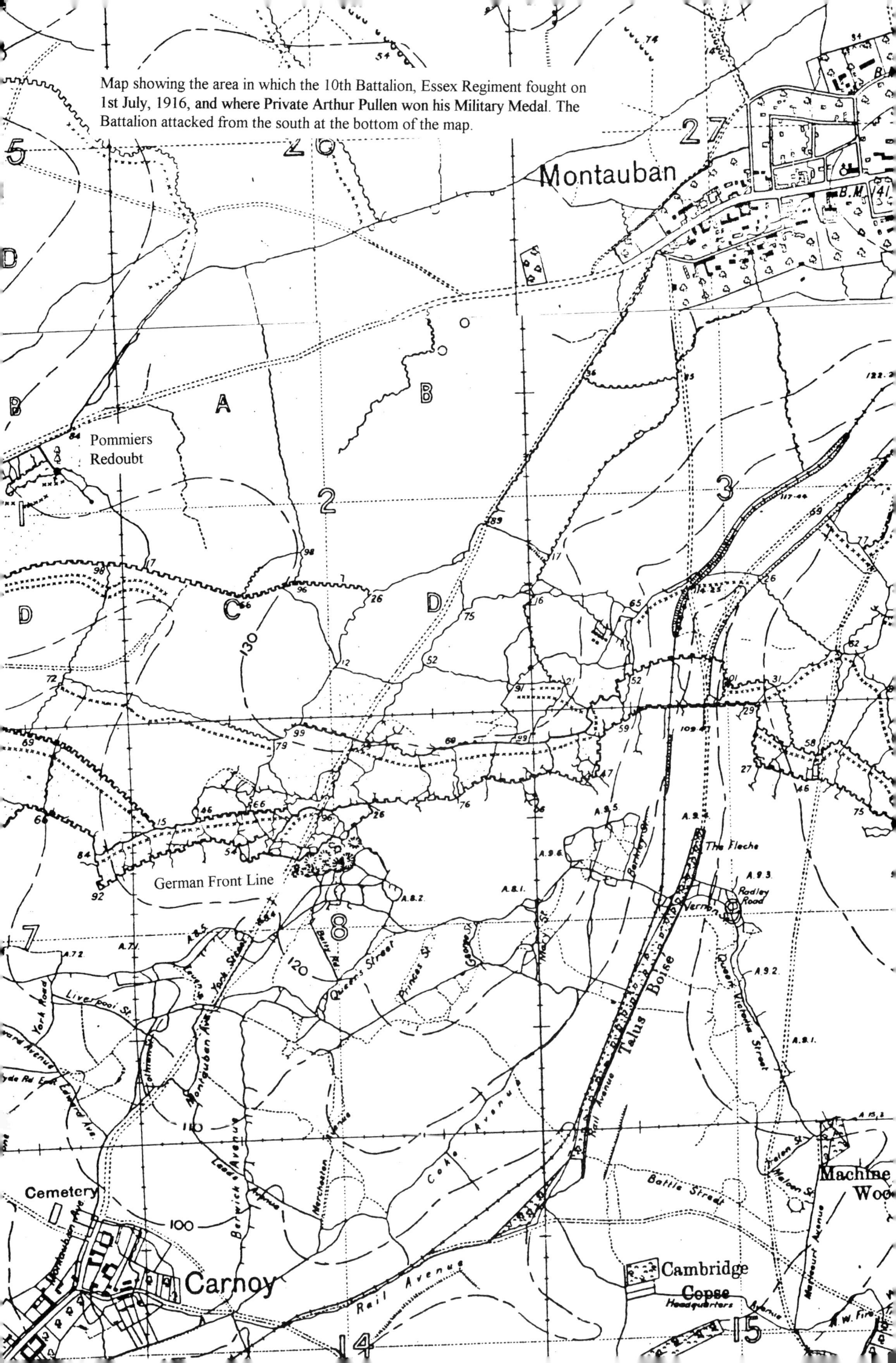

Map showing the area in which the 10th Battalion, Essex Regiment fought on 1st July, 1916, and where Private Arthur Pullen won his Military Medal. The Battalion attacked from the south at the bottom of the map.

then pushed on to Beetle Alley which was entered at 10.15 am with reinforcements of the 6th Northamptonshires.

Attempts to push further eastward along it and Montauban Alley were strongly resisted, and no further progress was made by the centre and left brigades of the 18th Division until 3.30 pm, when a bombing party of the 10th Battalion, Essex Regiment, reached White Trench, having cleared 400 yards of Montauban Alley, starting from Pommiers Redoubt. At 5.40 pm it met parties of the 6th Royal Berkshires and 8th Norfolks, which had come from The Loop Trench with great difficulty because of snipers. The entire Alley, the second objective of 18th Division, was now in British hands.

Private Arthur David Pullen, while serving in the 10th Battalion, Essex Regiment.

Earlier in the day, during these events, Arthur Pullen was wounded in the face and neck by shrapnel. Despite his wounds, he carried on towards the enemy trenches where he captured, single handed, seven Germans. He then proceeded to take them back to headquarters, which were two miles to the rear. One was shot as he tried to escape, but he was successful in bringing back the other six. For his gallantry he was awarded the Military Medal. He received the following letter as he recovered from his injuries at West Mersea.

*To 12866, Private A. Pullen, High Street, West Mersea.*
*It is with great pleasure that on behalf of the Commanding Officer I forward you a parchment awarded to you by the Divisional General for your gallant conduct in the early stages of the Somme Battle.*

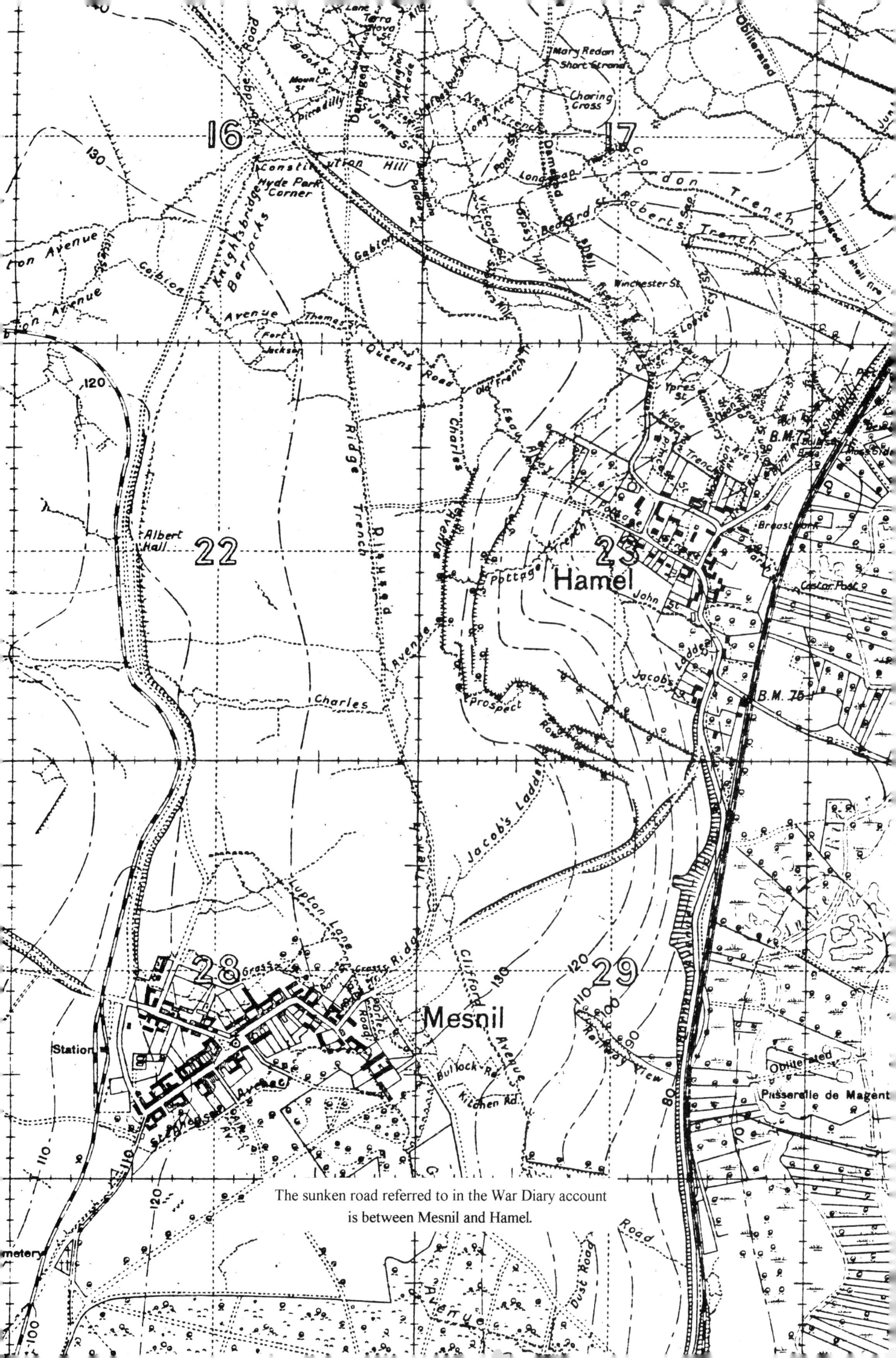

The sunken road referred to in the War Diary account is between Mesnil and Hamel.

*The Commanding Officer, Officers and men of the Regiment congratulate you and hope that you are now nearly fit to come and fight the Huns again. It may interest you to know that recently the Regiment has added still more glory to its name.*
*(Signed) R.A. Chell, Captain and Adjutant.*

The parchment reads:

*No 12866 Pte. A. Pullen ------ Battalion Essex Regiment.*
*I have read with great pleasure the report of your Regimental Commander and Brigade Commander regarding your gallant conduct and devotion to duty in the Field on July 1, 1916, during the Battle of the Somme. - F.I. Maxse, Major-General, Commanding 18th Division.*

Arthur Pullen returned to his Battalion and in 1917 was with them on the Ypres Salient where they arrived on 4th July. On 31st July, the Battalion took part in the Battle of Pilckem Ridge which resulted in him being gassed. The days events are described in the Battalion's War Diary.

*31/7/1917*
*Z Day. Our barrage opened at 3.50 am at zero + 3 mins, the enemy brought down a light barrage on our forward area, at zero + 25 mins, the enemy fired a few gas shells into Zillebeke. At 5.00 am, 'B' and 'C' Coys commenced to move from their positions north of Zillibeke Lake. At 6.00 am news was received that the 30th Division had captured blue and black lines.* (Battle lines as marked on the maps).

He was sent back to Base camp to recover, where he remained for three months. He was then attached to the 14th Battalion, Royal Welch Fusiliers, 38th (Welsh) Division.

On 23rd August, 1918, he was once again back on the Somme, taking part in what was known as the Second Battle of Albert. The day's action was described in the Battalion's War Diary.

*Zero hour was 4.45 am. 14th Bn followed close behind the 13th Bn. In a number of cases our men joined the 13th Bn & went on in the front wave to the far objective. Objective of battalion was sunken road in W.23.d & 29.b (Sheet 57.d S.E. (Beaumont)). Casualties were moderate. Three officers were wounded. Captain Humphreys Owen, acting 2nd in Command, was wounded while objective was being consolidated. Lt. K.O. Parsons was wounded during the attack & Lt D.D. Roberts at the assembly point. About 100 prisoners were taken and four machine guns. At 7 am 'A' Coy moved up on the right to support the 13th & 'B' Coy moved up on the left. Two platoons of 'C' Coy were sent to the left flank to hold the chalk pit. 2nd Lt. Seel moved this party to the flank and attacked a strong point, capturing a machine gun and 17 prisoners. The remainder of 'C' Coy & whole of 'D' Coy remained in objective as reserve.*

Arthur Pullen was killed during the attack and was buried in Bapaume Post Military Cemetery on the Somme. He is commemorated on the West Mersea War Memorial.

**Sources**

*Commonwealth War Graves Commission*
*Essex County Standard*
*Essex Regiment Museum*
*Mr Pullen*
*Regimental Museum Royal Welch Fusiliers*
*The Somme - The Day by Day Account by Chris McCarthy, published by Arms & Amour Press*
*Passchendaele - The Day by Day Account by Chris McCarthy, published by Arms & Armour Press*
*Essex Units in the War 1914-1919 by J.W. Burrows*
*10th Battalion, Essex Regiment, War Diary, PRO, Kew, Ref no: WO95/2038*
*14th Battalion, Royal Welch Fusiliers War Diary, PRO, Kew no: WO95/2555*

The grave of Private Arthur Pullen in Bapaume Post Military Cemetery on the Somme.

**SURNAME: Powell**

CHRISTIAN NAME(S): Charles Thomas

AGE: 32

RECRUITMENT OFFICE: Colchester

SERVICE NO: 74712              RANK: Bombardier

SERVICE/REGIMENT: 191st Siege Battery, Royal Garrison Artillery

DECORATIONS EARNED: War Medal, Victory Medal

DATE KILLED/DIED: 14th September, 1918   LOCATION: France

LOCATION OF GRAVE: Duisans British Cemetery

---

**BACKGROUND AND SERVICE HISTORY:**

Thomas Charles Powell was born in 1886, the son of John and Rose Powell of Parkstone, Dorset. He was one of six brothers.

Nothing is known of his early life, but he came to East Mersea as the resident professional at the Mersea Island Golf Club.

He married Mary (maiden name unknown). They lived at the Golf House, East Mersea and had two children.

On Friday, 31st March, 1916, at the Lexden and Winstree Tribunal, Second Lieutenant Edmund Percy Roberts, who was stationed at Felixstowe while recovering from jaundice contracted in France, made an application on behalf of a farmer, Mr Waterman, for the exemption of his son, W. Waterman, who was a stockman in the employ of his father, George Roberts. Also at the hearing was Thomas Powell, who for the duration of the war was working for Mr Waterman, as the Golf Club was closed because Mersea was a restricted area.

Thomas Powell advised the Tribunal, that he was willing to enlist instead of the stockman; he already had four brothers serving in France, all of whom had thrown up good businesses to join. He was quite willing to go so that the stockman could remain on the farm. The Tribunal chairman, Mr Fairhead, paid tribute to his patriotism. The case was adjourned so that Thomas Powell could be examined by a doctor to see if he was fit to serve.

Two weeks later on Friday, 14th April, 1916, it was reported at the Tribunal that he had passed the medical and had already enlisted. Second Lieutenant Roberts's father promised to look after Powell's wife and children while he was serving his country.

He enlisted at Colchester and joined the 191st Siege Battery, Royal Garrison Artillery. He embarked for France early in 1917.

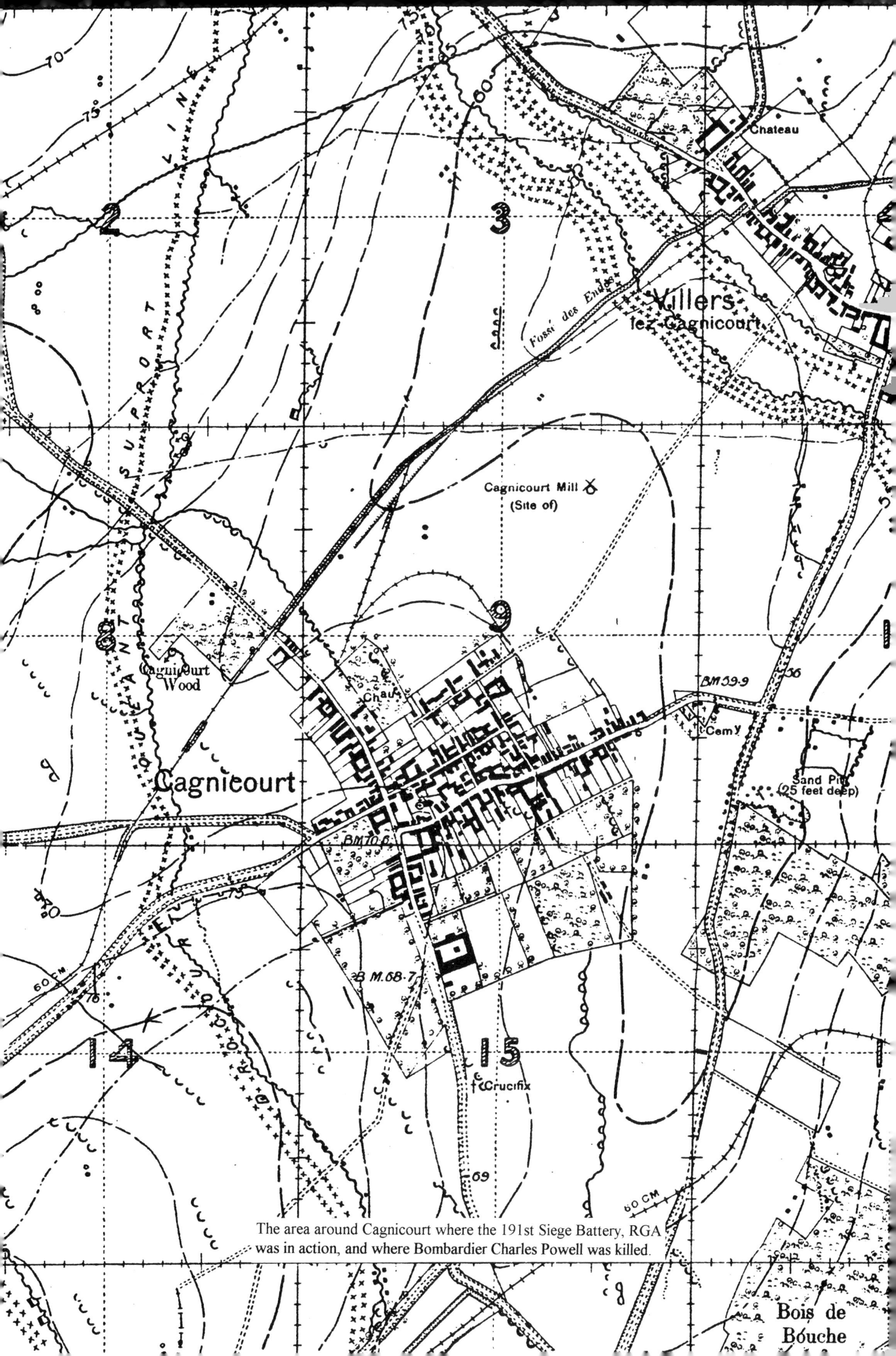

The area around Cagnicourt where the 191st Siege Battery, RGA was in action, and where Bombardier Charles Powell was killed.

On 13th September, 1918, the Battery was at Cagnicourt, and the Brigade War Diary describes the events of that day.

*13/9/1918 Cagnicourt*
*Hostile artillery considerable - Cagnicourt - severely harassed and battery positions attacked all day - The brigade suffered somewhat severe casualties.*
*191 Siege Battery - Capt Drewe M.C. wounded, 5 other ranks killed and 9 other ranks wounded.*
*26 Siege Battery - 10 other ranks wounded, some severely.*
*The Siege Batteries were called in to cover a minor local operation by the infantry which was entirely successful.*
*Only one section of 6" and 8" howitzers remain in forward positions, the remainder have been withdrawn to relieve the congestion of artillery around Villers and Cagnicourt - 2 guns of 191 Siege Battery will also be drawn back as the battery has suffered so severely.*

Bombardier Powell was one of those wounded, and he died of his wounds the next day. He is buried in Duisans British Cemetery, near Arras, and is commemorated on the East Mersea War Memorial in the church.

His widow and two children later left the Island to live in Barrack Street, Tallow, Co. Carlow, Ireland.

The grave of Bombardier Thomas Charles Powell in Duisans British Cemetery, near Arras.

**Sources**

*Commonwealth War Graves Commission*
*Essex Regiment Museum*
*Essex County Standard*
*Essex County Chronicle*
*77th Brigade, Horse Artillery War Diary, PRO, Kew, Ref no: WO95/324*

**SURNAME: Parkin**

CHRISTIAN NAME(S): Edward

AGE: 21

RECRUITMENT OFFICE: Ripley, Derbyshire

SERVICE NO: 200285      RANK: Private

SERVICE/REGIMENT: 11th Battalion Sherwood Foresters, Nottingham and Derbyshire Regiment

DECORATIONS EARNED: British War Medal, Victory Medal

DATE KILLED/DIED: October 5th, 1918      LOCATION: France

LOCATION OF GRAVE: Guizancourt Farm Cemetery, nr Gouy, Aisne

---

**BACKGROUND AND SERVICE HISTORY:**

Edward Parkin was born in 1897, at Ripley in Derbyshire, the second son of Mr Alfred and Jane Parkin of 7, Crossley Street, Ripley.

His elder brother was William Alfred, and he was subsequently to have a younger brother, John and three younger sisters, Sarah Ann, Florence Ellen and Hilda May.

In 1914 he enlisted at Ripley and joined the 11th Battalion, The Sherwood Foresters, Nottingham and Derbyshire Regiment.

It is not known how he became to be on Mersea Island, but it is possible that the Battalion was stationed at the Colchester Garrison, and that he met and married a local girl, Eva Ellen (maiden name unknown), while he was there. On 18th August, 1916, she gave birth to their son, Edward Arthur. Edward missed the birth of his son, and his baptism which took place on 24th September 1916, as he was sent out to France in early July, 1916. The family home was at 5, Council Houses, Barfield Road, West Mersea.

It was reported that he was badly gassed in May, 1917. However, the Battalion were not in line at that time. It is possible that this happened when the Battalion took part in an attack on Hill 60 on the Ypres Salient on 7th June 1917. Zero hour was at 03.10 pm when mines were exploded. The Battalion occupied their objectives with few casualties, the majority of these being from sniping and shell fire after the position had been gained.

He was sent back to England to recover, returning to France in September, 1917. Later the Battalion went to Italy to fight in the campaign there, returning to France on 18th August, 1918.

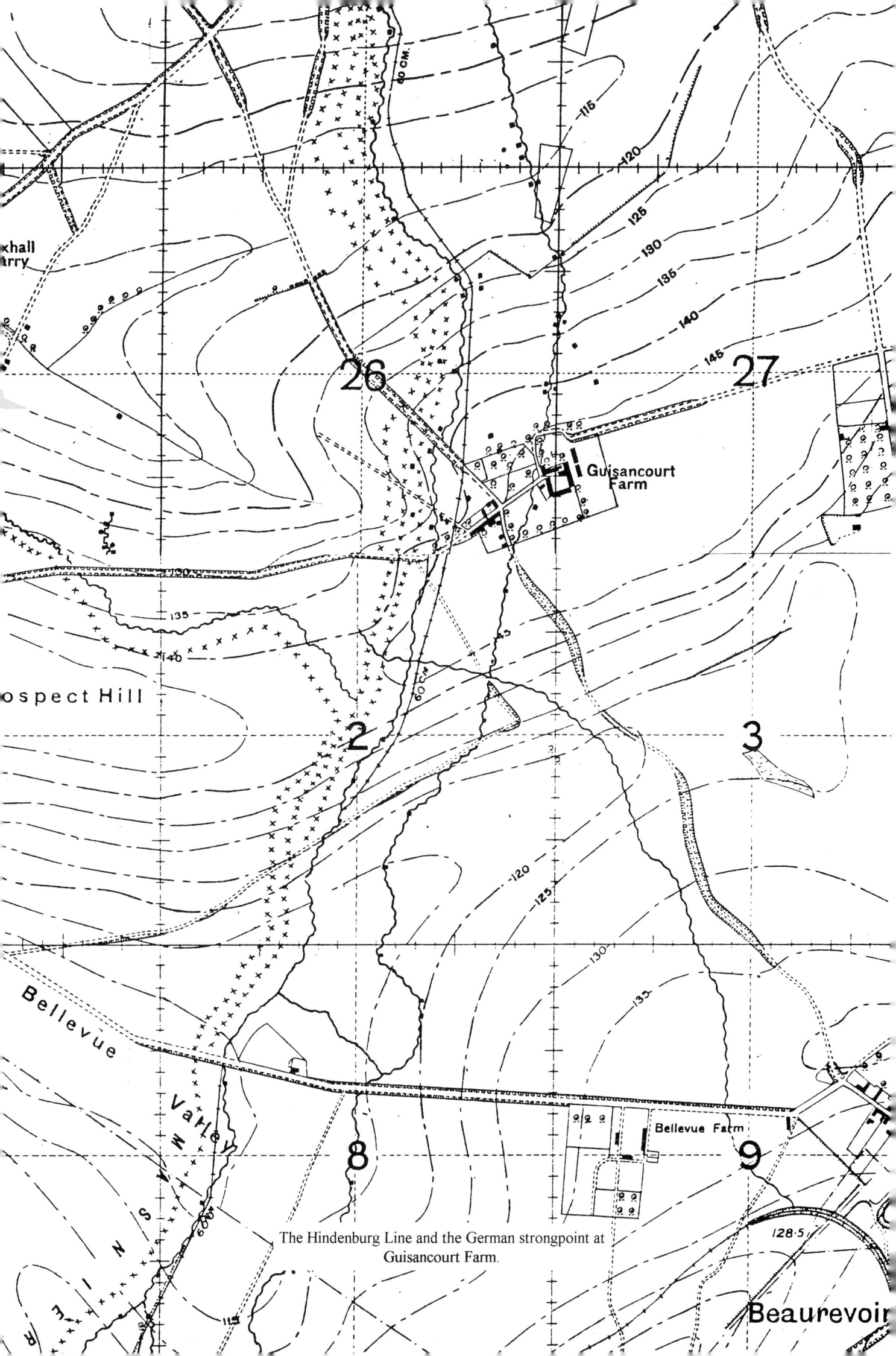

The Hindenburg Line and the German strongpoint at Guisancourt Farm.

On 4th October, 1918, the 11th Battalion, The Sherwood Foresters was at Mont St. Martin, north of St Quentin, standing by with the remainder of the Brigade in readiness to support the 7th Brigade (20th Division), who were attacking.

The following is the account of the action taken from the Battalion War Diary

*'At 8.00 pm orders were received stating that the Brigade would attack on a 3 Battalion frontage on the morning of Oct 5th. The 9th YORKS Regt. on the right, the 13th D.L.I. in the centre and the 11th S.F. on the left. The Brigade objective was a line running approximately from:- The centre of the eastern outskirts of BEAUREVOIR to LA SABBLONIERE ( inclusive) and thence along the high ground to GUISANCOURT FARM ( inclusive) to a point about 1,200 yards EAST, along the high ground. The actual frontage was about 1,500 yards. The Battalion moved into the assembly positions about 1,000 yards South of GUISANCOURT FARM and was in position by 3 am on the 5th.*

*During the assembly Lieut. G.E.McC. KEMBALL was slightly wounded in the leg, and 3 O.Rs were wounded by M.G. fire.*

*October 5th. ZERO hour was 6 a.m., at which hour the barrage opened and the battalion advanced on its objective:- 3 Coys. in the line, in order 'A', 'B' and 'C' from the right, with 'D' Coy. in support.*

*All objectives were gained with slighter opposition than was expected, considering that the left flank had to work up the MASMIERES - BEAUREVOIR LINE of the HINDENBURG defences, GUISANCOURT FARM being a strong point in this line and was strongly held by machine guns. All battalion objectives were captured by 7 a.m. and consolidation begun. 1 officer and 190 Germans were taken prisoners out of a total of 3 officers and 300 O.Rs taken by the Division. A number of Germans were killed and numerous machine guns, rifles etc were captured. The Battalion's left flank was always secure, PROSPECT HILL to the immediate west of it having been captured by the 50th Division the day before. The 13th D.L.I. however, failed to make good their objective with the result that the right flank of the Battalion was badly enfiladed from the high ground EAST of GUISANCOURT FARM and consequently at about 8.30 a.m., had to fall back and form a defensive flank to link up with the right Battalion. This eventually necessitated a withdrawal to the Southern edge of GUISANCOURT FARM and a line was occupied from there running in a S.E. direction towards BELLEVUE FARM, and was consolidated'*

During these operations, 2 officers were killed, 5 officers were wounded, 12 other ranks were killed, 130 other ranks wounded, 10 other ranks missing, and 2 died of wounds. One of the twelve other ranks killed was Edward Parkin. A contemporary report stated *'His death is mourned by his comrades as he was honoured and loved by all who knew him'*.

He is buried in Guizancourt Farm Cemetery, near Gouy, France, and is commemorated on the West Mersea War Memorial.

**Sources**
*Essex County Standard*
*Commonwealth War Graves Commission*
*Army Records Office, Ministry of Defence*
*The Sherwood Foresters Museum*
*11th Battalion, Sherwood Foresters, Nottingham and Derbyshire Regiment War Diary, PRO, Kew, Ref. no: 1915-1917 WO95/2187, Sept 1918 - Feb 1919 WO95/2247*

The grave of Private Edward Parkin in Guizancourt Farm Cemetery

**SURNAME: Lee**

CHRISTIAN NAME(S): Bertie

AGE: 26

RECRUITMENT OFFICE: Colchester

SERVICE NO: 3374  RANK: Private

SERVICE/REGIMENT: 'A' Squadron 8th Hussars (Kings Royal Irish)

DECORATIONS EARNED: 1914/15 Star, War Medal, Victory Medal

DATE KILLED/DIED: 16th October, 1918  LOCATION: France

LOCATION OF GRAVE: Doingt Communal Cemetary

---

**BACKGROUND AND SERVICE HISTORY:**

Bertie Lee was born in 1892 on Mersea Island, the son of Mr Alfred and Mrs Jessie Lee (nee Cook). His parents had married on 6th October, 1888, and his father was a labourer. Bertie was baptised in West Mersea church on 4th September, 1892.

In November 1908, at the age of seventeen, he enlisted at Colchester, and joined the 8th Hussars (The Kings Royal Irish). His brother, known on the Island as 'Did' Lee, was known to have walked to Colchester to assist Bertie with the cavalry horses. The Regiment later left Colchester to spend four years in India. At the outbreak of war, the Regiment was mobilised and embarked for Europe from Bombay on 10th October, 1914, arriving at Marseilles on 10th November.

On 2nd September, 1915, the Regiment were in the trenches at Authuille on the Somme. Like other cavalry units, they had relinquished their horses, and this would be the case until 1918, when the front became more mobile and the terrain more conducive to the use of horses in their cavalry role. The days events are described in the Regiment's War Diary.

*Dull morning - some rain. Enemy less active than usual during night. Our patrols repaired wire etc.*
*Enemy artillery active during morning and afternoon, shelling the village of Authuille and trenches. Enemy made use of rifle grenades at dusk causing casualties.*
*3374 - Private B. Lee - grenade wounds side, buttocks and legs.*

Private Bertie Lee was evacuated from France, convalescing in Ireland, and for over a year in England, before returning to France in February 1917.

In October, 1918,'A' Squadron of the 8th Hussars was in the area south of Cambrai. On 8th October, the Regiment was patrolling the area around Beaurevoir towards Premont. The War Diary gives an account of the day's events.

Above: Private Bertie Lee, on the right, while convalescing in Ireland.
Left: Private Bertie Lee, 'A' Squadron, 8th Hussars, (King's Royal Irish).
Below: Private Bertie Lee, standing on the right, beside the nurse, while convalescing in Ireland in 1915.

*8th October*
*South of Premont, Beaurevoir.*
*Fine morning, showers in the afternoon. Regiment paraded at 4.40 am and moved via Riqueval to valley south of Joncourt. Orders received about 8.15 am to move to valley, north of Wiancourt. Orders received about 11.00 am to support 19th Hussars who were south east of Premont. Regiment was shelled in crossing high ground south of Premont. Lieutenant D.W. Daly patrolled towards Maretz and reported armoured cars and machine gun on the main le Cateau road. Orders received about 15.00 to dis-engage enemy and come into Brigade reserve in valley, south of Premont. Regiment left about 17.45 to go to bivouac at Beaurevoir arriving at 18.00.*
*Casualties, other ranks - 1 killed, 11 wounded.*

Bertie Lee was one of those wounded, and he died at a Casualty Clearing Station on 16th October, 1918. He is buried in the Doingt Communal Cemetery, nr Peronne, France and is commemorated on the West Mersea War Memorial.

At the time of his death, his mother, Jessie Ellen Lee, now a widow, was living in East Road, near the Fox Inn.

**Sources**

*Commonwealth War Graves Commission*
*Essex County Telegraph*
*Headquarters, The Queen's Royal Hussars (The Queen's Own and Royal Irish)*
*Essex Record Office (Colchester)*
*8th Hussars (King's Royal Irish) War Diary, PRO, Kew, Ref. no: WO95/1164*
*Mr Keith Lee*

The grave of Private Bertie Lee in Doingt Communal Cemetery.

# The Royal Fleet Auxiliary *Industry*

On 22nd October, 1919, there appeared in the 'In Memoriam' columns of the local newspapers, a number of entries referring to Mersea men who had been killed when the Royal Fleet Auxiliary ship *Industry* was torpedoed. This was to be the first notification in the newspapers of the time that this incident had happened a year before, on 18th October, 1918. However, on the Island, they were well aware of the tragedy which had left six families without their men folk.

Why there was no report at the time remains a mystery. In official circles there was no Court of Inquiry, which was usual practice in these incidents. If there was, it has either been lost or withheld from release by the Admiralty. With regard to the newspapers, there was strict censorship at the time, but many of them, such as the *East Anglian Daily Times* issued a number of reports of ships sunk, once the Armistice had been signed. However, details regarding the attack on the *Industry* were not among them.

The *Industry* was formerly HMS *Glasgow*, and she was renamed in 1900. She was converted to a storeship by Beardmore of Glasgow and re-launched on 7th June, 1901. Her dimensions were 190 feet long and 30 feet wide, with a displacement of 1,460 tons. She was powered by a single screw, steam triple expansion engine.

Before 1914, she was manned by a 'Yard Craft' crew, but in that year she was taken over by the Royal Fleet Auxiliary. On 5th August, 1915, she was involved in a collision with the Dutch ship *Zealand* off the Wold lightship. In 1918, she was sailing between Ireland and mainland Britain. Her skipper was John Cormack, R.N.R. and the ship's officers were Lieutenant William Norman, R.N.R., Engineer Lieutenant Joseph C. Tait, R.N.R., and Engineer Sub Lieutenants Thomas C. Furness, R.N.R. and David B. Macalpine, R.N.R. The remainder of the crew consisted of men from the Mercantile Marine Reserve and a small number from the Royal Marine Reserve.

On 18th October, 1918, in the late evening, the *Industry* left Kingstown (now Dun Laoghaire) on the Irish coast escorted by the armed trawler *Persian Empire*. She had been preceded out of port by the merchant ship SS *Hundsdon*. It was bright moonlight, the weather was fine, and there was a moderate sea. There must have been some apprehension aboard the ships as an enemy submarine had been reported entering the area on 13th October, but a search by naval patrol vessels had failed to reveal anything.

Just before 21.30, the SS *Hundsdon* was torpedoed and sunk about three quarters of a mile south east of the Strangford Light Buoy. An S.O.S. signal was sent out, but because of a damaged aerial on the sinking ship, it was not picked up by the *Persian Empire* which, with the *Industry* was sailing one and a half miles ahead; also no explosion was seen. At about 22.10, presumably the same submarine torpedoed the *Industry*. The Naval Authorities at Kingstown reported that she sank at 22.10 at a position latitude 54.23, longitude 05.17.

The following report was issued by the headquarters of the Auxiliary Patrol Vessels.

*Friday, 18th October, 1918.*
*At 22.24, HMT Persian Empire reported that RFA Industry had been torpedoed and sunk 3 miles S. by E. from South Rock. She has picked up 4 survivors and taken them to Belfast, also 30 survivors from SS Hundsdon who was reported by Tara W.S.S. as having been torpedoed and sunk 8 miles S.W.b.S. from South Rock Light vessel at 21.30. Action taken - all available Auxiliary Patrol Vessels were ordered to proceed to the Southern Patrol Squares and use hydrophones there. HMS Platypus was informed of the presence of the submarine and informed HM Submarine R8 who was operating in the vicinity of South Rock.*

There are conflicting reports regarding the ultimate fate of the ship. Contemporary reports state that she sank, but in official Admiralty records for ships sunk, there is no mention of the *Industry*, and therefore it is possible that she was salvaged and towed into port. The Naval List has her on strength until August 1919. However, damage must have been considerable and devastating to the ship as twenty crew members were killed and their bodies never recovered, including six men from Mersea Island. The officers are commemorated on the Portsmouth Naval Memorial, and the other ranks on the Plymouth Naval Memorial.

**Sources**

*National Maritime Museum, Greenwich*
*Naval Historical Collectors and Research Association*
*Ships of the Royal Navy*
*Royal Fleet Auxiliary by Captain E.E. Stigwart, published by Adlard Coles*
*Royal Naval Museum, Portsmouth, Hampshire*
*Naval Lists 1914 - 1919*
*ADM137/808, PRO, Kew*
*ADM137/947, PRO, Kew*
*Irish Sea - German Submarines, July to November 1918, PRO, Kew, Ref no: ADM137/1517*

Royal Fleet Auxiliary Industry - Casualty List

| Name | Rank | Service | Service No | Age | Commemorated | Residence |
|---|---|---|---|---|---|---|
| Ambridge, B. | Fireman | MMR | 912971 | 23 | Plymouth | Swansea |
| Barlow, A. | Ordinary Seaman | MMR | 882966 | Unknown | Plymouth | Hoylake, Cheshire |
| Berridge, V.C. | Fireman | MMR | 881783 | 20 | Plymouth | Gravesend, Kent |
| Carney, J.J. | Ordinary Seaman | MMR | 836789 | 24 | Plymouth | St. Helens, Lancashire |
| Charlick, R. | Steward's Boy | MMR | 968576 | 17 | Plymouth | Bethnal Green, London |
| Coleman, H.P. | Sub Lieutenant | RNR | Unknown | Unknown | Portsmouth | Unknown |
| Foreman, T.H. | Leading Fireman | MMR | Unknown | Unknown | Plymouth | Unknown |
| Garrick, J.R. | Ordinary Seaman | MMR | 955637 | 18 | Plymouth | South Shields, Co. Durham |
| Goddard, C. | Stoker | MMR | 801031 | 22 | Plymouth | Southampton |
| Green, A.P. | Able Seaman | MMR | Unknown | 24 | Plymouth | West Mersea, Essex |
| Jones, J.A. | Stoker | MMR | 862937 | 22 | Plymouth | Liverpool |
| Lindsey, J.H. | Private | RMLI | PLY.8056 | 45 | Plymouth | Merton, Surrey |
| Mason, W.R. | Able Seaman | MMR | 857858 | 17 | Plymouth | Sunderland |
| Mole, A.J | Fireman | MMR | MFA18231A | 30 | Plymouth | West Mersea, Essex |
| Mole, F.W. | Able Seaman/Cook | MMR | Unknown | 36 | Plymouth | West Mersea, Essex |
| Mole, R.J. | Able Seaman | MMR | Unknown | 28 | Plymouth | West Mersea, Essex |
| Norman, W. | Lieutenant | RNR | Unknown | Unknown | Portsmouth | Unknown |
| Pullen, H. | Quartermaster | MMR | Unknown | 41 | Plymouth | West Mersea, Essex |
| Stoker, H.F. | Able Seaman | MMR | Unknown | 20 | Plymouth | West Mersea, Essex |
| Tait, J.C. | Engineer Lieutenant | RNR | Unknown | 42 | Portsmouth | Tynemouth, Northumberland |

**Abbreviations**
MMR: Mercantile Marine Reserve. RNR: Royal Naval Reserve. RMLI: Royal Marine Light Infantry

Royal Fleet Auxiliary *Industry* (Photo: *Royal Fleet Auxiliary* by Captain E.E. Sigwart).

**SURNAME: Green**

CHRISTIAN NAME(S): Archibold Percy

AGE: 24

RECRUITMENT OFFICE: Not known

SERVICE NO: Not known     RANK: Able Seaman

SERVICE/REGIMENT: Merchant Marine Reserve

DECORATIONS EARNED: Not Known

DATE KILLED/DIED: 18th October, 1918     LOCATION: Irish Sea

MEMORIAL IF NO KNOWN GRAVE: Plymouth Naval Memorial

---

**BACKGROUND AND SERVICE HISTORY:**

Archibold Percy Green was born in 1894, the son of Mr and Mrs Oscar Green of Moss Cottage, Queens Corner, West Mersea. He was baptised on 3rd October, 1897.

A contemporary postcard showing a view of Queens Corner and Moss Cottage.

He joined the Merchant Marine Reserve and on 29th September, 1916, he married Miss Lucy Hoy. The wedding was reported in the Essex County Standard dated 6th October, 1916.

*'A SAILOR'S WEDDING - An interesting wedding, which attracted a good deal of local interest, took place at West Mersea church, on Saturday, Sept. 29, when A.B. Percy Green, of the Royal Fleet Auxiliary Service, son of Mr Oscar Green, of West Mersea, was married to Miss Lucy Hoy, eldest daughter of Mr and Mrs Henry Hoy of the same parish. The ceremony was performed by the Rev. Ronald Dunn, of East Mersea, in the absence of the vicar (Rev. C. Pierrepont Edwards, M.C.), who was absent until the evening on war duties. The bride and bridegroom are both well known and esteemed in Mersea. The bridesmaids were Miss Ella Green and Miss Hetty Hoy, sisters of the happy pair. The bride was given away by her brother, A.B. Ernest Hoy, and A.B. Harry Pullen was best man. A.B. Mole assisted in the conveyance of the parties to and from the church in Mr Cudmore's waggonette. All the four sailors are shipmates on the same vessel.'*

The wedding of Able Seaman A. Percy Green and Lucy Hoy, the wedding party seen outside Moss Cottage, Queen's Corner, West Mersea.
Left to right are: Horace Green, Maud Mussett, Oscar Green, Ella Green, Bridegroom: Percy Green, Bride: Lucy Hoy, Peter Hoy, Mrs Peter Hoy, Hetty Hoy, Stony Pullen, Ivy Hoy, Mrs Bill Cook, Bert Hoy.

The couple set up home in Rainbow Road, West Mersea.

On 18th October, 1918, he was serving on the RFA *Industry* in the Irish sea with five other men from Mersea, when she was torpedoed by a German submarine. Percy Green was killed and his body was never recovered. Of the wedding guests who were on the same ship, two were to perish with Percy, the other, Able Seaman Ernest Hoy, was not on the casualty list and survived, unless he was not part of the crew on that particular voyage.

Percy is commemorated on the Plymouth Naval Memorial and on the West Mersea War Memorial. With Percy's death, the war had claimed another one of the Green's sons, the first being their elder son Edward Oscar Green who was killed on 24th December, 1917. (see page 120).

**Sources**

*Commonwealth War Graves Commission*
*Essex County Standard*

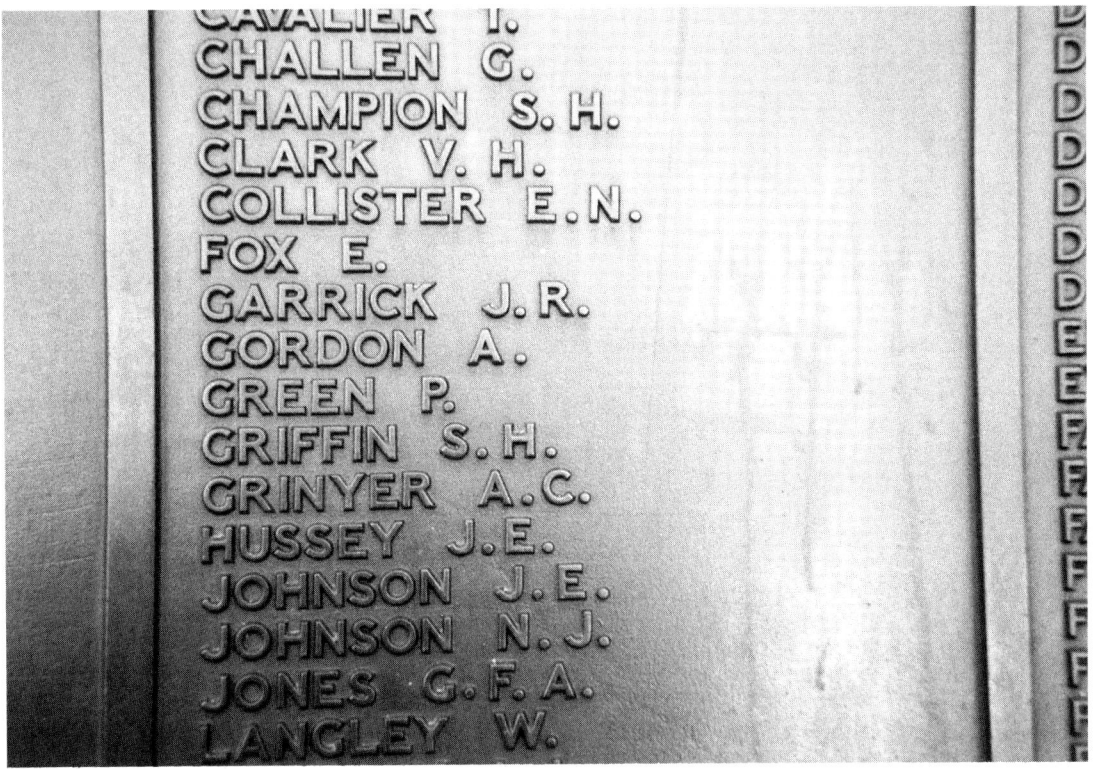

Able Seaman Percy Green's name inscribed on the Plymouth Naval Memorial.

**SURNAME: Mole**

CHRISTIAN NAME(S): Alfred John

AGE: 30

RECRUITMENT OFFICE: Not known

SERVICE NO: MFA/18231A            RANK: Fireman

SERVICE/REGIMENT: Merchant Marine Reserve

DECORATIONS EARNED: Not known

DATE KILLED/DIED: 18th October, 1918      LOCATION: Irish Sea

MEMORIAL IF NO KNOWN GRAVE: Plymouth Naval Memorial

---

**BACKGROUND AND SERVICE HISTORY:**

Alfred John Mole was born in 1888, second son of Mr Frederick Charles and Annie Mole of St Peters Road, West Mersea.

Nothing is known of Alfred's early life. He married Kate Ethel (nee Wright), and they had a daughter, Joan. The family home was at Laburnum Cottage, Seaview Avenue, West Mersea.

At the end of 1915, Lord Derby's Conscription Act came into force, and a number of Mersea men applied for exemption.

On 22nd July, 1916, a contemporary report of the Lexden and Winstree Tribunal quoted the following:

*'A West Mersea gardener, etc, Alfred J. Mole, 28, married in the employ of Mr Henry H. Hoblyn was claimed for exemption. The military representative said this was just the kind of man he wanted, he had been before the medical board at Weeley and had been passed for general service - One months temporary exemption was granted.'*

Alfred joined his brother Frederick in the Merchant Marine Reserve, and he was with him on the RFA *Industry* as a Fireman.

He was killed on 18th October, 1918, when the ship was torpedoed in the Irish Sea by a German submarine.

His body was never recovered and he is commemorated on the Plymouth Naval Memorial and on the West Mersea War Memorial.

**Sources**

*Commonwealth War Graves Commission*
*Essex Regiment Museum*
*Essex County Telegraph*
*Mr John Boon (Grandson)*

Fireman Alfred John Mole, Mercantile Marine Reserve

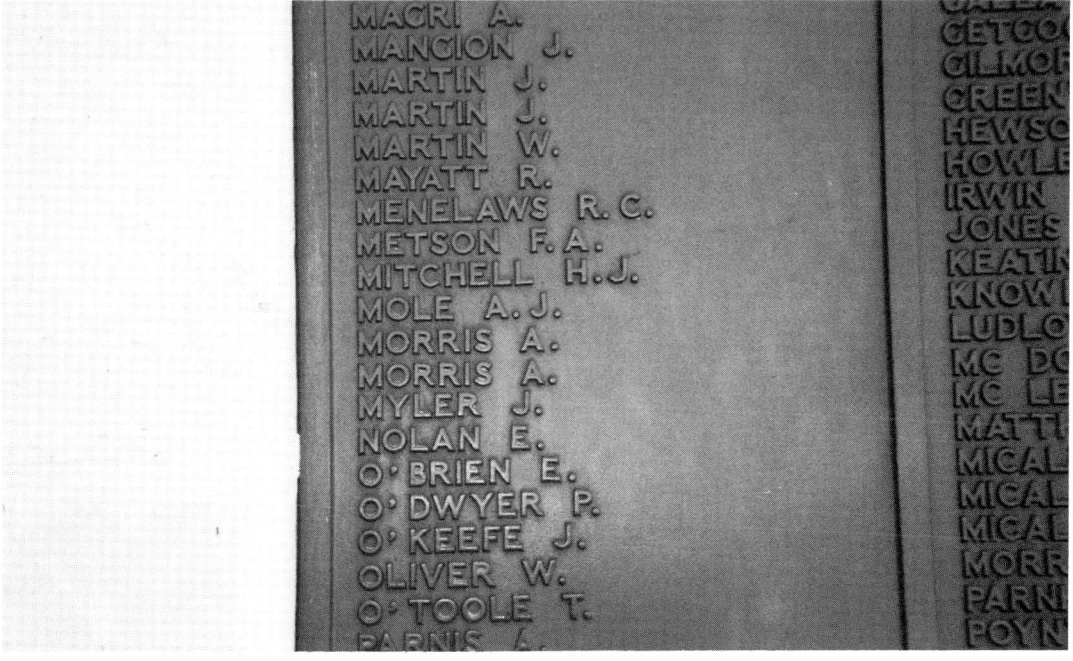

Fireman Alfred John Mole's name inscribed on the Plymouth Memorial

**SURNAME: Mole**

CHRISTIAN NAME(S): Frederick Westhorpe

AGE: 36

RECRUITMENT OFFICE: Unknown

SERVICE NO: Unknown     RANK: Cook/Able Seaman

SERVICE/REGIMENT: Merchant Marine Reserve

DECORATIONS EARNED: Unknown

DATE KILLED/DIED: 18th October, 1918     LOCATION: Irish Sea

MEMORIAL IF NO KNOWN GRAVE: Plymouth Naval Memorial

---

**BACKGROUND AND SERVICE HISTORY:**

Frederick Westhorpe Mole was born in 1882 on Mersea Island, the eldest son of Mr Frederick Charles and Annie Mole who lived in St Peters Road, West Mersea. Mr Mole was a fisherman by trade, but he had met his wife, who was from Cowes, Isle of Wight, when he was employed as a crewman on a luxury yacht.

The 1891 census recorded that there were five children in the family, Frederick aged 9, Harriet Mildred aged 7, Kathleen Jane aged 5, Alfred John aged 3, and Annie Emma aged 1. Later a further two children were born, Roy Wesley and Charlotte.

Nothing is known of Frederick's early life, but it is possible that he followed in his father's footsteps and became a fisherman. He married Susannah Ellen (née Wright) and they had one daughter, Ena Ruby. They lived at 'Fir Dene', City Road, West Mersea. He owned his own sailing boat, the *Skylark*. (After his death, the boat was sold, the proceeds being used to augment the income from a War widows pension).

With the introduction of conscription in 1916, he joined the Merchant Marine Reserve, and with his brother Alfred, was posted to the RFA *Industry*.

On 18th October, 1918, the RFA *Industry* was sailing in the Irish Sea when she was torpedoed by a German submarine. Frederick was killed and his body never recovered. He is commemorated on the Plymouth Naval Memorial and on the West Mersea War Memorial.

**Sources**

*Essex Regiment Museum*
*Commonwealth War Graves Commission*
*Mrs E.R. De'ath*

Frederick Westhorpe Mole, with his wife Susannah Ellen
and their only daughter, Ena Ruby.

Frederick Westhorpe's name inscribed on the Plymouth Naval Memorial

**SURNAME: Mole**

CHRISTIAN NAME(S): Reginald John

AGE: 28

RECRUITMENT OFFICE: Unknown

SERVICE NO: Unknown                     RANK: Able Seaman

SERVICE/REGIMENT: Merchant Marine Reserve

DECORATIONS EARNED: Unknown

DATE KILLED/DIED: 18th October, 1918   LOCATION: Irish Sea

MEMORIAL IF NO KNOWN GRAVE: Plymouth Naval Memorial

---

## BACKGROUND AND SERVICE HISTORY:

Reginald John Mole was born in 1890, the son of George and Phoebe Mole of West Mersea. He was baptised on 29th March 1891.

On 23rd May, 1916, he married Kate Elizabeth (nee Cundy), setting up home at 'Clandon', Mersea Avenue, West Mersea.

He joined the Merchant Marine Reserve and was an Able Seaman on RFA *Industry*. On 18th October, 1918, while in the Irish Sea, she was torpedoed by a German submarine, and Reginald John Mole was killed.

His body was not recovered and he is commemorated on the Plymouth Naval Memorial and on the West Mersea War Memorial.

**Sources**

*Commonwealth War Graves Commission*
*Essex Regiment Museum*
*Essex County Standard*
*Essex Record Office (Colchester)*

Able Seaman Reginald John Mole's name inscribed on the Plymouth Naval Memorial.

**SURNAME: Pullen**

CHRISTIAN NAME(S): Henry William

AGE: 41

RECRUITMENT OFFICE: Not known

SERVICE NO: Not known        RANK: Quartermaster

SERVICE/REGIMENT: Merchant Marine Reserve

DECORATIONS EARNED: Not known

DATE KILLED/DIED: 18th October, 1918    LOCATION: Irish Sea

MEMORIAL IF NO KNOWN GRAVE: Plymouth Naval Memorial

---

**BACKGROUND AND SERVICE HISTORY:**

Henry William Pullen was born in 1877, the son of Henry William and Julia Pullen of May Cottage, West Mersea. He was the elder brother of Alfred.

Prior to the outbreak of war he was a fisherman and served on the jury (committee) of the Tollesbury and Mersea Oyster Fishery Company.

He joined the Merchant Marine Reserve and served on the RFA *Industry* as a Quartermaster. He was killed when the ship was torpedoed by a German submarine on 18th October, 1918.

His body was not recovered and he is commemorated on the Plymouth Naval Memorial, and on the West Mersea War Memorial. Henry was the second son that the Pullen family were to lose in the war, the first being Alfred who died of wounds on 24th February, 1917. (see page 65)

**Sources**

*Commonwealth War Graves Commission*
*Essex Regiment Museum*
*Essex County Standard*
*Essex Record Office (Colchester)*
*Mr and Mrs Pontyfix*

Quartermaster Henry Pullen

Quartermaster Henry Pullen's name inscribed on the Plymouth Naval Memorial.

**SURNAME: Stoker**

CHRISTIAN NAME(S): Harold Frederick

AGE: 20

RECRUITMENT OFFICE: Unknown

SERVICE NO: Unknown         RANK: Able Seaman

SERVICE/REGIMENT: Merchant Marine Reserve

DECORATIONS EARNED: Unknown

DATE KILLED/DIED: 18th October, 1918    LOCATION: Irish Sea

MEMORIAL IF NO KNOWN GRAVE: Plymouth Naval Memorial

---

**BACKGROUND AND SERVICE HISTORY:**

Harold Frederick Stoker was born in 1898, the son of Thomas and Linda Stoker of Firs Avenue, West Mersea. He was baptised on 10th April, 1898.

He joined the Merchant Marine Reserve, and was an Able Seaman on the supply ship, RFA *Industry*. On 18th October, 1918, while serving in the Irish Sea, she was torpedoed by a German submarine. Harold was killed and his body was not recovered. George James Stoker, his cousin, was also a member of the crew, but on the day of the attack, was on sick leave on Mersea.

Harold Stoker is commemorated on the Plymouth Naval Memorial and on the West Mersea War Memorial.

**Sources**

*Commonwealth War Graves Commission*
*Essex Regiment Museum*
*Absent Voter's List, 1918*
*Robert Stoker*
*Mrs Evenden*

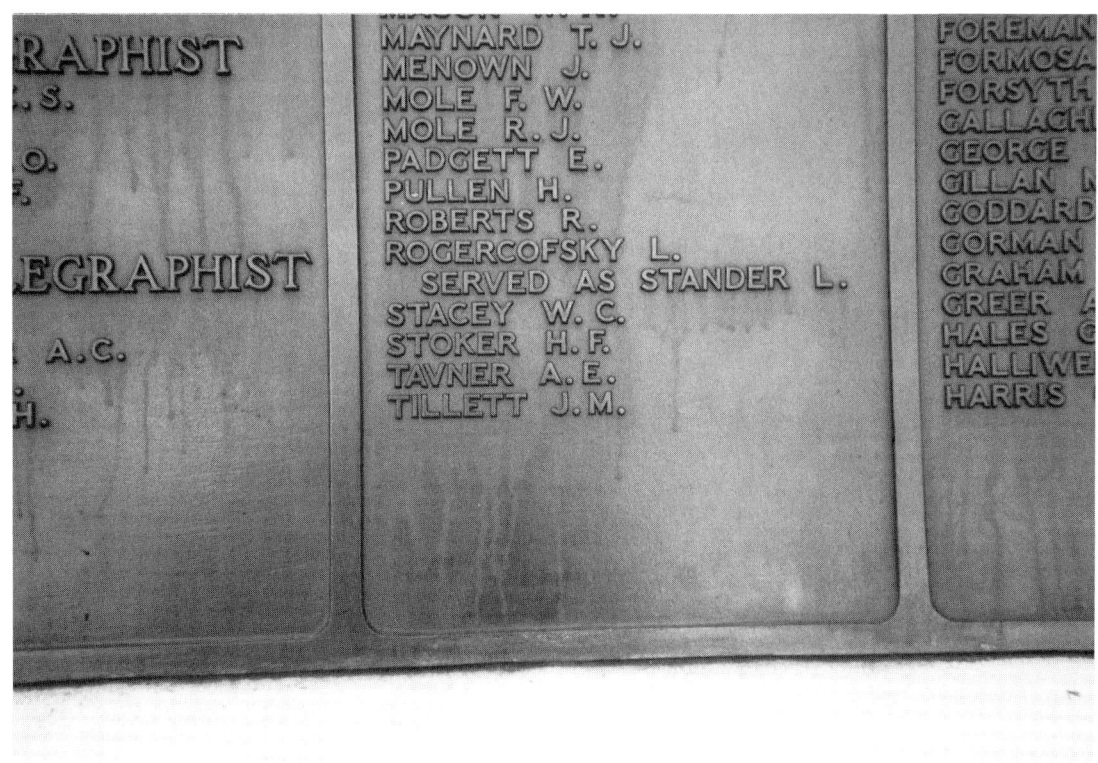

Able Seaman Harold Frederick Stoker's name inscribed on the Plymouth Naval Memorial.

The Plymouth Naval Memorial on which is inscribed the names of the six Mersea sailors who were killed when the RFA *Industry* was torpedoed in the Irish Sea.

**SURNAME: Hart**

CHRISTIAN NAME(S): Ernest

AGE: 29

RECRUITMENT OFFICE: Colchester

SERVICE NO: 47402?                    RANK: 2nd Lieutenant

SERVICE/REGIMENT: 3rd Battalion, Essex Regiment (service no: 599)
                           8th Hussars (Kings Royal Irish) (service no: 3998)
                           2nd Battalion, Essex Regiment (service no: 47402?)

DECORATIONS EARNED: 1914 Star, War Medal, Victory Medal.

DATE KILLED/DIED: 26th October, 1918   LOCATION: Near le Quesnoy, France

LOCATION OF GRAVE: St Souplet British Cemetery

---

**BACKGROUND AND SERVICE HISTORY:**

Ernest Hart was born in September, 1889, in the parish of Sawtry in Huntingdonshire, the third son of Henry and Martha Hart. He had an elder brother, Bertie, and two younger brothers, Frank and William. The family moved to Barrow Hill, West Mersea, the journey taking three days by horse and waggon, with the family spending the nights out in the open, sleeping under the waggons.

In August 1907, at the age of seventeen, he came under the employ of Mr Charles Brown of Barrow Hill Farm as his 'odd boy about the farm'.

On 15th October, 1908, he enlisted at Colchester, where he joined the 3rd Battalion, Essex Regiment (Special Reserve) for a six year period of service. On 6th February, 1909, he was discharged from the Reserve to join the regular army, his new regiment being the 8th Hussars (King's Royal Irish). With his brother Bertie following in his footsteps, they were posted to India on 29th September, 1908.

On 14th April, 1914, Ernest Hart, now a Corporal, had an unfortunate experience during a General's inspection at Ambala. During a display of jumping, his horse caught the top of a bush fence and fell, injuring Corporal Hart's right hip. A month later, on 15th May, a Court of Inquiry was held to determine whether he was negligent or whether it had been an accident. The recommendation was:

*'I am of the opinion that the injury named was sustained by the N.C.O. concerned whilst in the performance of his military duty, and he was not to blame. I recommend the remission of all Hospital Stoppages.*

                                       *Officer Commanding, 8th Hussars (King's Royal Irish)*

Ernest Hart (standing) and his brother Bertie. Probably taken when they were serving in India with the 8th Hussars (King's Royal Irish)

Soon after the war broke out, the Regiment was mobilised and was sent to France arriving, on 15th October, 1914. Ernest was promoted to Sergeant and served with the Regiment there until 8th November, 1917.

On 7th August, 1917, he applied for a commission, being strongly recommended by his then Commanding Officer. It was suggested that he be transferred either to the Essex Regiment or the Machine Gun Corps. On 8th November, 1917, he left France, and after a period of home leave, was ordered to report to the Officer Commanding, 2nd Reserve Cavalry Regiment at the The Curragh, Ireland. On 30th November, 1917, he received notification to join No. 16, Officer Cadet Battalion at Kinmel Park, Rhyl, where he gained his commission and was appointed a Second Lieutenant to the 3rd Battalion, Essex Regiment on 27th February, 1918. On receipt of his commission, he re-engaged to complete 21 years service in the army. He returned to France to join the 2nd Battalion, Essex Regiment on 12th September, 1918.

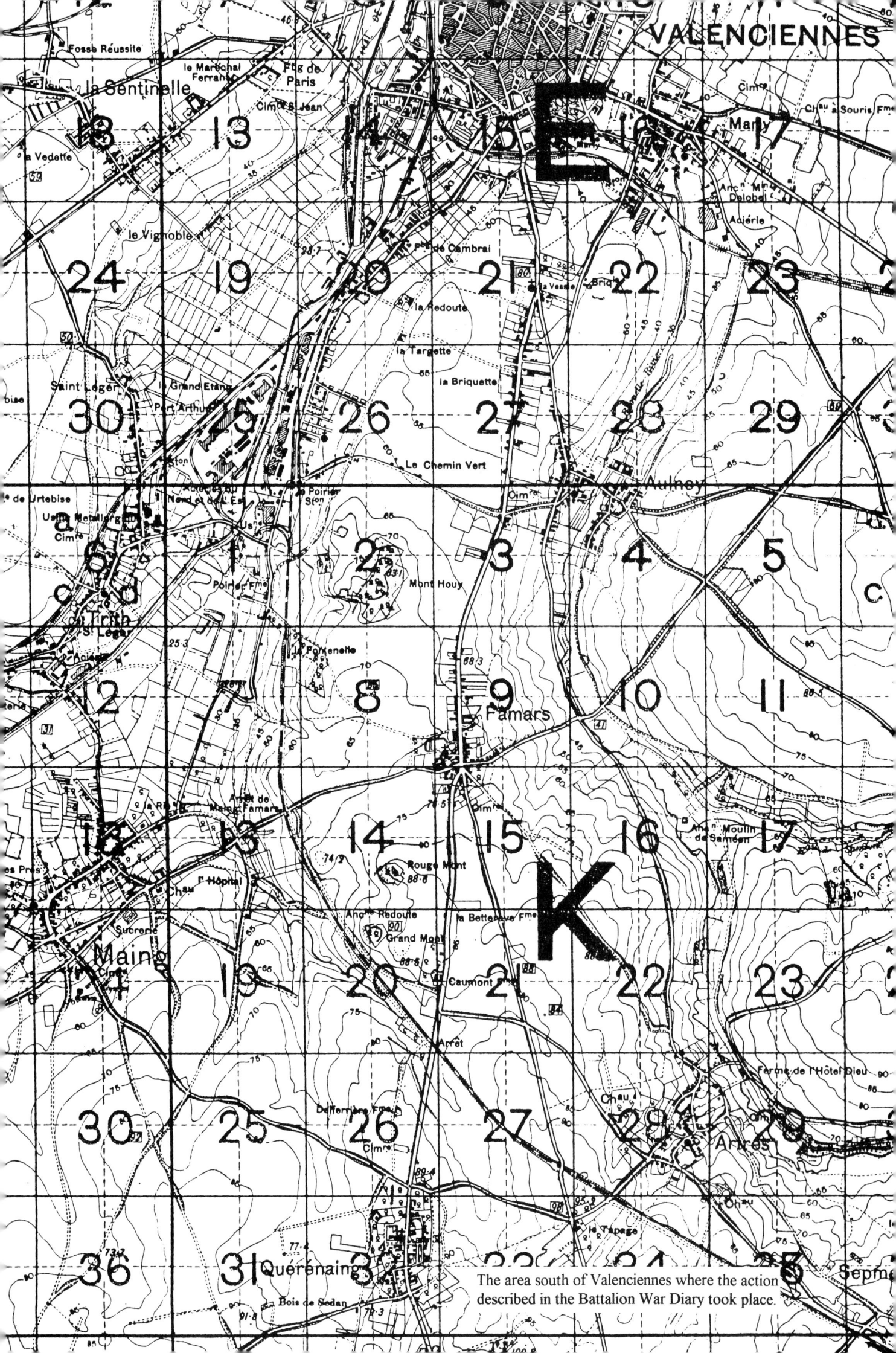

The area south of Valenciennes where the action described in the Battalion War Diary took place.

The final offensive of the 2nd Battalion, Essex Regiment, in 1918 was in the neighbourhood of Valenciennes. The action started on 25th October, 1918, and continued the next day. It is described with reference being made to the Battalion History and the Battalion War Diary.

The Brigade went in at 07.00 am, on a two battalion frontage in an effort to keep the enemy on the move and to secure the village of Querenaing and the Famars road running north-east as far as the halt at the level crossing over the railway. The 2nd Battalion, Essex Regiment were on the left, with the 2nd Battalion, Lancashire Fusiliers on the right and the 1st King's Own in reserve. The first named Battalion had two companies in front, 'B' and 'D' and two, 'A' and 'C' in support about 200 yards in the rear. The operation was designed with two objectives, the first being to secure the enemy trenches and then the road system south of the railway line. The barrage was provided by eighteen pounder guns which were stationary for nine minutes before advancing with the infantry following as closely as possible. The shell fire fell directly into the first objective and had the trench been occupied it would undoubtedly have caused many enemy casualties. However, it contained only one man, and he had been killed. Twenty feet in front of the trench was a wide belt of wire entanglement, uncut by the artillery fire, but the troops were able to pass through by the paths made by enemy carrying parties. When advancing upon the second objective, the Famars road, very little enemy resistance was encountered, and the few Germans who were met were very quickly dealt with. As soon as this point was reached, patrols were pushed forward to the Valenciennes-le Quesnoy railway line and posts established along it. Some difficulty was experienced in keeping direction during the advance due to the heavy smoke from the barrage. The enemy counter-attacked at 6.00 pm, but it was local and lacked enthusiasm, being easily repulsed.
Casualties: 1 other ranks killed, 25 other ranks wounded, and 3 other ranks missing.

The offensive was renewed the next day (26th October) at 10.00 am in an endeavour to take Artres and to secure to the east of the village a bridgehead over the Rhonelle. An enemy barrage came down about 250 yards away on the north eastern side of the railway and remained there for ten minutes. The barrage came down very short and our troops suffered casualties on the line of the railway. Our creeping barrage advanced at the rate of 100 yards every four minutes, the attacking troops following closely. The enemy offered much more resistance than on the previous day. Enemy machine guns were very active and caused casualties. The hostile barrage was placed more accurately and came down more quickly. About 3 enemy officers and 60 other ranks were captured, and about three times that number were killed. The prisoners seemed very dejected and stunned by the violence of our artillery. On reaching the high ground beyond the railway, our troops came under increased enemy machine gun fire, and some difficulty in advancing was experienced. Direct fire from enemy field guns was also brought to bear on the attacking forces. The objective was reached and posts established along the road. At about 4.30 pm a hostile counter-attack of more importance than that of the previous day was launched, and for a while the situation was critical. The enemy concentrated on our left flank, and on the right of the 51st Division at Famars. The enemy forces were beaten back by rifle, Lewis gun and machine gun fire. Touch with the 51st Division was maintained. The enemy counter-attack was made under a heavy gas and high explosive shell barrage. A heavy gas concentration arose and made the task of defending troops very difficult.
Casualties: 2 officers killed, 1 officer died of wounds, 2 officers wounded, 1 officer gassed. 1 other ranks died of wounds, 82 other ranks wounded.

Second Lieutenant Ernest Hart, 2nd Battalion, Essex Regiment

One of the two officers killed was 2nd Lieutenant Ernest Hart. After his death, his Company Commander wrote:-

*'I have been with him ever since he arrived at Felixstowe and saw him fight and fall leading his platoon to what ended in a glorious victory, in which we took positions commanding Valenciennes. I being his Company Commander feel his loss very, very keenly. He was a fine companion and friend. He was buried with full honour at Soulzior, the Colonel, Second in Command, several officers and some of his men being present. At the close, the bugle sounded the last post. He was one of the best and devoted sons'.*

He is buried in St Souplet British Cemetery, near le Cateau, and is commemorated on the West Mersea War Memorial.

**Sources**

*Commonwealth War Graves Commission*
*Essex Regiment Museum*
*Essex County Standard*
*2nd Battalion, Essex Regiment War Diary, PRO, Kew, Ref no: WO95/2247*
*Mr Ernest Hart, New Zealand*
*Mr T.J. Hart, West Mersea*
*Essex Units in the War 1914-1919 by J.W. Burrows*

The grave of Second Lieutenant Ernest Hart in St Souplet British Cemetery

**SURNAME:** Beynon

CHRISTIAN NAME(S): Walter James

AGE: 38

SHORE BASE: Portsmouth

SERVICE NO: 201889					RANK: Leading Seaman

SERVICE/REGIMENT: Royal Navy

DECORATIONS EARNED: Not known

DATE KILLED/DIED: 2nd November, 1918			LOCATION: Norway

LOCATION OF GRAVE: Faberg Churchyard, Norway

---

**BACKGROUND AND SERVICE HISTORY:**

Walter James Beynon was born on 11th November, 1880, at Brading, Isle of Wight, the son of William and Emily Beynon. On leaving school and until joining the Royal Navy, he was employed locally as a labourer.

On his eighteenth birthday, on 11th November, 1898, he signed on to join the Royal navy for a period of twelve years (see Naval Service Record). On 1st February, 1909, he signed on for a second term. On 19th September, 1912, he was posted to the Eastern West Mersea Battalion of the Coastguard, and he moved with his wife Florence Mary (maiden name unknown) to the Coastguard Cottages at West Mersea. Both Walter and Florence became involved in Island life, with Florence being part of the Methodist church congregation and Walter participating in the Athletic Sports Day in July 1914, where he came first in the jockey race and third in the wheelbarrow race.

With the outbreak of the First World War he, like many of his coastguard colleagues was called up for active service in the Royal Navy. On 1st August, 1914, he was posted to HMS *Hannibal* as a Leading Seaman. The ship was given the task of guarding the Humber approaches and Scapa Flow. There then followed a short term at HMS *Pembroke*, the shore station at Chatham from 20th February to 12th April. 1915.

On 13th April, 1915, he joined the newly converted armed merchant cruiser, HMS *India*, captained by Commander W.G.A. Kennedy R.N. The *India* was launched on 3rd September, 1896 by Caird and Co Ltd. of Greenock for the owners, the Peninsular & Oriental Steam Navigation Company. She was 499.9 ft long, 54.3 ft wide, with a gross tonnage of 7911 tons, and was powered by a triple expansion four cylinder engine with a speed of 18 knots. Her passenger carrying capacity was 317 1st Class and 152 2nd Class. Prior to the outbreak of war she was employed on the Indian and Australian services.

**201889**     Portsmouth     **201889**

Name in full: **Walter James Beynon**    10/6032 C.S.

Date of Birth: 11 November 1880
Place of Birth: Brading, I. of Wight
Occupation: Labourer

| Date and Period of C. S. Engagements. | Age. | Height Ft. in. | Hair. | Eyes. | Complexion. | Wounds, Scars, Marks, &c. |
|---|---|---|---|---|---|---|
| 11 November 1898 – 12 yrs | 18 / 18½ | 5' 8" / 5' 8¼" | Light / " | Grey / " | Fair / " | Scar on L. forefinger |
| Vol 1 February 1909 – to comp. | – | 5' 9" | LBro | " | Fresh | |

| Ships, &c., served in. | List and No. | Rating. | Sub-ratings Rating From To | Badges. | Period of Service From To | Character. | If Discharged, and for what Cause |
|---|---|---|---|---|---|---|---|
| Northampton | 15ᵃ 3886 | B 2c | LM 23.9.00 19.5.03 | G. 13.5.02 | 3 Nov 98 — | | |
| " " | " " | B 1c | 2G. 20.5.03 11.12.05 | G. 1.2.5.?? | 2 Feb 99 10 Feb 99 | | |
| Curacoa | 15ᶜ 1049 | Ord. | S.G. 12.12.05 22.2.06 | G,30.6.12 | 11 Feb 99 | | |
| D. of Well: I | 15² 4460 | " | SS. 23.2.06 ... | ⅓ | 3 May 99 10 July 99 | | |
| Monarch | 15 171 | " | 2L 1.10.07 7.10.09 | | 11 July 99 3 Nov 99 | NG 31.12.00 | |
| Terrible | 16 491 | " | S.G. 1.10.07 req. | | 4 Nov 99 31 Dec 99 | NG 31.12.01 | |
| Doris | 15 354 | " | S.G. 27.8.09 | | 1 Jan 00 3 Feb 00 | | 31.12.02 |
| " | | AB | | | 2 Feb 00 | | 31.12.03 |
| Monarch | 15 211 | " | | | 23 Sep 00 12 Oct 00 | | |
| D of Well: | 15² 239 | " | | | 13 Oct 00 9 Dec 02 | NG 31.12.05 | |
| Excellent | 15ᵈ 11168 | " | | | 10 Dec 02 4 Feb 03 | VG 31.12.05 | |
| D of Well: | 15² 17291 | " | | | 8 Feb 03 30 May 03 | VG 31.12.06 | |
| Boscawen | 5 239 | " | | | 31 May 03 3 June 03 | VG 31.12.07 | |
| " I | | | | | 4 June 03 31 Dec 03 | VG 31.12.09 | |
| Revenge | 15 1194 | " | | | 1 Jan 04 17 May 04 | VG 31.12.10 G-R.M.G. | |
| " " | " " | Ldg. Smn | | | 18 May 04 | VG 31.12.11 Sup R.M.G. | |
| Victory I | 15 3565 | " | | | 3 July 05 31 Aug 05 | VG 31.12.12 Sat R.M.G. | |
| Excellent | 15² 4908 | " | | | 1 Sep 05 — | NG 31.12.13 Sup. | |
| Prince of Wales | 5ᴱ 222 | " | | | 8 Sep 05 7 Sep 06 | VG 31.12.14 Sup | |
| Excellent | 15² 9803 | " | | | 8 Sep 06 24 Dec 09 | | |
| Victory I | 15² 6755 | " | | | 25 Dec 09 26 Oct 09 | | |
| Venerable | 5ᴴ 300 | " | | | 27 Oct 09 2 Nov 09 | | |
| Excellent | 15² 2780 | " | | | 3 Nov 09 30 Oct 11 | | |
| Victory I | 15² 8301 | " | | | 31 Oct 11 26 July 12 | | |
| Eastern. W. Mersea | | Btn | | | 27 July 12 18 Sep 12 | | |
| Hannibal | 5ᴳ 16 | Ldg Smn | | | 19 Sep 12 31 July 14 | | |
| Pembroke | 5ᴳ 305 | " | | | 1 Aug 14 19 Feb 15 | | |
| Arab India | 5 11 | " | | | 20 Feb 15 12 Apl. 15 | | |
| Pembroke | 14 4 | " | | | 13 Apl. 15 8 Aug. 15 | | |
| | | | | | 9 Aug. 15 Dec 18 X | D.D X | |

NP 13085 /18 X
D.D. 7 November 18. Pneumonia
Whilst interned in Norway.

TRACED WAR GRATUITY BY No. 14

| Clothing and Bedding Gratuities. | REMARKS. | |
|---|---|---|
| £6 7 6 | Op Grat for raising Vr 33 Northpton Nov 05 | L. Medal 20/3/14 |
| £3 Feby 99 | X for President V (P.O.W) March 19. | N.P. 4105/15 Interned in Norway |
| £3 Feb June 99 | | L. Grat 13.12.15 |
| £3.16 SCrB Midsr 1911. | | Paced Grat 27.11/? |

The Naval Record of Leading Seaman Walter Beynon

new S.C. written. 5-12-1?

PAID WAR GRATUITY

HMS *Hannibal*, the first ship that Leading Seaman Walter Beynon was to serve on, at the outbreak of the First World War.

The passenger ship *India* prior to her conversion into an armoured merchant cruiser.
*(Photograph courtesy of the National Maritime Museum G314)*

She was hired by the Admiralty on 13th March, 1915 for service as an armed merchant cruiser, and became part of the 10th Cruiser Squadron. On 8th August, she was patrolling off the island of Helligvaer, near Bodo, Norway, when she halted to examine a suspected blockade runner. While examining the suspect ship, HMS *India* was torpedoed by the German submarine U22 and sank. Out of the crew of 301, 160 were lost and 22 officers and 119 men were saved, being picked up by the SS *Gotaland* and taken into Narvik, assisted by HM armed trawler *Saxon*.

The German submarine U22 which attacked and sunk HMS *India*.
*(Photograph courtesy of the National Maritime Museum N5709).*

After the sinking and the subsequent rescue of the crew, there was confusion over who had survived and who had been lost. The file at the Public Records Office at Kew contains a number of letters from next of kin who were notified by the Admiralty that a husband or father had not survived, only to receive a letter from them in Norway advising that they had survived, prompting the Admiralty to apologise and confirm that they were alive. Leading Seaman Walter Beynon was one such case.

There was a flurry of communications from the British Consulate in Norway, the Admiralty in London, and the Norwegian authorities.

*Christinia, Monday 9th August, 1915*
*According to news received from Bodoe, a British auxiliary cruiser was torpedoed yesterday. One hundred and forty-two of the crew have been landed. It is believed that the captain is amongst those saved. The dead will be buried tomorrow.*

Accompanying this note was a list of survivors. Walter Beynon's name was not on the list.

Telegrams:—"Navy Accounts, London."

In any further communication on this subject, please quote

No. 9. N.P. 4105/15

and address letter to—
The Accountant General of the Navy,
Admiralty,
London, S.W.

Admiralty,

14 August, 1915.

Madam,

I regret to have to inform you that H.M.S. "India" was sunk on the 8th inst. and that the name of Walter James Beynon. Rating Leading Seaman Official Number 201889, who is believed to have been on board, does not appear in the lists of survivors received in this department. In these circumstances it is feared that, in the absence of any evidence to the contrary, he must be regarded as having lost his life.

Any application which the next of kin or legal representative may have to make in consequence of the foregoing information should be made by letter addressed to the Accountant General of the Navy, Admiralty, London, S.W.

I am, Madam,

Your obedient Servant,

Alfred Ryles

Accountant General of the Navy.

Mrs Florence Beynon
10 Hm. Cg Station
West Mersea
Colchester.

The notification sent by the Admiralty to Mrs Beynon advising her that her husband was missing presumed dead after the sinking of H.M.S. *India*.

On 12th August, 1915, a press release from the Admiralty contained the list issued by the British authorities at Christinia. On 13th August, the Norwegian Government decided that the survivors picked up by the HMT *Saxon* and those landed on the island of Helligvaer were to be interned at Trondheim, but that the eighty one men saved by the SS *Gotaland*, a neutral ship outside territorial waters, were free to go as from 21.00 on 12th August.

A further updated list of survivors was provided by the British Consulate on 14th August, with Walter Beynon's name added in pencil as unofficially reported saved. On the same day the Norwegian Government lodged a complaint with both the British and German authorities reported in the following press release.

*14th August, 1915 - Protest by the Norwegian Government*
*It is officially announced that just as the Norwegian Government previously insisted in face of the contrary contention of the British Government, that the West Fjord in its entirety was a Norwegian territorial water, the Norwegian Government now on the occasion of the torpedoing of the British auxiliary cruiser India has informed the German Government that the West Fjord has been from time immemorial been regarded as belonging to Norwegian sea territory. This is specifically the fact with the part of the fjord where the India was attacked.*

*The funeral of twelve more English sailors from the India took place yesterday afternoon with full military honours. There were many wreaths on the coffins, including offerings from the Norwegian Navy and the British Legation. A company of Norwegian soldiers paid the last honours by the graveside.*

On 16th August, another list of survivors was issued, the original having Walter Beynon's name on it, but on the duplicates, which would have been issued to the press, it had been omitted.

With still no firm news on the fate of her husband, Mrs Beynon asked the Soldiers' and Sailors' Families Association to write a letter on her behalf to the Admiralty.

*The Director,*
*Greenwich Hospital,*
*Admiralty*
*August 20, 1915*
*Sir,*
*I am writing on behalf of Mrs Beynon, staying at 130, Goldhawk Road, previously of Coast Guards, West Mersea, near Colchester, Essex. She had a notice from the Admiralty that her husband, Leading Seaman Walter J. Beynon, 201889, H.M.S. 'India' was reported dead. A friend of hers, Mrs Wright, 18, Northcote Road, whose husband, J.T. Wright, A.B., H.M.S. 'India' whose husband is also reported missing, has had a letter from her husband dated August 11, saying that he is alive and also his friend Beynon, the above man. The letter had a Norwegian stamp on it.*

*I think that Mrs Beynon is calling at the Admiralty this afternoon with Wright's letter. I hope enquiries will be made to find out whether the men are alive or not. I shall be much obliged for any information on the subject.*
*I am, Sir, Your obedient servant, D.L. Cappel, Asst. Secretary, Naval Side.*

On 25th August, the Admiralty adjusted their records, and it was officially confirmed that he was one of the survivors, and the following report appeared in the Essex County Standard of August 28th, 1915.

**Coastguard on Torpedoed Vessel**
*Walter Beynon, late coastguard of Mersea, who was on the India when she was torpedoed on August 8th, was mourned by all Mersea as lost, but to the joyful surprise of his wife and his many friends a letter has just been received by Mrs Beynon dated three days after the vessel was lost, saying that he has been saved and had landed in Norway. He is very popular in Mersea.*

At the end of August, the British authorities were still in some confusion as to how to deal with such a large number of internees in a neutral country as shown by Mrs Beynon's correspondence with them.

*August 28th, 1915*
*Dear Sir,*
*I should be greatly obliged if you could kindly give me any information as to correspondence with seamen interned in Norway.*

*My husband was saved from HMS India, and has written to me from Joerstadmoen, Faaberg, Norway; but my letters to him, have been opened and returned by the Censor, marked as being contrary to the regulations, and merely accompanied by a printed circular regarding correspondence for Prisoners of War. If no regulations have been issued dealing with Men interned in a Neutral Country, I should be glad to know if any newspapers or books may be sent, and whether postage has to be paid on letters. Also, if I should address them c/o G.P.O. London, or send direct to the address given in Norway.*
                                               *Yours obediently, Mrs Beynon.*

British sailors from HMS *India* interned at Joerstadmoen, Norway, 1915 - 1918.

Walter Beynon and his fellow crewmen now settled down to life as internees for the duration of the war. An allowance of 10s 6d per week was paid to their dependants including Mrs Beynon. The Norwegian authorities established a separate British camp at the northern end of Joerstadmoen guarded by forty men from the Gudbrandsdalens Battalion.

By all accounts, the interned were treated well, with good food, together with a supply of English books and magazines. One of their pastimes was football which they introduced into the area. The camp regime was quite relaxed relying on gentleman's agreements to keep to the rules, and the interned were allowed to move freely in the area. Walter Beynon was to spend the next three years in the camp. At the end of October 1918, he caught pneumonia and despite medical treatment died on 2nd November. He was buried in Faberg churchyard near Lillehammer on 6th November. He is commemorated on the West Mersea War Memorial.

The grave of Leading Seaman Walter Beynon in Faberg churchyard, nr Lillehammer, Norway.

**Sources**

*Commonwealth War Graves Commission*
*Essex County Standard*
*Pastor Terje Raddum, Faberg Church, Norway - photograph of grave*
*History of Joerstadmoen, 1995*
*ADM116/1440, PRO, Kew*
*National Maritime Museum, Greenwich*

**SURNAME: Whiting**

CHRISTIAN NAME(S): Percy Louis

AGE: 24

RECRUITMENT OFFICE: Colchester

SERVICE NO: 48289  RANK: Private

SERVICE/REGIMENT: 3rd Battalion, Wiltshire Regiment

DECORATIONS EARNED: Not known

DATE KILLED/DIED: November 24th, 1918   LOCATION: Aylesford Military Hospital, Kent.

LOCATION OF GRAVE: Melksham Church Cemetery, Melksham, Wiltshire

---

**BACKGROUND AND SERVICE HISTORY:**

Percy Louis Whiting was born on 6th August, 1894, the son of Horace Louis Farthing and Rosina Whiting. His parents married on 6th April, 1896, and they had two more children, a son, Clifford James, born on 16th May, 1897, and a daughter, Grace Ethel, born on 28th July, 1898. All three children were baptised on 11th June, 1899.

Nothing is known of his early life, but at the outbreak of the war, he was employed by a Mrs Sargent, who ran a hairdressing and newsagent's business in Melrose Road, West Mersea. By 1916, he had married a Miss Marks.

At the beginning of 1916, conscription came into force, and Tribunals were set up to hear cases of those who claimed exemption. The local Tribunal was the Lexden and Winstree, named after the local authority in which it had jurisdiction. As reported in contemporary newspapers, Percy Louis Whiting appeared a number of times.

February 1916
*Mrs Sargent, hairdresser and newsagent, West Mersea, applied in respect of P.L. Whiting, stating that he completely managed her business and she was absolutely dependent on him. Whiting wrote stating that he was married, but in the single groups, and he had been passed only for home service. A month's postponement was granted to enable a medical certificate to be obtained.*

March 1916
*Mrs Sargent, widow, West Mersea, again applied for P.L. Whiting, a single man (?), aged 21 manager of a hairdressing business, and the case was adjourned for a medical examination, it being stated that Whiting had defective eyesight.*

The shop in Melrose Road owned by Mrs Florence Sargent, which was managed by Percy Whiting, and where he had his hairdressing business. This photograph was taken in 1908, prior to his involvement *(Brian Jay Collection)*

October 1916
*Percy L. Whiting (22) married, hairdresser, newsagent, and Stationer, West Mersea, who had passed in Class C3, consented to withdraw the claim on permission to claim if ever he was called up. Mr C.E. Page, solicitor, supported the application.*

July 1917
*Mr. C.E. Page, Colchester represented P.L. Whiting, a hairdresser etc (22, married) of West Mersea who had passed C3. Mr Page said the man on the strength of the previous rejection, took over the business, which would have closed if he now went. Three months temporary exemption was granted.*

October 1917
*The only hairdresser at West Mersea appealed for exemption through Mr Page who stated that the man's wife 'was in poor health'. He had been passed C3, six months exemption was allowed.*

May 1918
*Percy L. Whiting (married, 23), a West Mersea hairdresser was supported by Mr C.E. Page and the case was adjourned.*

<u>July 1918</u>
*Mr C.E. Page, solicitor supported the application of Percy L. Whiting (23, married), hairdresser and newsagent, West Mersea, for conditional exemption, and until August 1st was granted.*

His son, Kenneth, was born in June, 1918

On 1st August, 1918, he finally enlisted, and he joined the 3rd Battalion, Wiltshire Regiment. During training, he contracted bronchial pneumonia and died on Sunday 24th November in Aylesford Military Hospital in Kent.

On 6th December, 1918, he was given a military funeral at the Congregational Church, Melksham, in Wiltshire. The Reverend W.G. Farr officiated and the Local Volunteer Regiment together with wounded from the Local Red Cross Hospital formed a guard of honour. An Australian soldier played the Last Post. He was buried in Melksham Cemetery, close to St Michael's Church.

He is commemorated on the West Mersea War Memorial. His widow and son left Mersea Island to live in Melksham at No 4, Canon Square. His name appears on the War Memorial in the Square opposite the house. His brother, Clifford Farthing had been killed the previous year on 3rd May, 1917 (see page 97).

The grave of Private Percy Louis Whiting in Melksham Church, Cemetery, Wiltshire.

## Sources

*Commonwealth War Graves Commission*
*Mr Darren Crook*
*Essex County Standard*
*Essex Chronicle*
*Essex County Telegraph*
*Essex Record Office (Colchester)*

**SURNAME: French**

CHRISTIAN NAME(S): Percy

AGE: 27

RECRUITMENT OFFICE: Not known

SERVICE/REGIMENT: Merchant Marine Reserve

SERVICE NO: Not known          RANK: Deckhand/Sea Gunner

DECORATIONS EARNED: Not known

DATE KILLED/DIED: 14th December, 1918     LOCATION: Unknown

LOCATION OF GRAVE: Barfield Road Cemetery, West Mersea

---

**BACKGROUND AND SERVICE HISTORY:**

Percy French was born on Mersea Island in 1891, the fourth son of William and Laura French who lived at Elm Dene, City Road, West Mersea. He was baptised on 5th June, 1892.

When he was ten, in 1901, Percy's mother died at the age of 35. Nothing is known of his early life, but it is assumed that he was involved with the sea in his civilian occupation. In June, 1914, it was reported that he was part of the crew of Mr C Perkin's yacht *Pride* in the Mersea to Heybridge race. On its return to Mersea, the yacht sank and the crew nearly drowned before being rescued by the crew of the *Anonyma*. Mr William Mussett was awarded a specially struck medal for his part in the rescue. In 1915, Percy was presented with a cigarette case inscribed,

>'Sarita'
>1915
>to
>Percy French
>from
>P. Frost Smith
>Torquay to Mersea

He joined the Merchant Marine Reserve, possibly in 1916. One of his first postings was as a Leading Seaman on the Auxiliary Patrol vessel HMS *Zaria*.

He survived the war, but became a victim of the influenza epidemic while serving as a deckhand/sea gunner on the Patrol Yacht *Medusa II* and died on 14th December, 1918.

He is buried with his mother and father in Barfield Road Cemetery, West Mersea. The inscription on the gravestone tells us that he died on board HMS *Agadir* which was a hospital ship. He is commemorated on the West Mersea War Memorial.

**Sources**

*Commonwealth War Graves Commission*
*Essex County Telegraph*
*Essex County Standard*

The grave of Percy French in West Mersea Cemetery, Barfield Road, West Mersea.

**SURNAME: Russell**

CHRISTIAN NAME(S): Alfred Edward

AGE: 30

RECRUITMENT OFFICE: Colchester

SERVICE NO: 160354           RANK: Private

SERVICE/REGIMENT: 17th Battalion, Essex Regiment (Service no: 400155) transferred to Labour Corps

DECORATIONS EARNED: War Medal, Victory Medal

DATE KILLED/DIED: 23rd December, 1918     LOCATION: Colchester Military Hospital.

LOCATION OF GRAVE: East Mersea Churchyard

---

**BACKGROUND AND SERVICE HISTORY:**

Alfred Edward Russell was born in 1888, the son of Albert and Mary Russell of 43 East Road, West Mersea. He was baptised on 21st June, 1889. At the time of the 1891 census, he had one brother, Harry, aged one month.

After attending the local school, he left to help his father who was a thatcher. He married Katie (nee Clark) on 4th November, 1911, and lived in East Mersea opposite Weir Farm. At the outbreak of war he volunteered with his friend, Frank Pullen. Unfortunately, he was not fit enough for service abroad and he joined the 17th Battalion, Essex Regiment which was on the home front.

Their task was to guard coastal installations, and it is thought that he was posted to Sheringham on the Norfolk coast. During his service, he transferred to the Labour Corps.

In December 1918, he returned home on leave feeling ill. This developed into influenza, and finally to pneumonia. He was admitted to Colchester Military Hospital and died there on 23rd December 1918. He was buried in East Mersea churchyard on 29th December, 1918.

During the research for this book, it was discovered that Private Alfred Russell's name was not on the village War Memorial inside East Mersea Church. At the time of his death the family were told that because he had died on the Home Front he was not eligible to have his name added to the Memorial. Later it was agreed that his name could be added, but nothing was done. An approach was made to the family to ascertain whether they still would like his name added, which they did, and on Sunday 27th February, 2000, an additional plaque carrying the name of Private Alfred Edward Russell was added below the War Memorial in the church and dedicated at a special service.

Overleaf: Photograph of either the 17th Battalion, Essex Regiment or the Labour Corps on the North Norfolk coast.

Private Alfred Edward Russell

The grave of Private Alfred Edward Russell in East Mersea churchyard.

**Sources**

*Essex Regiment Museum*
*Commonwealth War Graves Commission Cemetery Register for North Essex*
*Mrs Sams (daughter)*

**SURNAME:** Hewes

CHRISTIAN NAME(S): Albert

AGE: 28

SHORE STATION: Portsmouth

SERVICE NO: 13146/D.A.        RANK: Deck Hand

SERVICE/REGIMENT: Royal Naval Reserve

DECORATIONS EARNED: War Medal, Victory Medal

DATE KILLED/DIED: 31st December, 1918    LOCATION: Southampton

LOCATION OF GRAVE: West Mersea Cemetery, Barfield Road, West Mersea

---

**BACKGROUND AND SERVICE HISTORY:**

Albert Hewes was born on 7th June, 1890, the son of George 'Odge' and Isabella (nee Ennew) Hewes, who lived in Smithfield Cottage, Firs Chase, West Mersea. He was baptised on 14th September, 1890.

He joined the Royal Navy on 17th August, 1916, his civilian occupation at the time being oyster fishing. He was posted to *Pembroke 1*, the shore station at Chatham before transferring to the Special Trawler Reserve on 20th October, 1916. His first posting was to *Victory 1*, the shore station at Portsmouth Barracks. By February 1917, he had joined a Motor Launch Squadron operating from their Eastern Mediterranean base at Taranto in Italy and served on ML501. On 31st October, 1917 he was admitted to sick quarters with Pyrexia (high temperature) and stayed there until 17th November when he rejoined his ship. He transferred to ML440 and survived the war. On 22nd November 1918, his Naval Record shows that he was admitted to No. 79 General Hospital, Taranto, and on 5th December his condition was serious enough to warrant the long journey home by Ambulance train. On 11th December, it was reported that he was seriously ill with tubercle of lung (tuberculosis) and was in Stationary Hospital, Marseilles. By 22nd December, he had reached England and was in the University Hospital, Southampton with reports that he was no longer seriously ill. Unfortunately, this situation was not to last and on 31st December, 1918 he died from phthisis (pulmonary tuberculosis). He is buried in the West Mersea Cemetery, Barfield Road, and is commemorated on the West Mersea War Memorial.

**Sources**

*Commonwealth War Graves Commission*
*Mr A. Hewes*
*Essex County Telegraph*
*Ministry of Defence DR2A - Navy*
*Essex Regiment Museum*

Group photograph of the West Mersea Pirates football team taken before the outbreak of the First World War. Albert Hewes is in the left hand corner, sitting down. (*Brian Jay Collection*)

The grave of Albert Hewes in West Mersea Cemetery, Barfield Road, West Mersea

**SURNAME: Mussett**

CHRISTIAN NAME(S): Ezra John

AGE: 29

RECRUITMENT OFFICE: Not known

SERVICE NO: G/27722     RANK: Private

SERVICE/REGIMENT: Queen's Own Royal West Kent Regiment transferred to Labour Corps (service no: 819337)

DECORATIONS EARNED: War Medal, Victory Medal

DATE KILLED/DIED: 12th February, 1919     LOCATION: Marlborough, Wiltshire

LOCATION OF GRAVE: West Mersea Cemetery, Barfield Road, West Mersea

---

## BACKGROUND AND SERVICE HISTORY:

Ezra John Mussett was born on 4th September, 1889, the son of Herbert Samuel and Sophia Mussett of Ruby Cottage, West Mersea. He was baptised on 14th November, 1889. He had three sisters and one brother. His father, Herbert died on 19th March, 1912.

He married Maud (maiden name unknown) in 1914, and their daughter Joy was born in 1915. In civilian life he was an insurance clerk working for a company in London. He took part in amateur athletics and ran for the West London Harriers. Apparently, his running contributed to a strained heart which meant that when he enlisted and joined the Queen's Own Royal West Kent Regiment, he was transferred to the Labour Corps. On 12th February, 1919, he died of influenza at Marlborough in Wiltshire.

He is buried in West Mersea Cemetery, Barfield Road, and is commemorated on the West Mersea War Memorial.

**Sources**

*Commonwealth War Graves Commission*
*Essex Regiment Museum*
*David Mussett*
*Mr Hines*

Private Ezra John Mussett

The grave of Ezra John Mussett in West Mersea Cemetery, Barfield Road, West Mersea

## *Aftermath*

*Have you forgotten yet?...*
For the world's events have rumbled on since those gagged days,
Like traffic checked while at the crossing of city-ways:
And the haunted gap in your mind has filled with thoughts that flow
Like clouds in the lit heaven of life; and you're a man reprieved to go.
Taking your peaceful share of Time, with joy to spare.
*But the past is just the same - and War's a bloody game...*
*Have you forgotten yet?...*
*Look down, and swear by the slain of the War that you'll never forget*

Do you remember the dark months you held the sector at Mametz -
The nights you watched and wired and dug and piled sandbags on parapets?
Do you remember the rats; and the stench
Of corpses rotting in front of the front-line trench -
And dawn coming dirty-white, and chill with hopeless rain?
Do you ever stop and ask, 'Is it all going to happen again?'

Do you remember that hour of din before the attack -
And the anger, the blind compassion that seized and shook you then
As you peered at the doomed and haggard faces of your men?
Do you remember the stretcher-cases lurching back
With dying eyes and lolling heads - those ashen-grey
Masks of the lads who once were keen and kind and gay?

*Have you forgotten yet?...*
*Look up, and swear by the green of the spring that you'll never forget*

SIEGFRIED SASSOON
March, 1919